Visit the *Literacy for QTLS* Companion Website at
www.pearsoned.co.uk/hickey to find valuable student
learning material including:

- Skills-audit test and answer sheet
- Individual Learning Plan (ILP) template
- SWOT analysis template
- Key spellings for professionals
- Additional exemplary material

PEARSON
Education

We work with leading authors to develop the strongest
educational materials in education studies, bringing
cutting-edge thinking and best learning practice to a
global market.

Under a range of well-known imprints, including Longman,
we craft high-quality print and electronic publications which
help readers to understand and apply their content,
whether studying or at work.

To find out more about the complete range of our
publishing please visit us on the World Wide Web at:
www.pearsoned.co.uk

LITERACY FOR QTLS
Achieving the Minimum Core

Julia Hickey

Sheffield Hallam University

PEARSON
Longman

Harlow, England • London • New York • Boston • San Francisco • Toronto
Sydney • Tokyo • Singapore • Hong Kong • Seoul • Taipei • New Delhi
Cape Town • Madrid • Mexico City • Amsterdam • Munich • Paris • Milan

Pearson Education Limited
Edinburgh Gate
Harlow
Essex CM20 2JE
England

and Associated Companies throughout the world

Visit us on the World Wide Web at:
www.pearsoned.co.uk

First published 2008

ISBN: 978-1-4058-5946-2

British Library Cataloguing-in-Publication Data
A catalogue record for this book is available from the British Library

Library of Congress Cataloging-in-Publication Data
Hickey, Julia.
 Literacy for QTLS / Julia Hickey.
    p. cm.
 Includes bibliographical references and index.
 ISBN-13: 978-1-4058-5946-2 (pbk.)
 1. Teachers--Training of--Great Britain. 2. Effective teaching--Great Britain. 3. Occupational training--Great Britain.
 4. Individualized instruction--Great Britain. I. Title.
  LB1725.G6H43 2008
  370.71'1--dc22

                      2007028196

10 9 8 7 6 5 4 3 2 1
11 10 09 08 07

Typeset in 9.5/12.5pt Palatino by 30
Printed in Great Britain by Henry Ling, Ltd., at the Dorset Press, Dorchester, Dorset

The publisher's policy is to use paper manufactured from sustainable forests.

For my Daddy who breathed life into words and gave me stories of outlaws, heroes, villains, derring-do and happy-ever-after.

Brief contents

Supporting resources

Visit **www.pearsoned.co.uk/hickey** to find valuable online resources

Companion Website for students

- Skills-audit test and answer sheet
- Individual Learning Plan (ILP) template
- SWOT analysis template
- Key spellings for professionals
- Additional exemplary material

For more information please contact your local Pearson Education sales representative or visit **www.pearsoned.co.uk/hickey**

Contents

Preface

Background

Since 2000 it has been expected that Initial Teacher Training (ITT) programmes should equip all trainee teachers in the post-compulsory sector with the knowledge and skills needed to develop inclusive approaches to addressing the language and literacy needs of their own learners. The minimum core specifications rolled out in 2003 strengthened the importance of inclusive approaches to literacy within vocational and academic programmes. It also gave emphasis to the personal literacy knowledge and skills required by tutors and trainers working in a post-compulsory setting.

Following on from the government White Papers *Equipping our Teachers for the Future* (DfES, 2004a) and *Further Education: Raising Skills, Improving Life Chances* (DfES, 2006a), a number of reforms, effective from September 2007, were made to the Teacher Qualifications Framework including Qualified Teacher and Learning Skills (QTLS) status for practitioners with full teaching roles in the lifelong learning sector.

Since September 2007 all QTLS courses for lifelong learning practitioners have been expected to support and assess trainees' personal language and literacy skills as identified by the *New Overarching Professional Standards for Teachers, Tutors and Trainers in the Lifelong Learning Sector* (Lifelong Learning UK, 2006) and more specifically detailed in the minimum core. These literacy and language skills are then assessed through nationally administered tests.

The *New Overarching Professional Standards for Teachers, Tutors and Trainers in the Lifelong Learning Sector* (Lifelong Learning UK, 2006) and the minimum core also require trainee teachers to recognise some of the personal, social and cultural factors influencing language, literacy learning and development in their own learners. The minimum core provides a frame of reference to 'ensure sufficient emphasis on how to teach vocational and other subjects in ways which meet the needs of learners whose levels of language, literacy and numeracy would otherwise undermine their chance of success' (FENTO, 2004a). The standards also identify the need for trainees to develop strategies to promote inclusivity.

The aim of *Literacy for QTLS* is not to prepare academic and vocational teachers to be literacy specialists. It is designed to ensure that their levels of literacy reflect the professional nature of the role and to enable practitioners to support the literacy and language needs of their own learners. No matter how proficient an individual's literacy and language knowledge and skills, there are always areas that will be less familiar than others.

Literacy for QTLS

Literacy for QTLS is designed for all prospective practitioners working in the lifelong learning sector.

The text is primarily designed to enable you to identify your areas of strength and weakness, to then develop personal knowledge and skills in order to pass the nationally administered literacy test. The text is also designed for you to consider some of the strategies that could be used to support the language and literacy skills of your own learners. It can be read in its entirety or dipped into as required based on your own needs and professional interests.

● Skills audit

Chapter 2 of *Literacy for QTLS* is a skills audit designed to help you assess your own literacy and language needs, set SMART targets and monitor your progress as you work towards the national tests. The first section of the skills audit will help you to identify your current levels of language/literacy qualification and suggest routes that you may wish to follow in order to prepare to undertake the language and literacy requirements of the minimum core. The second part of the audit is a self-assessment containing forty-four questions covering different aspects of literacy and language; they can be found on the Companion Website to accompany this book at **www.pearsoned.co.uk/hickey** along with the answers. The third part of the skills audit is a SWOT analysis to help you consider your strengths and weaknesses as you work towards the minimum core requirements. The final section of this chapter will help you to create an action plan so that you can develop skills and close knowledge gaps that you have identified.

The questions and the blank documents identified in this chapter can also be found by following the weblink. There is no need to worry if you do not have access to the Internet. *Literacy for QTLS* provides all the questions, answers and information you need to complete the skills audit.

● The structure of *Literacy for QTLS*

The text is designed to be user friendly and contextualised where appropriate.

- Each chapter begins with an introductory paragraph followed by an identification of which elements of the minimum core will be addressed in the chapter.
- **Key definitions** are given in the margin alongside some of the terminology which you will encounter. There will be a minimal definition of a few words alongside the text and a more full explanation along with examples where appropriate in the glossary at the back of the book.
- Each chapter is interspersed with **tasks** where appropriate to enable you to engage with the text and also to identify where you can implement your skills and knowledge in your own working environments. Tasks relating to developing knowledge and skills are contextualised to the teaching profession where possible.

- Examples or recommendations for **best practice** are given where appropriate. Illustrations of best practice are drawn from reports to demonstrate where and how language and literacy support and development can be successfully embedded into academic and vocational programmes.

- **Snippets** giving relevant quotations and facts are offered where appropriate in some of the chapters to help you contextualise the experiences of your own learners.

- At the end of each chapter there is a **summary** of key points.

- A **Test your knowledge** section in each chapter gives you the opportunity to rehearse skills and knowledge gained. Some of the tasks and questions in the Test your knowledge section will require you to apply your personal knowledge and skills to case studies, scenarios and looking at your own practice. Questions with an asterisk (*) indicate that an answer has been provided at the back of the book.

- Each chapter concludes with a **Where next?** feature indicating further reading and useful websites. The scope of the minimum core is such that you would be advised to access other resources signposted at the end of each chapter to further develop knowledge and skills depending upon your needs. There is a Where next? at the end of this preface directing you to the Lifelong Learning UK website where you can find links to the White Papers identified in this preface and to the standards required of practitioners for QTLS.

The structure and content of the text are shaped by the twin concerns of the minimum core: personal language and literacy skills and knowledge, and suppporting learners to develop their language and literacy skills and knowledge in an academic or vocational context.

● Chapter content and the 'overarching professional standards' covered

The standards covered are indicated by emboldened text. All the chapters encourage the following professional values in practitioners working in the lifelong learning sector:

AS 4 **Reflection and evaluation of their own practice and their continuing professional development as teachers.**

AS 7 **Improving the quality of their practice.**

Chapter 1 is about the scale of the need covering the changing definitions of literacy and defining what it means to be literate in a modern society. It offers an overview of some of the complex effects of low levels of literacy and the impact of low levels of literacy upon participation in and access to society and the modern economy.

AK 3.1 **Issues of equality, diversity and inclusion**

Chapter 2 covers a skills audit.

Chapters 3–9 cover personal skills and knowledge including: reading, writing, grammar, punctuation, spelling, speaking and listening and finally non-verbal communication as well as identifying some strategies to help develop these language and literacy skills in your own learners. Each chapter helps teachers in the lifelong learning sector to:

AK 5.1   **Know and understand ways to communicate and collaborate with colleagues and/or others to enhance learners' experience.**

BK 3.1   **Know and understand effective and appropriate use of different forms of communication informed by relevant theories and principles.**

BK 3.2   **Know and understand a range of listening and questioning techniques to support learning.**

BK 3.3   **Know and understand ways to structure and present information and ideas clearly and effectively to learners.**

BK 3.4   **Know and understand barriers and aids to effective communication.**

CK 3.4   **Know and understand the language, literacy and numeracy skills required to support own specialist teaching.**

Chapter 10 is about the different factors affecting the acquisition and development of language and literacy. It summarises some of the key theories on the acquisition and development of language in children and adults, as well as looking at some of the barriers to language and literacy development such as age, gender, language and cultural background.

AK 3.1   **Know and understand issues of equality, diversity and inclusion.**

BK 2.2   **Know and understand ways to engage, motivate and encourage active participation of learners and learner independence.**

BK 2.3   **Know and understand the relevance of learning approaches, preferences and skills to learner progress.**

BK 5.1   **Know and understand the impact of resources on effective learning.**

BK 5.2   **Know and understand ways to ensure that resources used are inclusive, promote equality and support diversity.**

Chapter 11 is about the range of specific learning difficulties and/or disabilities that can hinder language learning and skill development. It suggests some strategies for supporting learners with specific learning difficulties and disabilities as well as identifying the legal requirements for inclusive practice within the lifelong learning sector.

Chapter 12 is about the role of world English and some of the issues arising from multilingualism.

AK 3.1   **Know and understand issues of equality, diversity and inclusion.**

BK 2.3   **Know and understand the relevance of learning approaches, preferences and skills to learner progress.**

BK 5.1   **Know and understand the impact of resources on effective learning.**

BK 5.2   **Know and understand ways to ensure that resources used are inclusive, promote equality and support diversity.**

CK 3.3   **Know and understand the different ways in which language, literacy and numeracy skills are integral to learners' achievement in own specialist area.**

CK 3.4 Know and understand the language, literacy and numeracy skills required to support own specialist teaching.

FK 1.1 Know and understand sources of information, advice, guidance and support to which learners might be referred.

FK 1.2 Know and understand internal services which learners might access.

FK 2.1 Know and understand boundaries of own role in supporting learners.

Chapters 13 and 14 are specifically about identifying, mapping to the Adult Literacy Core Curriculum and embedding language and literacy skills and knowledge within vocational or academic programme areas.

BK 5.1 Know and understand the impact of resources on effective learning.

BK 5.2 Know and understand ways to ensure that resources used are inclusive, promote equality and support diversity.

CK 3.3 Know and understand the different ways in which language, literacy and numeracy skills are integral to learners' achievement in own specialist area.

CK 3.4 Know and understand the language, literacy and numeracy skills required to support own specialist teaching.

Where next?

Texts

Lifelong Learning UK (2007) *Addressing Literacy, Language, Numeracy and ICT Needs in Education and Training: Defining the Minimum Core of Teachers' Knowledge, Understanding and Personal Skills - A Guide for Initial Teacher Education Programmes*, London: Lifelong Learning UK.

Website

www.lifelonglearninguk.org

Acknowledgements

My thanks go to all the people who helped and supported me during every step of this process: Elaine Owen who allowed me to use her as a sounding board for ideas about the content and structure of the text; Claire Roddison for her advice on floral symbols; Jemma Ingram for her advice about working with hearing-impaired learners; Nina Weiss for her eye for detail and excellent suggestions during the review process; Catherine Yates for her support, guidance and patience during the drafting process; Emma Easy and Ruth Freestone King for their expertise and attention to detail; and finally, Kyle Hewgill for his proofreading skills and belief in me.

Publisher's acknowledgements

We are grateful to the following for permission to reproduce copyright material:

Unnumbered figure on p. 3 from 'Get-on' with Gremlins poster – Department for Education and Skills website. © Crown Copyright material is reproduced with the permission of the Controller of HMSO and Queen's Printer for Scotland; Unnumbered figure on p. 24 from the *National Primary Strategy*, Department for Education and Skills. © Crown Copyright material is reproduced with the permission of the Controller of HMSO and Queen's Printer for Scotland; Unnumbered table on p. 36 from *Extending Literacy: Developing Approaches to Non-Fiction*, Routledge (Wray, D. and Lewis, M., 1997); Unnumbered figure on p. 47 from 'A cognitive process theory of writing', *College Composition and Communication*, Vol. 32: 4 (Flower, L. and Hayes, J.R., 1981). Copyright 1981 by the National Council of Teachers of English. Reprinted and used with permission; Unnumbered figure on p. 121 from *If You Take My Meaning: Theory into Practice in Human Communication*, Hodder & Stoughton (Ellis, R. and McClintock, A., 1991). Reproduced by permission of Hodder & Stoughton Limited; Unnumbered figure on p. 137 from *The Dynamics of Human Communication – A Laboratory Approach*, The McGraw-Hill Companies (Myers, G.E. and Myers, M.T., 1985); Unnumbered figure on p. 162. © 2007 Cath Smith. DEAFSIGN from the LET'S SIGN SERIES, www.DeafBooks.co.uk. Tel: 01642 580505.

In some instances we have been unable to trace the owners of copyright material, and we would appreciate any information that would enable us to do so.

1 The scale of the need

Literacy
Ability to read
and write.

Sir Claus Moser catalogued the scale of poor **literacy** in the report *A Fresh Start* (DfEE, 1999a). He estimated that approximately 7 million adults in England had poor literacy skills. Of those, about 20 per cent had less literacy than might reasonably be expected of an 11-year-old child. A survey published in 2007 identified that this percentage rises to 50 per cent for army recruits. An earlier survey comparing literacy levels between nations was equally worrying: it discovered that only Poland and Ireland had poorer levels of literacy than the UK (*The International Adult Literacy Survey*, Office for National Statistics, 1998). More recently the Confederation of British Industry (CBI) identified that literacy skills impacted on the individual and the employer in many different ways and identified a 'worrying shortfall' (CBI, 2006: 7) in the different literacy skills required by an effective workforce. Leitch's report (HM Treasury, 2006) confirmed this when it identified that one-seventh of the adult population (5 million) had insufficient literacy skills to be able to function in a modern working environment, raising the possibility of long-term industrial and economic decline because 'our nation's skills are not world class' (HM Treasury, 2006: 1). The report also indicated that, unless drastic measures were taken to up-skill the workforce, to motivate non-traditional learners and increase motivation, 'the UK risks a lost generation' (HM Treasury, 2006: 61).

This first chapter of *Literacy for QTLS* invites readers to consider what is meant by the word literacy; how the concept of literacy has changed over time and to reflect on the impact of low levels of literacy both to the country and to the individual. It is the starting point for recognising the scale of the need and the different strategies for supporting learners including embedding literacy, numeracy and language skills within vocational and academic subject areas.

Minimum core element

A1
- The importance of English language and literacy in enabling users to participate in public life, society and the modern economy.

The changing importance of literacy

A changing importance of literacy can be illustrated by the following snapshot dating to the beginning of the twentieth century. It is staged to tell a story. The couple are

The changing face of literacy

standing outside a house: their home. The woman is holding an open book: the Bible. So far there is nothing particularly significant about the story. Now let's add some additional information. The man is a farm manager, an important role in an agricultural community, but it is his wife who is holding the book. Remarkably she could read and write whereas the farm manager could not. The book she held was the only book the couple owned. Her literacy is situated in her religious beliefs and the language of King James.

So what does the picture tell us about the importance of literacy at the beginning of the twentieth century?

- It was valued by those who were able to read and write.
- The ability to read was worthy of note within this strata of rural society.
- It was unnecessary to be literate in order to function successfully within society.

Other evidence indicating the way in which the importance of literacy has changed can be seen in this wedding certificate dating from 1891. One witness, unable to sign her own name, has made her mark.

Kesiah was effectively illiterate but had not felt it necessary to disguise her lack of basic writing skill. Fifty years earlier in 1841, in England, 33 per cent of men and 44 per cent of women signed their marriage certificates using their mark rather than signing their names.

1891 wedding certificate

Get-On campaign gremlin encouraging adults to improve their literacy and numeracy skills

Source: Department for Education and Skills, http://www.dfes.gov.uk/get-on/downloads.shtml. © Crown copyright material is reproduced with permission of the Controller of HMSO and Queen's Printer for Scotland.

These pieces of evidence, whilst anecdotal, reveal the way in which compulsory education and the importance of functional literacy have developed since the introduction of key Education Acts in 1870, 1891 and 1944. The concept of literacy is one that has changed over time and context. Today, in the UK, people may be *prepared* to admit to not being good at mathematics but are less likely to openly admit to their lack of literacy skills. The government's gremlin advertising campaign commencing in 2001 following the launch of **Skills for Life** highlighted the secrecy and stigma attached to poor literacy today.

Love them or loath them, the various gremlins that feature in TV and radio advertising created by the government's Get-On campaign highlight the difficulties faced by individuals with poor literacy skills in the twenty-first century.

Skills for Life
Provision for adult literacy, numeracy and English for non-English speakers.

Defining basic skills and literacy

There are different definitions of basic skills and also of literacy.

Stop and reflect

What do you understand the meaning of the phrase 'basic skills' to be and what do you think is meant by the word 'literacy'.

3

The Basic Skills Agency defines basic skills as

the ability to read, write and speak English and to use mathematics at a level necessary to function and progress at work and in society in general (www.basic-skills.co.uk).

The White Paper *21st Century Skills: Realising Our Potential* (DfES, 2003a) identified ICT as the third skill. The word literacy is harder to define even though its dictionary definition is the ability to read and write (www.askoxford.com). Research indicates that there are different kinds of literacy. The CBI defines functional literacy as:

Each individual being confident and capable when using the skills of speaking, listening, reading and writing and is able to communicate effectively, adapting to the range of audiences and contexts (CBI, 2006: 104).

Domain
Context where a particular form of language is used.

Context is an important consideration. People use different kinds of literacy depending upon their situation. Some people may speak using a specific regional dialect when they are communicating with their family and friends but they may switch to a more standard form of the language when they are at work or meeting someone unfamiliar. They use different literacies depending on the **domain** they are communicating within (Barton, Hamilton and Ivanic, 2000: 6). In effect this means that most people have multiple and identifiable literacies bound up in their cultural, economic, social and personal lives. The most straightforward form of multiple literacy use is the case of a bi- or multilingual speaker. The language that the speaker uses at home may be different from the language they are required to use in an educational or workplace context. It may be that English is a second or even third language. Other literacy domains include home, work, education, the media, the Internet, religion and professional, in fact all, occupations – consider some of the specialist language used by estate agents, lawyers, accountants, hairdressers, beauticians, doctors and practitioners within the lifelong learning sector.

Snippet

She [Lenny Henry's mother] told us we had to speak like everyone else, because in our house we spoke Jamaican all the time which is a kind of patois. I lived in a strange bifurcated world where the doormat was the sign for me to switch from Dudley Len to Jamaican Len, till eventually I became a weird morph of everything.
Comedian Lenny Henry speaking of his multiple language domains during an interview with Giles Hattersley for the *Sunday Times*, 11 March 2007, News Review, p. 5.

● Situated and transportable literacies

Situated literacy
Language and form that belong to a specific location.

Some literacy practices are associated with particular locations such as work or religious beliefs, for example. These are **situated literacies**. The language and format of some reading and writing are readily recognisable as belonging to a specific location. Within an educational environment it often appears that situated literacy is secondary to the skill or practice being developed within vocational subject areas. This can be an advantage because learners do not see the situated literacy as a development of their literacy skills e.g. following instructions for a specific purpose, such as making play dough on a childcare course or following verbal directions in order to complete a manicure on a beauty therapy course. The disadvantage is that the situated literacy can often be ignored because the emphasis is on the vocational skill. This means that learners who do not have the skills necessary to follow the instructions will not achieve the vocational task successfully.

Transportable literacies are the elements that can be moved between contexts and practices. Processes tend to be transportable as do the frameworks of language. Understanding that instructions are sequenced and that instructions can be used differently depending on their context are transportable skills.

Transportable literacy
Skills/knowledge that can be used in different situations and contexts.

● Dominant and marginalised literacies

Dominant literacy
Form of language used by dominant organisations within a society.

Standard English and RP (Received Pronunciation) represent the **dominant literacy**. They have prestige. In order to access and succeed within society, education and the workplace, individuals need to be able to access a standard variety of the language that is accepted by society in general. Hamilton and Hillier (2006) comment that Standard English and RP 'are privileged by their association with formal organisations, such as those of the school, the church the workplace, the legal system, commerce, medical and welfare bureaucracies.'

Marginalised literacy
Non-sandard forms of language.

Marginalised literacies are more fluid in their form and structure. They are not valued by influential institutions within society. People who speak and write in a strong dialect format are unable to access and succeed within wider social institutions; 'when questioned about them [marginalised literacies], people did not always regard them as *real* reading or *real* writing' (Hamilton and Hillier, 2006). Marginalised varieties of the language are not taught at school or in the lifelong learning sector; they are learnt at home and amongst cultural and social peer groups.

Marginalised literacies tend to have smaller audiences because of their non-standard nature. They may give social cohesion or identity to a specific group. Consider 14–19-year-olds. There is a definite language domain for this group and the language accepted by this group changes rapidly as individuals grow and change. It may have been 'hip' and 'groovy' to use these words in the 1960s but modern adolescents would not regard them as appropriate.

The most important thing about these definitions of literacy for vocational and academic tutors is the concept of language within the context of a specific culture.

The concept of being able to switch literacy domains is important for vocational and academic tutors. Users share a common understanding of language in a specific context. Assumptions are made about the way in which things are done and the occasions that specific forms of language are used. So, beauticians teaching within the lifelong learning sector may use different vocabulary and language structures with a client from those they would with a colleague, a learner or a manager within the teaching and learning organisation but outside the beauty profession. The same tutors will be able to understand and communicate effectively with learners who may habitually use non-standard or marginalised forms of language to communicate within a class setting. To communicate effectively practitioners must be able to switch language, structure and content to meet the needs of the audience and purpose for the communication.

Personal and professional literacy skills

Task

How important are literacy skills in your life? Note down - in a table format similar to the example provided - a typical day in your life. Begin with the alarm clock going off and finish when you can think of nothing else (you may for example go to sleep but the following morning recall a dream in which you heard something or spoke to someone). Choose an average day.

Speaking	Listening	Reading	Writing
Asking for directions	Listening to the answer to the request for directions	Reading emails.	Creating a worksheet or handout

Stop and reflect

Jobs and professions often have additional literacy requirements. Consider the essential literacy skills that you need in order to be an effective professional. If possible, once you have reflected on the skills and knowledge that you feel that you need, discuss this question with a group of practitioners working towards QTLS.

You may have discussed the academic skills that you require in order to achieve QTLS. This will include a range of reading and note-taking techniques; the ability to use the Harvard referencing system for resources that you have referred to; writing in different formats; contributing to discussion and giving presentations as well as researching the available literature and carrying out investigations. You may have mentioned the skills that you need in order to get a job in the sector, including skimming and scanning the job columns; filling in application forms; CV writing; good interview techniques. At work you need to apply literacy skills in meetings – to take notes and give your point of view during discussions; read a variety of official documentation using an appropriate range of skimming, scanning, detailed reading, critical reading; plan and prepare sessions using the correct documentation; create handouts and other teaching and learning activities; respond to memos, emails and circulars. All of these writing skills involve being able to choose the correct format; adopt an appropriate register and style; apply grammar and punctuation conventions; spell words, including technical terms, correctly and proofread what you have written.

In addition you may have identified speaking and listening skills that you require to function within your organisation, and others that you use for classroom management and interacting with our own learners. *Success for All* (DfES, 2002a) committed all vocational and academic tutors to addressing the literacy needs of their learners within the subject or vocational area. So this means that, to be an effective professional, tutors must also have some knowledge of the frameworks of language and **miscue analysis** skills. The list seems almost endless and it is inevitable that there are some skills that you feel confident about and others that you recognise need to be developed. You may do this because you enjoy learning for the sake of learning or

Miscue analysis
Diagnostic assessment used to identify language processing difficulties.

else you may wait until you have to improve a skill because you need to use it for a particular purpose.

What are the essential literacy skills that your learners may require in order to succeed within your vocational or academic subject area?

The scale of the need

How much do you know about the development of the *Skills for Life* (DfES, 2003b) agenda and the scale of the need in the UK? Test your knowledge with this multiple choice quiz. The data is taken from Sir Claus Moser's report, *A Fresh Start* (DfEE, 1999a); from an earlier report called *It Doesn't Get Any Better* (Bynner and Parsons, 1997) which investigates the impact of poor literacy and numeracy skills on the lives of 1,711 37-year-olds; from the CBI report *Working on the Three Rs* (2006) and from the DfES document *Skills for Life: Focus on Delivery to 2007* (2003b).

Multiple choice quiz

1   *Skills for Life* was launched in:

   1999 ☐
   2001 ☐
   2003 ☐

2   Having poor essential skills means that you could earn considerably less over your working life. On average, how much less?

   £15,000 ☐
   £25,000 ☐
   £50,000 ☐

3   How much do poor literacy, language and numeracy skills cost the country each year?

   In excess of £10 billion ☐
   In excess of £15 billion ☐
   In excess of £20 billion ☐

4   According to Sir Claus Moser's report, *A Fresh Start*, how many adults cannot locate the page reference for plumbers using the Yellow Pages?

   1 in 3 ☐
   1 in 4 ☐
   1 in 5 ☐

▶

5 In July 2003 the government produced a White Paper *21st Century Skills: Realising Our Potential*. It announced the introduction of a third basic skill to go alongside literacy and numeracy. The third basic skill is:

A second language ☐

ICT ☐

Health matters ☐

6 What percentage of this number had difficulty or could not deal with forms or paperwork in a job?

33 per cent ☐

43 per cent ☐

53 per cent ☐

7 42 per cent of women with good literacy skills had never been promoted. How large a percentage of women with poor literacy skills had never been promoted?

35 per cent ☐

75 per cent ☐

84 per cent ☐

8 How likely was it that people with low literacy would be in a household where both partners were out of work as compared with someone with good levels of literacy?

Twice as likely ☐

Five times as likely ☐

Eight times as likely ☐

9 Based on a Malaise Inventory of yes/no questions how much more likely were women with low levels of literacy to be depressed than those with good levels of literacy?

Twice as likely ☐

Five times as likely ☐

Eight times as likely ☐

10 What percentage of men with low literacy levels were likely to be involved with some public role such as a residents' association or parent-teacher association?

3 per cent ☐

6 per cent ☐

9 per cent ☐

The answers to the multiple choice questionnaire are located in the paragraph that follows.

The *Skills for Life* strategy was launched in **(1)** 2001 following the report delivered by Sir Claus Moser, *A Fresh Start* (DfEE, 1999a), which revealed the extent of low levels of literacy and numeracy skills in the United Kingdom. It is estimated that poor basic skills could cost an individual **(2)** £50,000 during their working life. This does not take into account other factors, e.g. a report found that girls with low reading levels were twice as likely to smoke as those who had secure reading levels (Parsons and Bynner, 2002). In addition it is estimated that poor basic skills cost the country in excess of **(3)** £10 billion each year and this cost is likely to increase as the skills required for twenty-first century jobs are raised. The UK has significantly fewer appropriately qualified workers than other European countries such as Germany. **(4)** 1 in 5 adults were unable to use the Yellow Pages effectively, let alone use literacy at levels required by modern industry. **(5)** The third essential skill that the government identified was ICT, reflecting the changes that modern society and workplaces are undergoing. **(6)** About 53 per cent of people had difficulty filling in forms at work; **(7)** 75 per cent of women with poor literacy skills had never been promoted; **(8)** it was eight times as likely that both partners would be out of work if they had low levels of literacy. In addition to impacting on economy, low levels of literacy impact on health and participation in the wider community; **(9)** women with poor levels of literacy were five times as likely to be depressed as those with higher skill levels; **(10)** only 3 per cent of men with low levels of literacy had some public role.

Evidence suggests that individuals who have literacy needs fall into one of three categories: those who are aware that they need to improve their skills; those who have a 'latent need'; and those individuals who have an 'invisible need' (Parsons, 2002a). The people who fall into the last two groups are unlikely to seek support to improve their literacy skills. Those who have a latent need believe that their skills are satisfactory and those individuals with an invisible need believe that their skills are stronger than they actually are. This means that very few people with needs perceive them or seek to improve their skills.

Stop and reflect

Individuals with poor levels of personal literacy face a range of different costs to themselves, their employers and to the country as a whole. What might some of these costs be?

Low levels of literacy impact at a variety of personal and social levels, disempowering individuals (Parsons and Bynner, 2002). It is therefore evident that people with low levels of literacy are in poorly paid jobs with few life chances.

People with poor levels of personal literacy:

- Are often employed in low-skilled and low-paid jobs. The DfES document *Skills for Life*: *Focus on Delivery to 2007* (2003b) identified that people with low levels of literacy earn, on average, 11 per cent less than their more qualified peers. They are also less likely to seek or gain promotion.

- Are more likely to experience more frequent and longer periods of unemployment. Leitch (HM Treasury, 2006) emphasises the findings from one survey that found that people holding literacy skills at level 1 are up to 10 per cent more likely to be in work than those with lower levels of literacy.

- Have less spending power and may face debt as a consequence.
- Are less likely to own their own home. There is evidence to suggest that people with low levels of literacy are more likely to be homeless than those who have higher levels of literacy.
- Are more likely to be dependent on state benefits. In 2003 approximately 3.5 million people were in receipt of benefits, of whom 40 per cent were likely to have basic skills needs (DfES, 2003a: 11).
- Are less likely to have private pensions.
- Are less likely to take part in community activities such as parent-governor roles or even voting.
- Are more likely to have children who also have difficulties with literacy. This can have several consequences. Parsons (2002b) conducted a survey that found that male criminal offenders were more likely to have come from a home where there was little interest or involvement in their education.
- Are more likely to be a part of the prison population. It has been found that nearly 80 per cent of prisoners have some literacy difficulties and function below level 1. The link between low levels of literacy and crime have been widely researched (Parsons, 2002b).
- Are more likely to suffer from ill health, lack of confidence and poor self-esteem.
- It is likely that literacy skills decline when they are not used. Adults with poor literacy skills who have difficulty accessing employment were found to have reduced skills as time passed. This phenomenon was found to be more noticeable amongst men than women (Bynner and Parsons, 2000).

Little wonder then that Leitch identifies the importance of functional literacy as a means of 'reducing income inequality' and improving people's 'life chances' (HM Treasury, 2006: 36).

Snippet

Language expresses identity, enables cooperation, and confers freedom.

The Kingman Report (DES, 1988: 7)

Meeting the challenge

Since the 1970s a variety of strategies have been developed to support learners as they improve their literacy skills. The chronology included in this section includes key developments regarding the teaching of English as part of compulsory education as well as within the lifelong learning sector because they are important steps to the current understanding we have of the way that English and literacy should be taught. There are many different factors involved in identifying and supporting adult learners with literacy needs. Current policies have grown from wider political and cultural developments including the concept of social justice, equality, employment and funding (Hamilton and Hillier, 2006).

● Chronology of key developments

- The Bullock Report – *A Language for Life* (DES, 1975) investigated English teaching in the compulsory sector.

- *English from 5 to 16* (DES, 1984): this document divided English teaching into four parts: speaking and listening, reading, writing, and knowledge about language (KAL).

- The Kingman Report – *The Report of the Committee of Inquiry into the Teaching of English Language* (DES, 1988) recommended a model of English language to be used within compulsory education.

- The Cox Report – *English for Ages 5–11* (DES, 1989) developed a framework for English teaching in the compulsory sector.

- The Further and Higher Education Act 1992.

- The Tomlinson Report – *Inclusive Learning* (Further Education Funding Council, 1996) investigated provision and learning experiences for learners with specific disabilities and/or difficulties. The report identified strategies for inclusive learning.

- The National Literacy Strategy (1998) produced an outline of how literacy should be taught in the compulsory sector.

- The Kennedy Report – *Learning Works: Widening Participation in Further Education* (Kennedy, 1997) investigated widening participation and the post-16 teaching and learning environment.

- The Moser Report – *A Fresh Start* (DfEE, 1999a) was published revealing the extent of the basic skills needs in the UK.

- The government White Paper *Learning to Succeed* (DfEE, 1999b) identified the fact that individuals with learning difficulties and disabilities were twice as likely to be unqualified or unemployed as their peers.

- *Skills for Life* was launched in 2000 following the publication of the Moser Report. This included nationally recognised standards, qualifications and targets for learners and tutors within the sector.

- *Breaking the Language Barriers* (DfEE, 2000a) reported on the findings of the working group set up to find out about numbers and the type of provision available for speakers of languages other than English (ESOL).

- *Freedom to Learn: Basic Skills for Learners with Learning Difficulties and/or Disabilities* (DfEE, 2000b) was published by the working group set up to identify skills needed and barriers faced by adults with learning difficulties and/or disabilities.

- This was followed in 2003 by the White Paper *21st Century Skills: Realising Our Potential* (DfES, 2003a). Explanation of the differences between basic skills and key skills was provided. Basic skills relate to underpinning skills at text, sentence and word levels whereas key skills are more closely linked with the way in which the underpinning skills are applied in vocational and academic subject areas.

- The Leitch Report – *Review of Skills: Prosperity for All in the Global Economy: World Class Skills* (HM Treasury, 2006) and the government White Paper *Further Education: Raising Skills, Improving Life Chances* (2006a). A demand-led system is being developed to ensure employers are able to access training and support to train their workforce to meet the challenges of the twenty-first century and the global economy.

In addition to recognising requirements for structured support in order for learners to develop their literacy and numeracy needs within the lifelong learning sector, an increasing recognition of the need for support situated in specific literacy domains, such as the workplace and targeted groups of individuals at risk of suffering from their lack of literacy skills, has resulted in an increasing range of innovative and carefully targeted programmes of study as well as the publication of resources designed to develop underpinning literacy skills in vocational contexts. Vulnerable groups at risk of social exclusion have been identified and supported as they develop their literacy skills. For example, the Home Office require offenders to be assessed to identify their level of literacy, and provision is offered to support their learning needs (Parsons, 2002a: 9). Campaigns such as Sure Start have targeted specific groups of learners. In the case of Sure Start, literacy and numeracy skills have been provided to enable parents to support their children as they develop their own skills at school.

Snippet

 Literacy as Freedom.
Slogan for UNESCO's United Nations Literacy Decade 2003-2012

Summary

- The importance of literacy has changed as the demands of society have developed.
- There are different definitions of literacy.
- Context is a key feature of the way in which literacy is used.
- People who have access to dominant or formal literacies have access to society.
- People who rely on marginalised literacies are often disempowered.
- People switch literacies depending upon the audience, purpose and context in which communication is taking place.
- Strategies to support literacy development are bound by social, political and economic contexts.

Where next?

Texts

Crowther, J., Hamilton, M. and Tett, L. (2001) *Powerful Literacies*, Leicester: NIACE

Shrubshall, P. and Roberts, C. (2005) *Case Study Four: Embodying Literacy and Making Movement Literate in Complementary Therapy and Personal Care Classes*, London: NRDC

Websites

www.basic-skills.co.uk

www.dfes.gov.uk/readwriteplus

www.lifelonglearning.co.uk

www.literacytrust.org.uk

www.niace.org.uk

www.nrdc.org.uk

1

Skills audit

There is an expectation that vocational and academic tutors in the lifelong learning sector should be able to demonstrate literacy skills that will enable them to support the needs of their own learners, or be certified to a minimum of at least level 3. The minimum core was introduced by FENTO in 2003 to all post-16 teacher education programmes. The core outlines the knowledge and personal skills that are required of all tutors working in the lifelong learning sector. The minimum core was reviewed in 2006 and a new set of guidelines introduced in 2007. Knowledge and understanding of the core skills were assessed through national testing for the first time in the same year.

This chapter is a starting point for you to identify and reflect upon your individual language and literacy needs on the journey towards QTLS. The literacy and language questions forming Part two of the audit can be found at **www.pearsoned.co.uk/hickey**. The questions are designed to help you identify areas for further study and lead towards an **action plan** that will help you work towards achieving the literacy requirements of QTLS.

Action plan
Document to plan progress towards learning goals.

Stop and reflect

> Why do you think that literacy requirements for practitioners in the lifelong learning sector have been established? It may help to discuss this question with a group of peers.

Educators need to be able to communicate effectively with a range of people in different circumstances and contexts. Practitioners come into contact with learners, colleagues, managers and representatives of other organisations, such as external verifiers and inspectors, and clear communication is important. In addition to delivering sessions, where modelling good practice is also a factor, there are all sorts of meetings that a practitioner must attend. Good-quality written work, demonstrating an awareness of grammar, writing techniques and the appropriate conventions, is essential for a trainee working towards QTLS and as a professional in the lifelong learning sector. The ability to read and interpret texts (both fiction and non-fiction) is also an expectation at this level; think about all those memos, emails, course documents and textbooks that practitioners read. In addition, vocational and academic subject tutors who have achieved QTLS must be able to support their own learners as they acquire the essential skills necessary for them to achieve their own goals.

> ## Standards for teachers, tutors and trainers in the lifelong learning sector
>
> Domain A: Professional values and practice.
>
> AS 4   Reflection and evaluation of own practice and continuing professional development as teachers.
>
> AS 7   Improving the quality of practice.

Why complete a skills audit?

A personal skills audit identifies the level and type of skill demonstrated by individuals. A skills audit is also a term used in an educational setting to identify the levels and skills required to achieve a particular learning programme. The personal skills audit found in this chapter requires consideration of language and literacy skills integral to QTLS outlined in the literacy elements of the minimum core. It provides an opportunity for reflection upon individual strengths and weaknesses and an opportunity to create a plan in order to develop personal skills and knowledge as necessary.

The audit is self-assessed. There are different forms of self-assessment including 'self testing, self rating and reflective questioning' (Boud, 1995). This skills audit contains components of all three types of self-assessment. Part one of the audit is about identifying current levels of qualification. Part two, comprising questions on language and literacy skills or knowledge, is self-testing and self-rating. This means that some of the questions have correct answers, or an example of a correct answer, whilst others require reflection upon current states of knowledge or skill. Part three of the audit is a **SWOT analysis**. It offers an opportunity to explore individual strengths and weaknesses as well as perceived opportunities and threats on the journey towards achieving the literacy requirement of the minimum core.

SWOT analysis
Reflecting on strengths, weaknesses, opportunities and threats of individuals/ organisations.

The final part of this chapter is about action planning and strategies for developing the language and literacy skills that have been identified during the audit, additional **diagnostic assessment** undertaken elsewhere, during the course of the teacher-training programme and during time at work.

Diagnostic assessment
Focused assessment identifying strengths, weaknesses and knowledge/skills gaps.

Many educators do not possess a level 3 English language qualification; others have higher level qualifications than those identified as essential but may have completed their studies some years ago. Everyone has strengths and weaknesses. We all have **spiky profiles**! An audit of language and literacy skills at level 3 is a useful initial indicator of the areas that need to be developed in order to achieve the minimum core literacy criteria. For trainees who have level 3, or higher, a skills audit is a useful way of identifying skills that may need a brush-up to enable effective learner support within particular academic or vocational curriculum areas.

Spiky profile
Indicates that individuals have different skills, strengths and weaknesses.

Effective self assessment, reflection and action planning will help:

- Develop self-awareness
- Identify learning needs
- Set challenging yet realistic goals
- Monitor progress.

When should I undertake the skills audit?

You can undertake the audit now and begin action planning for your language and literacy development as soon as you are ready.

If you have just started working towards QTLS you may not be entirely sure about what is expected of you yet so you may wish to wait for a few weeks until you have settled into the course and have some experience of the kinds of spoken and written communications that are required of you before completing the SWOT analysis. However, there is no reason why you should not complete it now if you wish: it may help you to feel more confident about the skills you already possess as a trainee and also as an educator in the lifelong learning sector.

It is important to review the SWOT analysis and the action plan throughout the year as skills and knowledge develop. A new skills or knowledge need may be identified and, hopefully, the early targets on the action plan will be achieved.

Remember! The skills audit is a form of self-assessment. It is a proven fact that when people undertake **ipsative assessment** they are more likely to underestimate their knowledge and skills. Try to be realistic and fair to yourself when you undertake the skills audit.

Ipsative assessment
Independent self-assessment of an individual's strengths and weaknesses.

Part one: Current qualifications

This part of the skills audit will help you identify and reflect on your current levels of language and literacy qualification. Make a note of the answers to these two questions.

1. What is the highest English language or communication qualification you hold?

2. How long ago did you gain the qualification?

● Part one: feedback

Levels
Nationally recognised standards of skill/knowledge required for qualifications and their recognition by employers/education providers.

The National Qualifications Framework (NQF) identifies the **level** of skill and knowledge that different qualifications require and the levels at which qualifications will be recognised by employers and educational providers. Qualifications are grouped together by level. For example, level 1 is pre-GCSE; level 2 is GCSE grade C and above; level 3 relates to qualifications such as A levels and BTEC Nationals. Further information can be found by visiting the Qualifications and Curriculum Authority (QCA) website. The QCA offers information about the types of qualifications that exist, the National Qualifications Framework and the way in which awarding bodies are regulated.

If you have no formal English or communication qualifications you should identify the skills that you currently have at level 2 before progressing to level 3. The website for the Move On National Project for numeracy and literacy will help you to assess your current skills; brush up on areas of knowledge and understanding; take up to nine practice tests to help you gain a level 2 qualification and finally help you to find a test centre if you wish to gain a level 2 literacy certificate. You can register at this website to develop your literacy knowledge and skills at your own pace. Alternatively, the organisation delivering your QTLS programme may offer additional support or tuition to help you improve your literacy. It should be a priority on your action plan to find out what resources are available to you to upgrade your literacy skills.

If you have: a GCSE or GCE-O level at grade C or above; CSE grade 1; a communications key skills award at level 2; a recognised ACCESS 2 qualification; Irish Leaving Certificate or appropriate Scottish Qualifications Authority awards then you have attained a level 2 qualification. If you have a different qualification the Qualifications and Curriculum Authority website may be able to provide an explanation of how your qualification relates to the different levels. If your certificate is an overseas qualification you may need to refer to the National Academic Recognition Information Centre (NARIC). Qualification equivalence may also be determined by the organisation where you are studying. Depending upon how long ago you attained your qualification you may wish to take the assessment to be found on the Move On website to find out whether you need to revise some knowledge and skills before progressing to level 3. The longer ago that you gained your qualification the more likely it is that you will have forgotten some of the material that you covered.

If you have a communications or English literature or language A level then you have a level 3 qualification which covers elements of the minimum core but which does not cover all aspects of the curriculum. Even if you have a degree in English or a related subject you will still need to pass the literacy test to achieve QTLS. Complete Parts two and three of the skills audit to find out what areas you need to revisit in order to pass the literacy component of QTLS and to best support your own learners.

Part two: Self-assessment

There are forty-four questions divided into seven sections to reflect the structure of Part one of *Literacy for QTLS* which can be found on the Companion Website to accompany this book at **www.pearsoned.co.uk/hickey**. The assessment is not a race or a test to catch people out. It is designed to stimulate reflection and to help individuals identify their own learning goals if a skills or knowledge shortage is identified. It can be completed as a whole or section by section.

Part two can be either self marked or peer marked. If a number of trainees are working in a study group the skills audit can be used as the basis of a discussion about the kinds of knowledge and skills required and the levels of confidence that individual trainees have.

Initial assessment
Indicator of the levels that a learner is currently working at.

The self-assessment can be used rather like an **initial assessment** to identify broad areas of knowledge or skill that are sound or that need to be acquired. There may be some areas that can immediately be identified for development. If there is a particular section that remains uncompleted because of prior negative experiences or because you 'know' that you will find it difficult, add this topic to your action plan but remember to break it down into manageable chunks. The self-assessment may also have helped you to identify specific skills and knowledge in need of development. Turn to the relevant chapters to address the learning goals that have been identified.

Alternatively, the results from the skills audit will have identified areas that are strengths. The chapters of *Literacy for QTLS* covering these areas of the minimum core may benefit from a skim read – just as a refresher.

Part three: SWOT analysis

Originally a SWOT analysis was developed as a business tool. It can also be applied to the needs of individuals. The upper boxes are about internal factors whilst the two lower boxes require participants to reflect on perceived external factors.

The results from the second part of the audit and from any diagnostic assessment you have carried out should enable you to identify your strengths and weaknesses in the two upper boxes. The two lower boxes offer an opportunity for you to reflect upon the external influences in your journey towards QTLS. What are the 'opportunities' that are available to you? E.g. Formalising prior knowledge and experience or sharing good practice. The box headed 'threats' is a chance for you to consider the barriers that may exist to developing language and literacy skills, such as time pressures and availability of resources. A template for a SWOT analysis is available on the Companion Website. Alternatively create your own using the model provided here:

Strengths	Weaknesses
Opportunities	Threats

SWOT analysis diagram

Creating an action plan

Having completed all sections of the skills audit you have now assessed whether your knowledge and skills are secure or not. The next step is to identify actions to develop, extend or consolidate the skills and knowledge that you require to achieve the literacy minimum core.

An action plan is rather like a route planner. Having reflected on existing levels of skill and knowledge an effective action plan will outline realistic learning outcomes (what you are going to do), identify how you are going to achieve your outcomes (resources, people who may be able to help, processes) and set a date for when you will achieve each outcome.

Outcomes are sometimes described as goals. Goals can be short-term or long-term depending upon how important they are and how many steps you will have to make in order to achieve them. Goals should be broken down into manageable chunks. Other ways of describing these chunks are steps, targets or milestones. The word used depends on the environment where the action plan is created.

Sometimes **soft goals** are set. These goals/targets are subjective and harder to measure because they are related to emotions – often, confidence. For example, a trainee has bad memories of learning grammar from their school days. The trainee may feel concerned that they cannot tackle grammatical frameworks successfully. The action plan that this trainee produces will require them to break grammatical frameworks into small but manageable chunks. One of their long-term goals will be to overcome their confidence barrier.

An action plan should set SMART targets that lead towards learning goals. SMART is a commonly used acronym standing for:

Soft goals/ targets
Subjective goals usually related to emotions such as confidence.

2

Specific — Targets should be specific. It is not SMART to identify 'learn about punctuation' as a target. It is much more SMART to identify 'list the eight uses of a capital letter'. Some of the outcomes identified may be soft outcomes. This means that they are psychological rather than concrete. If you have faced a barrier to learning about grammar ever since primary school then you will need to include some soft targets to help you build your confidence and overcome your barriers.

Measurable — What are the criteria for success? Consider the verbs that you use to describe your targets. For example, the word 'understand' is too vague. How can you identify whether you have understood something or not? The verb 'list' on the other hand is much more specific and can be demonstrated.

Achievable — It is important to set targets that will challenge you as you develop skills and knowledge but it is also important to break skills into manageable chunks so that you do not become disheartened.

Realistic — Sometimes the word relevant is used here. In both cases the words are about keeping motivated. A target demanding that you know everything there is to know about punctuation by next Tuesday would be unrealistic and irrelevant unless you happened to be teaching punctuation.

Time-bound — It is useful to have a date by which tasks should be completed. A series of dates progressing from target to target en route to your goal will help keep you on track.

You can find a template for an action plan on the Companion Website at **www.pearsoned.co.uk/hickey**. You can print this out or download and customise it to suit your own needs.

An action plan is a tool to help you progress towards your learning goals. Use it like a map to help you keep on track with your learning. This means that it should be reviewed regularly. Celebrate targets that you have achieved and goals when you reach them. Review those targets and goals you have not fully met by their deadlines. Decide what action you will take to meet them. Add new goals broken down into manageable targets as your professional development continues. Remember to keep the targets SMART.

Summary

- Literacy at level 3 is one of the three minimum core strands that must be achieved in order to attain QTLS.
- Elements within the minimum core have been identified as necessary for professional practice and in order for practitioners to support their learners as they develop their own literacy skills within academic and vocational settings.
- The personal skills audit is designed as a tool to encourage reflection leading to the creation of an action plan for the development of literacy and language skills and knowledge.
- The skills audit covers the personal elements of the minimum core. These include: reading, writing, grammar, punctuation, spelling, speaking, listening and non-verbal communication.
- The skills audit is an indicator. Further, more focused, diagnostic assessment may be required. It may also be a requirement of the course trainees undertake in the journey towards QTLS.
- An action plan outlines what needs to be done, how it will be achieved and when it will be done.
- Action plans should set SMART targets in order for short-term or long-term learning goals to be achieved.
- The action plan is a working document. It should be reviewed and updated regularly.
- New goals may be added as professional development continues.
- Celebrate achievements.

Where next?

For a fuller diagnostic assessment you may need to access other assessment tools. Many organisations and institutions have developed their own level 3 assessments to help trainees identify skills and knowledge gaps; these may be mandatory to the course. There are also commercially available assessments, paper-based and interactive, such as bksb (basic and keySKILLBUILDER) subscribed to by many lifelong learning sector providers.

There are other sources of assessment available on the Internet. Many of these assessments are free, such as the ones offered by the government for secondary and primary school teachers. Other sites contain assessments that are specific to particular areas of language and literacy, such as punctuation or spelling.

Texts

Johnson, A. (1998) (2nd edn) *English for Secondary Teachers: An Audit and Self-Study Guide*, London: Letts

Websites

www.move-on.org.uk Move On

www.naric.org.uk National Academic Recognition Information Centre (NARIC)

www.qca.org.uk Qualifications and Curriculum Authority (QCA)

3 Reading

Snippet

>
> It was after I joined the army as a boy soldier. The army education corps told all us new recruits that the only reason we couldn't read (we had an average reading age of 11 year olds) was because we didn't read. He held up a book we should have read at school, *Janet and John*, and told us all, 'From today, that all changes.'
>
> Andy McNab, Reading Champion for the National Literacy Trust – involving boys and men in creating a reading culture.

This chapter focuses on the reading skills that you use to engage with texts as a trainee working towards QTLS, as a professional working in a teaching and learning environment and on the essential reading skills that you may need to help your own learners to develop in order to complete their academic or vocational course successfully. The way that you use this chapter will depend upon your current levels of skill and knowledge. You may wish to work through the chapter to rehearse the skills identified or to brush up on specific techniques. Alternatively you may wish to use the chapter as a stimulus to support the reading skills of your own learners or to develop materials using some of the strategies described here. Having read through this chapter and completed the activities, you should be able to provide evidence for the following standards.

Minimum core elements

A2

- Interpreting written texts.
- Knowledge of how textual features support reading.
- Understanding the barriers to accessing text.

Part B Personal Language Skills

- Find, and select from, a range of reference material and sources of information, including the Internet.
- Use and reflect on a range of reading strategies to interpret texts and to locate information or meaning.
- Identify and record key information or messages contained within reading material using note-taking techniques.

Fluent reading skills

Reading is rather like driving a car. Experienced drivers do not think about the different skills involved in the act of driving. When asked to describe the different stages involved, drivers are often unable to break driving into its component parts. Drivers have, or should have, **automaticity**. This means that drivers follow through a sequence of mechanical activities in order to control their cars without having to think about what comes next in a sequence of actions. Fluent readers know what they want from the text they are reading, ask questions that engage with the text and then use different reading strategies depending on the **purpose** of the text and what they want to get out of it. However, fluent readers do not consciously identify strategies before looking at the material nor are they necessarily conscious of switching strategy when their purpose for reading changes.

Automaticity
A skill that is automatic.

Purpose
The writer's intention.

Task

Read this extract and then answer the questions that follow.

Consonantal articulation necessitates manipulation of the eggressive airstream in the vocal tract. The pulmonic eggressive airstream is either compressed or rarified. Articulation is either active or passive. There are eleven articulators of which speech formed in the pharyngeal manner is more common to languages such as Arabic. Post-alveolar classification is a subclassification of alveolar articulation but can be classified separately.
   Effective formulation of speech requires anticipatory coarticulation including labialization, palatalization and velarization.

a. How did you feel about reading the passage?

b. Briefly explain what the paragraph is about.

c. Identify the strategies that you used to work out the meaning of the passage.

d. How did you tackle any words that you had not previously encountered? Consider the sound of the word and the meaning of the word.

Reading a difficult text requires concentration and several rereadings in order to make sense of the contents: it can be tiring and time consuming. It can also be frustrating and if a learner struggles to make sense of a text often enough it can lower self-confidence, which in turn impacts upon motivation. The paragraph in the task explains the way in which consonant sounds are made by air being forced from the lungs. The problem is that the explanation is filled with specialist terminology derived from Latin and Greek roots. There is no background **context** to help work out meaning and no images, diagrams or captions that might have made the passage easier to understand. Look at this alternative explanation of the same passage:

Context
The situation in which the text is used.

The organs can be either passive - the air flows over them - or active in that they change the airflow. Air flow is changed by eleven organs of speech, though some organs such as the pharynx are more commonly used in languages such as Arabic. Sound produced by the alveolar ridge (the hard part of your mouth directly behind your front teeth) is sometimes divided into two groups of sound depending where on or near the ridge the sound is made. Sounds overlap. The organs of speech anticipate sounds that follow one another and shape themselves accordingly.

In this passage the language is much more straightforward. Some sentences are shorter and one of the specialist words is explained: a diagram or illustration would have made this passage even easier to follow.

People use many different strategies to make sense of a difficult text. You may have scanned the whole passage to gain some sense of meaning and then returned to the start for a more detailed reading. Some readers may have been able to apply previous knowledge and understanding to the passage. Other strategies may have included looking for readily identifiable words, using a dictionary or asking someone who can understand the text to explain it. Readers often reread a difficult passage many times; fluent readers predict content forwards and backwards. This means that as well as working out what might be coming next, a fluent reader will identify where they are struggling to understand a text, and, if information is provided later that helps interpret the difficult section, the reader will refer back to work out unfamiliar words or complicated sentences that came earlier and then read forward again so that they gain a sense of the whole passage. This is a form of contextualisation because it builds understanding on existing knowledge.

Sounding out new words also draws on a range of strategies and may vary according to personal preference; they can be matched to known words that look similar to the new word; they can be broken down into prefixes, roots and suffixes; or syllables; or even individual sounds. The way that a word sounds can then be worked out by fitting the various parts back together. Readers who are not fluent may vocalise these strategies if they use them at all whereas fluent readers internalise the sounding-out and rehearsal of the complete word. Some readers may prefer to use a dictionary that provides guidance on pronunciation and a key to pronunciation based on the **international phonetic alphabet** (IPA). Meaning of new words can be gained from a dictionary. During the course of reading, meaning is more likely to be derived from applying knowledge of context; from similar looking words on the principle that the word is likely to have a similar meaning; or words are broken down into their separate parts – roots and affixes – readers drawing on their knowledge of the separate parts to deduce meaning.

International phonetic alphabet Provides a symbol for each sound that is made.

The four-searchlights model for reading provides a diagrammatic overview of the different strategies or cues that fluent readers use to decode texts.

A model for reading – the four searchlights

There are a number of models that have been developed to explain the process by which we decode or read the words and sentences on the page and make sense of the ideas contained in them. The four-searchlights model has been supporting learners as they develop essential reading skills since 1998 when the National Literacy Strategy was introduced (now part of the National Primary Strategy; DfES, 2006b). It has been applied across the curriculum from primary level through to supporting adult learners.

Cue Means by which a reader is able to decode the text.

Each searchlight or **cue** provides some information about the text. Fluent readers use a range of strategies enabling them to switch between cues to comprehend a text as required. The fewer the searchlights that a reader can effectively use the more likely it is that they will struggle because they are dependent on a limited number of cues, so when they become stuck they cannot supplement their knowledge using another cue to work out meaning.

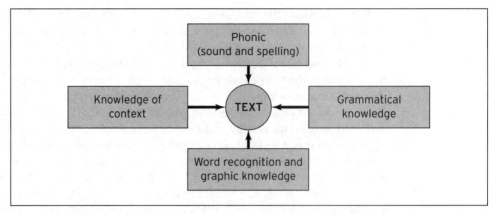

The four-searchlights model for reading

Source: Department for Education and Skills (2006b: 4), *National Primary Strategy*. © Crown copyright material is reproduced with the permission of the Controller of HMSO and Queen's Printer for Scotland.

Semantic cues
Knowledge of context that helps reader understand meaning of a text.

Syntactic cues
Knowledge of grammar/word order that help work out text's meaning.

Fluent readers use their knowledge of a subject or topic – or the **semantic cues** – to predict what is coming next or to work out the meaning of text. Knowledge of context also involves using headings, subheadings and illustrations to predict what a text is about. They are able to apply their understanding of grammar and word order – the **syntactic cues** – to identify the relationship between words and ideas and they are able to use the grapho-phonic cues (the way letters correspond to sounds) to work out difficult words.

The Rose Report (DfES, 2006c), developing conclusions first drawn by Ofsted in 2002, identifies that beginner readers need to learn to recognise words and develop language comprehension skills rather than rely on knowledge of context. Word recognition and language comprehension are distinct processes. Comprehension draws on knowledge, an understanding of the language system and an understanding of the vocabulary in the text. Understanding of individual words is part of the language process. Readers have to be able to draw on a store of familiar words and apply phonic rules in order to decode words and add to their store (DfES, 2006b).

● Whole words

Readers do not always need to read every word or indeed every letter in every word to know what a word says.

Task

Read the passage below. It first made its appearance on the Internet in 2003.

Aoccdrnig to a rscheearch at Cmabrigde Uinervtisy, it deosn't mttaer in waht oredr the ltteers in a wrod are, the olny iprmoetnt tihng is taht the frist and lsat ltteer be at the rghit pclae. The rset can be a toatl mses and you can sitll raed it wouthit porbelm. Tihs is bcuseae the huamn mnid deos not raed ervey lteter by istlef, but the wrod as a wlohe.

www.mrc-cbu.cam.ac.uk/~mattd/Cmabrigde/

According to a researcher at Cambridge University, it doesn't matter in what order the letters in a word are placed, the only important thing is that the first and last letter be in the correct position. The rest can be jumbled but you can still read the word without problem. This is because the human mind does not read every letter by itself but the word as a whole.

Although the passage above is a spoof, research undertaken at Nottingham University has identified that fluent readers take in the first and last letters of words and often do not notice if middle letters are 'randomized' (Rawlinson, 1976).

Fluent readers recognise words by a variety of methods, including shape and letter patterns or strings. Where whole words are recognised the reading process progresses smoothly. However, when readers come across words that they are unfamiliar with, in terms of the links between sound and letter shape or word meaning, the process of reading slows whilst the reader breaks the word down, sounds it out, reconstructs it and repeats it. The reader then has to understand the meaning of the new word by context, by deconstructing the main part of the word from any prefixes and suffixes or by matching the word to another word that looks the same and that the reader knows about. The flow of the text has been interrupted. The reader has to retrace their steps to take up the threads of the text once more. Specialist or technical terminology often slows readers down because they are unfamiliar with the words. Vocational and academic subjects often use specialised technical terms. QTLS is no exception to this.

● Semantic cues

Fluent readers identify information about a text before they start reading. They make an analysis of the text so that they can begin to work out what the content might be about. It is easier to recognise the textual features of some types of text than others.

> ### Task
>
> Create a mind map or a list, on your own or with a group of peers, identifying some of the different types of text you come into contact with as a professional working in the lifelong learning sector (e.g. syllabuses and emails).

Hopefully you will have identified a diverse range of texts that you come into contact with as a professional working in the lifelong learning sector. One of the overarching standards (AK 6.1) for practitioners working towards QTLS requires knowledge of relevant statutes and codes of practice. This means that if they are not already on your list you should add summaries, reports and regulations. Information, analysis and debate of educational issues are found in professional journals and newspapers. Add these to your list or mind map if they are not already there.

Each of the different kinds of text provides a fluent reader with information to help them predict how to read a text and about the contents of a text. This information is gained from the appearance of the text, from layout, from images, from sentence structure and from the kind of language that the text uses.

● Purpose and audience

Texts have a range of different purposes including: describing, entertaining, explaining, informing, instructing and persuading:

- **Description** This kind of text uses describing words such as adjectives and adverbs (words that describe the way that actions are completed e.g. *slowly*) in order to create a sense of what something or someone is like. Descriptions can be very detailed or else they can give an overview. In both cases the description enables the reader to create a picture of what something is like in their mind.

- **Entertainment** This type of text can take many forms such as short stories, novels or even play scripts. These kinds of entertainment texts are fiction and tell a story. Other kinds of entertainment texts include poetry, humour, biographies and travel writing. The last two examples on this list are also informative because they provide information about a person or a place. People read all these different kinds of text for enjoyment.

- **Explanation** This kind of text explains how something happens, how something works; details the causes of an event or provides a definition for something. Explanation texts can also explain the reason for events. Explanation texts can make use of charts and diagrams. The first part of an explanation text will provide a statement about the content of the text and a definition of key words. Explanations are often written in the present tense. The difference between an explanation and an instruction is that an instruction tells the reader how to do something although some of the features of the text may be the same, such as using sequence words like 'first', 'then' and 'next' because it is important for both text types that information is presented in a series of logical steps. Other features of information are words that indicate cause such as the words 'because' and 'so'. This paragraph about explanations is an example of an explanation!

- **Information** This form of text includes memos, notices and reports. They both tell the reader something they need to know. Notices answer questions: how, why, what, where and when. This form of writing includes facts and may use headings, subheadings and bullet points to make the content clear to the reader.

- **Instruction** This type of text tells the reader how to do something.

- **Persuasion** This kind of writing uses language and often image to put forward a particular point of view in the hope of persuading the reader to agree with the writer. Advertising is a good example of persuasive writing. Speech writers also use language and **rhetorical devices** to persuade people to their point of view.

Rhetorical devices
Techniques used to persuade listeners/readers towards viewpoint of the text.

Genre
In literature, the type of written text.

Audience
Intended readership of a text.

Writers choose the best **genre** for their purpose and their intended audience. Texts can have primary and secondary purposes. For example, the writer may intend to persuade you of something but will do it in an entertaining way. The primary purpose is to persuade whilst the secondary purpose is to entertain. The structure, layout and content will also depend on the intended **audience**.

In addition to layout you may have noticed pictures, diagrams, tables and illustrations. Other structural features include: headings, subheadings, bullet points and

Stop and reflect

Think about some of the reading that you have undertaken during the last week. It does not matter whether it was a textbook you are using for your teacher-training course, an email at work, the novel you are currently reading, the advert you read whilst you were waiting for the bus or even the back of the packet of cereal you found yourself reading this morning. Think about the different types of textual features you might have noticed about each genre (e.g. layout).

numbered points. You may have also noticed some information about the language. The textual features you may have identified include: specialist or technical vocabulary, use of first person (I) or second person (you), adverbs and adjectives, **rhetorical questions**, slang, direct speech, short or long sentences. Different kinds of writing make use of different features. For example, instructions make use of short sentences, **imperative** forms of the verb, numbers, bullet points and words like 'first', 'next' and 'finally' to sequence the text. By contrast, persuasive texts are more likely to make use of lists of three, to use quotations, plays on words, rhetorical questions and more use of 'we' and 'you' in order to involve the audience. Fluent readers can scan a piece of writing and recognise the textual features to work out what type of text they are going to encounter. It is easier to think of the indicative features of some types of texts more quickly than others.

Rhetorical question
It does not expect an answer from the reader/listener.

Imperative
Form of verb that gives orders, commands and instructions.

3

Best practice

Readers need knowledge about language in order to access different types of text. According to the *Adult Literacy Core Curriculum* (DfES, 2001a) readers need to 'recognise how language and other textual features are used to achieve different purposes.' They should also be able to 'understand that choice of language and textual features reflect the purpose of a text.'

Quotes from www.dfes.gov.uk/curriculum_literacy/tree/reading/readingcomp/l1/2/ (accessed 22 April 07)

Reading strategies

There are several different reading strategies that are commonly used to interpret texts and locate information or meaning in different kinds of material. Fluent readers choose the most appropriate reading strategy automatically; less able readers tend to believe that they need to read each word in turn.

● Skimming

Skimming
Reading a text quickly to gain the gist of what it's about.

Skimming involves looking over the surface of a text quickly to see whether it is likely to be of interest or not. Readers use clues such as the layout, headings, key words and illustrations to help them decide whether they wish to read the text in more detail or not.

Group task

Work with a group of 8-10 peers if possible. Each find a news, journal or magazine article about an education related topic. Photocopy the article onto A4 paper. Carefully remove the headline or title from the article. Ideally both the article and the headline should be re-photocopied so that the following matching activity cannot be based on appearance and paper type. The group should mix their articles and headlines together. The next step is to identify which headline belongs to which article – obviously members of the group should refrain from identifying their own choice of article and headline. Talk about the strategies that you used to match the headlines with their respective paragraphs.

Readers should identify the key words or ideas in the headlines then skim the articles looking for the key words and ideas. Many readers look for information which stands out from the rest of an article such as subheadings and words that have been emboldened or italicised. Quotations can provide useful information as can pictures and their captions.

● Scanning

Scanning
Reading a text in search of specific words or information.

Key words
Those essential for specific understanding and communication.

Readers use this technique when they are looking quickly for specific information. **Scanning** means that readers check a text for a **key word** or words. The reader identifies the term or word that is being searched for and looks quickly over the page for the term or word. This technique is often used when readers look at newspapers, newsletters, emails, memos and textbooks. Meaning in whole paragraphs can often be scanned by reading the first sentence of the paragraph. This sentence is usually the topic sentence which explains the main point of the paragraph whilst the body of the paragraph expands or exemplifies the point. A scan of the text allows readers to decide whether the material is relevant or not.

Skimming and scanning both involve rapid eye movement, immediate word recognition and ability to use layout, headings and illustrations to provide clues. Readers scanning for information may also use an ability to pick out numbers, capital letters, spelling patterns or key words.

Fluent readers identify words by shape, by letter strings and patterns. Remember, using block capitals to emphasise a key word or term will not help your learners to memorise or recognise the word again because block capitals do not offer the same visual cues as words presented in a lower-case format.

Task

Skimming and scanning both involve whole word recognition. Complete this word search of ten words frequently used in planning. As you complete the search identify the strategies that you employ to recognise the whole words. The solution to this word search can be found at the back of the book.

activity	aims		assessment	criteria	evaluation
method	outcomes		smart	strategy	resources

```
E  T  N  E  M  S  S  E  S  S  A
V  S  O  V  E  M  D  G  A  D  Y
A  R  T  A  N  O  U  T  C  G  O
L  U  A  T  H  O  D  I  E  O  U
U  S  Y  T  I  V  I  T  C  A  T
A  S  E  T  E  R  A  I  M  S  C
T  M  R  A  T  R  G  O  A  T  O
I  A  C  R  T  E  R  I  A  L  M
O  R  E  S  O  U  R  C  E  S  E
N  T  C  R  I  T  E  R  I  A  S
```

● Detailed or close reading

Detailed reading is about comprehension of the text. This means that the reader has to interact with the text. Detailed reading means active reading. It may mean that readers go back over sections of the text to check that they have really understood the content. Consider the assignments that you are currently working on as part of your course. It is sensible to read everything contained in an assignment brief to find out exactly what you need to do. The steps for detailed reading include a preliminary skimming of the text to get the gist of what it is about. The reader will then interact with the text considering what they already know about the subject and what it is that they wish to know. If there are questions to be answered the reader will identify the key words within the questions and look for the answers in the text based on the key words.

When a reader is making a detailed reading, eye movement will be slower and may involve the reader going back over material to check meaning and also to make links between ideas.

There are a number of useful strategies to use when making a detailed reading. You may find them useful in your own reading. Modelling the strategies in your classes will help your learners read for detail more effectively.

KWL This is a mnemonic for the steps to a successful detailed reading of a text. First make a list of what you already **know** about the topic. Next identify some of the things that you **want** to know about the topic and finally, having read the text, identify what you have **learnt** from the text. A KWL grid is set out like this:

What do I **know** about reading strategies?	What do I **want** to know?	What have I **learnt**?

SQ3R This stands for **survey, question, read, recite** and **review**. It explains how fluent readers think their way through a text when they are reading.

Fluent readers gain an overview of a text that they are going to read by making a **survey** of the text. They may skim through the text reading titles and subtitles. Pictures, diagrams and graphs can also help fluent readers gain an overview of what a text is about. Sometimes layout provides useful clues because information is placed in different fonts, underlined, italicised or placed in a box so that it stands out from the rest of the text. In academic papers there is often an abstract at the start of the document that provides an overview of the content. Sometimes there are summaries containing key points at the end of a text. These features help a reader to decide what the author thinks is key content in the text.

Having gained an overview of the text, fluent readers then ask **questions** of the text. The readers are actively engaging with the text. Some of the questions they ask

Literal
Words interpreted in a way which everyone understands.

Infer
Read meaning into words beyond what's written.

themselves may be **literal**. This means that the answer is explained in the text. Other questions may be **inferential** because although the text does not state the answer explicitly it is inferred by the language that the writer uses. Other questions may be there to activate the reader's own knowledge of the topic; some questions may be raised to help the reader make an evaluation of the text whilst other questions may be raised to help the reader to apply conclusions drawn from the text to another situation. Fluent readers do not necessarily start and finish a text with the same set of questions. Reading and reflection can raise new questions.

Readers should then **reread** the text in detail looking for specific answers to their questions and generating new questions as necessary.

These answers are 'recited'. Quite simply this means that the reader makes a note of the answers in their own words or recalls them to mind.

The **review** stage of the process is when the reader goes back to the questions that have been generated and decides whether or not the text has provided the answers or if further clarification is required.

● Critical reading

Implicit
When meaning can be understood from the language used.

Bias
Favouring one point of view.

This type of reading involves identifying **implicit** information or reading between the lines. Some texts may be **biased** in a particular direction or towards a specific viewpoint. Critical readers distinguish between fact and opinion. They identify whether the text is biased or not. For example, to some people a guerrilla may be a hero, to others a guerrilla is a criminal – it depends on viewpoint. The language that a writer uses will let the reader know what the writer's viewpoint is. This means that by looking at the language the reader can infer what is not necessarily explicitly stated.

Readers should ask these kinds of questions of a text:

● **What?** What is the text about? What does the content tell you? Is it accurate?

● **Why?** Why did the writer create this text? Or in other words what is the writer's intended purpose?

● **Where?** Is the text relevant? Is there anything about the location of the writer, the text or the material being covered that you should take into consideration?

● **When?** Is the text current?

● **Who?** Who is the writer? What is their relationship to the topic being covered?

● **How?** How has the writer structured the text? How has the writer used language? For example, if the language is emotive is the writer biased? How is the text relevant to my needs?

This rhyme by Rudyard Kipling (1990) may be more memorable for people with a more auditory learning preference:

> I keep six honest serving-men
> (They taught me all I knew);
> Their names are What and Why and When
> And How and Where and Who.
>
> Rudyard Kipling from *The Elephant's Child*

Note-taking techniques

Reading for study and research means taking notes. The first thing to do is to familiarise yourself with the material. This may involve skimming over it to get the gist. Then read through it again looking for the key points. It is important to filter information as it is being read. Is it a key point or is it a supporting example?

Some key word/topic identification can be done using a highlighter or by underlining, provided the text is yours. This is the time to apply SQ3R. By generating questions, reading relevant sections of text and by recalling key points, information can be filtered and classified. The only thing that remains to be done is for it to be organised.

There are different ways of organising notes. Preferred note-taking style may depend on prior experience and practice, preferred learning styles and the purpose of the note-taking:

- **Linear notes** This kind of note-taking uses sentences and paragraphs.

- **Mind maps** This is a very visual way for creating notes. Key words are placed on the page and then joined together with lines to show their relationship.

- **Spider diagrams** The key topic is placed in the centre of the page. Words and phrases related to the key topic radiate outwards from this point like the legs of a spider.

- **Diagrammatic representation** Sometimes it is easier to draw something in a simplified form and show what happens through labels, arrows and key words. Science experiments and geographical cycles are often recorded in this way.

- **Flow charts** A process can be recorded by a flow chart that identifies key ideas and their relationship to one another.

- **Storyboarding** A narrative or cycle can be recorded using a storyboard. The page is divided into a number of boxes. Each box represents a stage in the story or the process and is given a title. The boxes should show logical progression. Then it becomes a simple matter to place key words and brief sentences in the correct 'box'.

- **The Cornell System** of note-taking uses a tabular format. The table consists of two columns like this:

Key word or cue	Notes

The reader identifies key words which are written in the left-hand column. This takes the place of highlighting or underlining material. The note-taker must then recall what they have read using the key words or cues in the left-hand column. This is the recite stage of SQ3R. They can then reflect on and review what has been written adding additional detail from a further reading or from inferences that they have drawn.

31

Clarity and ease of reference are important factors. You may know what your notes say when you first write them but it is important that they still make sense when you refer back to them. Some of the features that a good set of notes may demonstrate are shown in the figure below.

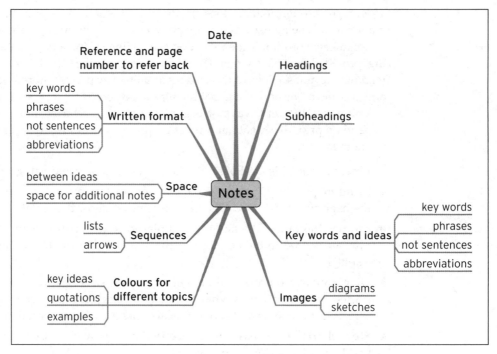

Effective notes

Writing a summary based on a reading

There are different ways of remembering the information that you have read. You could create a mind map, make a list of points or write a summary. Summarising is an important skill. A successful summary, or précis, puts the main points of a text into a smaller number of words without losing or adding meaning.

Here is a set of instructions for writing a summary:

a. Read the text carefully.

b. Make a note of the main ideas contained in the material that you have read.

c. Check for links between ideas and delete any unnecessary details such as specific examples.

d. Now write your summary using your own words. Remember, a summary of a piece of text should not develop your own ideas. It should not contain any new information.

Group task

Work with a group of eight to ten peers for this activity.

1 Select a text related to a lifelong learning sector issue. It should be between 250 and 300 words long.

2 Write a summary of the text in no more than 100 words.

3 Type it out.

4 Divide the whole group in half so that there are two groups of four or five members. Each member of the half-group must provide a copy of the original material and their summary. These should be mixed up and then swapped with the texts and summaries of the other half-group.

5 Match the texts to their correct summary.

6 After the activity is complete discuss what ingredients make a good summary.

3

Citations, references and a bibliography

Harvard referencing
System for identifying literature by name and date.

It is important to acknowledge the use of a text during research or for study. **Harvard referencing**, also known as the name-and-date system, is one of the methods that can be used to identify texts that have been read during the formative stages of any piece of writing. It is really just an alphabetical list providing essential information about the text that has been identified. This means that someone else could follow the reference trail if they were interested in the topic that is contained in a specific text. It also means that there is no question of **plagiarism**.

Plagiarism
Accidental/ intentional use of other writers' works as one's own.

Citations are references you make to someone else's work within the body of your writing. This could be an idea or a short direct quotation like this:

> **Incorporating a quotation from someone else's work into your own text, 'quote' (Author, year of publication: page number).**

The quotation is in quotation marks – these can be single or double. The author is then cited. The name, date of publication and page number are given in parentheses (brackets).

> **Research by author (year of publication) identified strategies for extending learner interactions with texts**.

The author or authors are named and the year of the text publication follows in brackets. It would also be acceptable to place the authors in brackets alongside the year like this: **Research (author or authors, year of publication) identified strategies**. It is a matter of personal preference. If the text is by two or more authors it is important to present the information cited in a consistent format or else readers may think there is more than one text being referred to.

Bibliography
List of literature that
has formed
background reading
during research.

References and bibliographies must provide all the information possible about a text so that someone else could find it if they wished. The minimum amount required is the author's name, date the book was published, the title of the book, where it was published and who published it:

> **Author, A.N. (1999)** *Title of book*, **Location: Publisher**

Note the way that the author's surname is presented first, followed by their first name or initials. This is followed by a full stop.

There are other types of text that may be referred to:

- Journals should show:

> **Author, A.N. (Date of publication) Title of the article.** *Journal Name.* **Vol. 3 (15), pp. 127–130.**

Reference list
Identifies works
cited in a piece of
writing.

The author's details are presented in a standard format so that it can go into the **reference list**. The title of the article is in plain text with a full stop at the end. The title of the journal should stand out so that it can be easily identified. For this reason it is presented in italics and there is a full stop after it. The volume number of the journal, if this is available, is then provided followed by the issue number in brackets. Then the page numbers should be given. All of this information will enable another reader to locate the same information.

- Newspapers should show the name of the author, the date of publication, the title of the article in plain text followed by the italicised title of the paper, the date of publication, the page and if possible the column.

- An Internet reference should give the author's name or the owner of the site where possible, the full URL (the part starting http://) and finally the date that it was accessed. This information is usually present on a printout but check to make sure because the full address is not always given in which case it should be copied and pasted into a list for future reference.

Task

Harvard referencing can differ slightly from institution to institution in that some places prefer full stops after the date for example whereas others do not. Find Harvard referencing guidelines from the organisation delivering the QTLS programme where you study.

Supporting your learners as they develop their reading skills

Adult learners can face many barriers to achieving an academic or vocational pro-gramme. One of the barriers can be lack of reading skills. There may be many reasons for this, including English being a second or even third language, dyslexia or other processing difficulties. Adult readers can struggle with their reading on many levels.

The NRDC report *Adult Literacy Learners' Difficulties in Reading: An Exploratory Study* (Besser et al., 2004) identified problems with whole-word recognition or failure to recognise words in the context of the text being studied. Lack of automaticity slows down the reading process. Other learners may not know about the different reading techniques or when to apply them to different texts for different purposes.

Best practice

'Content area teachers are best equipped to show students how to read the texts unique to their subjects. This means they must first become familiar with the rudiments of comprehension to make sense of what they are reading and then guide students to using these strategies.'
(Fordham, 2006: 390)

3

Vocational and academic subject tutors need to be able to support their learners to develop their own reading skills. This can be achieved by a variety of methods.

- Activating prior knowledge prior to reading. This could be done in the form of a mind map, a spider diagram, through discussion or by a KWL grid.

- Modelling different reading techniques and strategies. The tutor leads the learners through the process: show them how it should be done.

- Developing comprehension skills using DARTs. This stands for 'Developing Independent Readers'. The aim of DARTS is to encourage readers to look more carefully at the meaning and implied meaning of texts. This is done by making analysis of the texts and by reconstruction of texts. Reconstruction activities include completing **cloze exercises**, rearranging texts into the correct order – this may be done by sorting processes described in the text into the correct order in a separate activity or by sorting the text itself into the correct order; this could involve rearranging paragraphs or sentences by looking for sequence cues such as 'first', 'then' and 'next'. Other types of reconstruction involve completing tables and diagrams. Analysis is where learners take a complete text and look more closely at the underlying ideas. This could be underlining key words, dividing the text into paragraphs or ranking ideas in their order of importance.

Cloze exercise
A passage with key words removed.

- Reformulating texts for different audiences and purposes or summarising texts.

- Using a frame or scaffold to create notes. Rather than starting with a blank page the learners are presented with a grid, diagram or a skeleton for notes on a particular text.

Acronym
Initial letters of phrase/name used to form new word.

- Tutors can draw on the EXIT model for supporting reading. EXIT is an **acronym** for extending interactions with texts. The model identifies different stages in the processes of reading and producing text. It is accompanied by suggested teaching strategies.

Process stage	Teaching strategies
1. Activating of prior knowledge	Brainstorming, concept mapping, KWL grids.
2. Establishing purposes	Question-setting, KWL and QUADS (questions, answers, details, source) grids.
3. Locating information	Situating the learning in meaningful contexts, teacher modelling.
4. Adopting an appropriate strategy	Metacognitive discussion, teacher modelling.
5. Interacting with the text	Text marking and restructuring, genre exchange (changing the purpose, audience and format), cloze activities, sequencing (DARTs).
6. Monitoring understanding	Teacher modelling, strategy charts.
7. Making a record	Writing frames, grids, teacher modelling.
8. Evaluating information	Discussion of biased texts.
9. Assisting memory	Review, revisit, restructure.
10. Communicating information	Different types of writing frame, alternative outcomes.

Source: Wray, D. and Lewis, M. (1997) *Extending Literacy: Developing Approaches to Non-Fiction*, London: Routledge. Reproduced with permission of Routledge.

Summary

- The purpose and intended audience of a text affect the way it is read.
- Readers need to actively engage with the text they are reading.
- There are a number of different reading strategies that fluent readers use automatically depending upon the purpose of their reading.
- Effective readers are able to question texts, identify key points, then review their knowledge and reflect on the content of the text.
- Critical readers look beyond the text to identify fact, opinion and bias.
- There are many different note-taking strategies. Preferred methods depend upon the type of material to be noted, the purpose of the notes and the personal preference of the note-taker.
- Summaries are a condensed form of the original text. A good summary does not add new ideas or delete key points: it simply expresses the text in the reader's own words.
- Written output drawing on reading should be referenced using an appropriate referencing system such as Harvard referencing. This enables readers of the new text to follow ideas, concepts and issues back to their original source should they wish and it also avoids the problem of plagiarism.
- Fluent readers approach texts systematically. Readers who are not so confident require a framework to assist them to read a text carefully and critically.
- There are various strategies available to support learners as they develop their own reading skills within vocational and academic settings.

Test your knowledge

3.1* Working on your own, with a partner or as part of a study group begin to identify key words that are essential for you to understand and use:

a. Consider vocabulary that trainees progressing towards QTLS need to be familiar with in terms of: programme design e.g. *learner cohort*, *schemes of work* and assessment e.g. *ipsative assessment*.

b. Identify some of the strategies that you could use to improve your understanding of key words related to teaching and learning.

3.2* Working on your own or with another subject specialist from your curriculum area:

a. Identify key words that are essential for your own learners to understand in order to achieve in your curriculum area. You may wish to identify a specific course and topic.

b. Identify some of the strategies that you could embed into your scheme of work to help learners recognise and use key words more effectively.

3.3 List as many additional text types that fit into each of the following categories of purpose as possible. These should link to your professional practice or the expected reading of your own learners where possible. Confer with your peer group.

Text purpose	Examples of texts
Describe	A case study
Entertain	Cartoon in the *Times Educational Supplement's* FE Focus.
Explain	A handout
Inform	Dictionary
Instruct	Front sheet of an examination
Persuade	Flier for additional literacy sessions to support academic or vocational subject

3.4* Consider some of the different textual features that readers might expect to find in the following types of text. It may help to find some examples of the different kinds of text. Create a table like the one shown below so that you can compare the different features found in different kinds of text.

Text	Primary purpose	Layout	Structure	Language	Intended audience
A syllabus	Inform.	Condensed, regular typeface.	Paragraphs, headings, subheadings, bullet points and numbered points. Tables and diagrams. May have examples.	Technical terms and specialist vocabulary. Formal. Use of present tense, passive verbs.	Tutors, course managers and programme teams.

Text	Primary purpose	Layout	Structure	Language	Intended audience
A newspaper article					
An advert					
An email					
A fire notice					
A class handout					

3.5* Answer True or False to these statements.

    a. If there is more than one author for a text it is only necessary to identify the first author listed. *True/False*.

    b. The reference beginning Other, A.N. (ed.) (2007) … means that the text has an editor. *True/False*.

    c. The year a book was published usually appears on the back of a text's title page. *True/False*

    d. An abbreviated form of the title may be used. *True/False*

    e. Titles should be *italicised* if a document is word-processed and <u>underlined</u> if handwritten. *True/False*

    f. If a text has been updated it becomes a new edition. The edition number should be shown before the author. *True/False*

    g. If a chapter within a text is being referenced it is indicated by page numbers e.g. pp. 23-56. *True/False*

3.6 Adapt an existing text related to a specific vocational or academic curriculum area of your choice to support your own learners as they develop their own reading skills. Discuss the ways in which the adapted resource could be used during a taught session.

Where next?

Texts

Basic Skills Agency (1989) *Making Reading Easier*, London: Basic Skills Agency

Buzan, T. (1982) *Use Your Head*, London: BBC Publications

Buzan, T. (2006) *Speed Reading*, London: BBC Active

Fairbairn, G. J. and Winch, C. (1991) *Reading, Writing and Reasoning: A Guide for Students*, Buckingham: Open University Press, pp. 7-22

Wainwright, G. (2005) (2nd edn) *Read Faster and Recall More*, Oxford: How To Books

Winfield, J. (n.d) *How to Teach Skimming and Scanning*, London: Basic Skills Agency. Available at www.basic-skills-wales.org/bsastrategy/en/resources/secondary_how_to.cfm.

Website

www.bbc.co.uk The material at the BBC Skillswise website offers a useful introduction to various reading strategies including skimming, scanning and summarising.

4 Writing

Text
Any written form ranging from a few words to a novel.

Understanding the purpose for writing, considering intended audience and thinking about the processes involved in the production of **text** are just three of the factors that writers take into consideration. The way that you use this chapter will depend upon your current levels of skill and knowledge. You may wish to work through the chapter to rehearse the skills identified or to brush up on specific techniques. Alternatively you may wish to use the chapter as a stimulus to support the writing skills of your own learners or to develop materials using some of the strategies described here. Having read through this chapter and completed the activities, you should be able to provide evidence for the following standards.

Minimum core elements

A2
- Communicating the writing process.
- Using genre to develop writing.
- Developing spelling and punctuation skills.

Part B Personal Language Skills
- Write fluently, accurately and legibly on a range of topics.
- Select appropriate format and style of writing for different purposes and different readers.
- Use spelling and punctuation accurately in order to make meaning clear.

Text type, purpose and audience

There many different reasons for writing.

Stop and reflect

Consider the kinds of text have you written during the last month. It may help to create a list or a spider diagram of the different types of text that you have written or collaborated with at work, at home and during study for QTLS, e.g. *emails*.

Practitioners in the lifelong learning sector create many different types of text including: schemes of work, session plans, teaching and learning activities, handouts, worksheets, activities and other resources, OHTs (overhead transparencies), PowerPoint presentations, ILPs (individual learning plans); they may fill in registers, notes of concern, assessment feedback and reports, send emails, write agendas, minutes of meetings and memos, contribute to newsletters and write references for learners. As trainees working towards QTLS, there are other kinds of writing that are required including: note-taking from lectures, seminars and texts; compiling research and writing reports; writing journals and teaching logs; traditional essays and completing forms, to name but a few. Then there is the writing that we may do as individuals, depending upon our personal preferences: lists, letters, postcards, greetings cards, diaries, creative writing and poetry, article writing and notes of all kinds.

4

Stop and reflect

There are three questions that should be asked of any text:

- **Who is it intended for?** Consider the needs of the intended audience.
- **Why is it being written?** What is the **mode** or purpose of a piece of writing? Writing can have more than one purpose – for example, something can be informative but also entertaining.
- **How are you going to construct it?** Consider format, layout, structure, content and language. These are called textual features.

Mode
Another word for purpose.

If you have not yet done so it may be useful to refer to Chapter 3 which contains some information about the different textual features that readers may expect to see in a range of different text types commencing on page 25.

Task

Find examples of some different types of text such as instructions, information, explanations, persuasion and entertainment.

Identify some of the different textual features that they contain. Here are some examples of what you might notice: layout; use of images, diagrams and illustrations; headings, subheadings and bullet points; language, including sentence length, whether the writer refers to 'I', 'you', 'we' or is more formal and names the subject of the sentence e.g. *trainees*; vocabulary – is it straightforward, repetitive or are the words longer and harder to follow.

Discuss your research with a peer group in order to identify regular textual features in different groups of texts.

Context
Situation in which a piece of writing is used.

One of the conclusions that may be drawn from this activity is that **context** plays an important role in the writer's choice of format, style and language. It is, for example, unlikely that many people would write a memo to their spouse or partner reminding them to collect something. It would be far more likely that the text would take the form of a scribbled note.

The difference between speech and writing

Writing differs from speech in that the reader of the completed text will not be able to seek immediate clarification in the way that a listener may be able to seek clarification from the speaker through non-verbal communication or further questioning. The writer is also able to review what has been composed in a way that a speaker is unable to review what they have said.

Stop and reflect

Consider the factors that writers have to take into account as being different from a face-to-face or speaker/listener situation. It may help to create a table like the example shown here.

Speaking/listening	Reading/writing
Gesture/body language	Punctuation/paragraphing

Paralanguage
Speakers add meaning to their words by the way they speak.

Speakers can clarify their words through **paralanguage**. Speakers also watch their listeners to ensure that the listener comprehends what they are saying. If the listener does not understand what has been said the speaker can clarify what they have to say by using another form of words to re-express themselves. Listeners can also ask questions of the speaker if they are unclear about something. Writers are often not able to clarify their words at all if the reader has misinterpreted them. Writers must use punctuation and grammatical constructions to make their meaning clear. Punctuation provides some of the signposting that paralanguage offers to the spoken word. Writers sequence their words in a logical order and may have to abide by a specific or limited format.

The way that speakers use language and the way that writers use language also differ. We do not speak in complete sentences, we often repeat ourselves and we may use informal language including **idiom**, **dialect** and **slang**. By contrast most forms of writing tend to be more formal. This means that writers need to use complete sentences and use a more standard vocabulary.

Idiom
Phrases that do not literally mean what they say.

Dialect
Words/phrases/ grammatical constructions peculiar to geographical region/social strata/occupation.

Slang
Words that are considered to be non-standard.

Style
Way in which language, structure and content are organised.

Layout

Fluent readers can often predict the content and **style** of a text just by looking at the layout of a text. Writers use the same cues to help structure their writing. There are certain types of writing that follow accepted conventions. For example a memo is always set out in a specific format to help make sure that the reader cannot misunderstand the content of the text.

The conventions of layout or format and style for particular texts can help writers plan what they are going to write and how they are going to write it. The conventions also help to show the reader what the content of the text is going to be like.

MEMO

TO: The memo recipient   **DATE:** 10/05/07
FROM: The memo writer   **TIME:** (*this is not always included*)

SUBJECT: What the memo is about

The message is written in a short straightforward form which outlines key information, explanations or instructions.

4

Sometimes the layout is readily apparent, on other occasions the layout and structure is more subtle. For example, worksheets often make use of planned repetition. The same information is presented three times in three slightly different ways in order to reinforce the information contained in the text and to ensure that learners use the information provided at the start of the worksheet in a context appropriate to their vocational or academic study.

Style and language

● Register

Register
Level of formality/informality of a piece of writing

The language styles that people use vary according to what they are talking about, the formality of the situation and whether we are speaking or writing. This is called **register**.

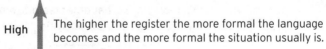

High The higher the register the more formal the language becomes and the more formal the situation usually is.

Colloquial
Informal style of speaking.

Our language becomes more **colloquial**, or informal, when we are in an informal situation. We may talk using idiom but we would not write something using idiomatic expressions. It is more likely that we will include contracted forms of word such as 'can't'.

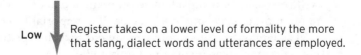

Low Register takes on a lower level of formality the more that slang, dialect words and utterances are employed.

Lexis
Another word meaning vocabulary.

The ability to use appropriate vocabulary, or **lexis** as it is also known, and appropriate tone is an important communication skill for a professional practitioner.

● Addressing the audience

Texts can be made more formal or informal depending on the way the writer address the audience and the **pronoun** that is used.

Pronoun
Words used to replace nouns in sentences.

1st person singular = **I** e.g. *I think the best way to approach this issue is to . . .*	• This is very informal because it is a very personal way of writing. It can be used in diaries and journals but should not be used in formal academic essays. • It is used in persuasive writing because it sounds personal. • The reader knows that it will contain opinion.
2nd person singular = **you** e.g. *You need to use a variety of different teaching and learning activities.*	• Still quite informal but it has a friendly tone that makes the reading easier. • The verbs can be direct and active. This makes the text more straightforward. • It is not gender specific so does not discriminate or create any barriers.
3rd person= **he, she, it**, or, in terms of a text, the use of a third-person impersonal noun - **the reader, learners, trainees** e.g. *Trainees in the lifelong learning sector need a broad knowledge base.*	• A formal approach to writing. • Sentences are more likely to contain passive verb forms (refer to Chapter 5). • The formal approach is necessary for academic essays and official reports. • Instructions or advice often use the third person.
1st person plural = **we**	• This is informal and is often used in persuasive texts because it draws the reader into the text and creates a shared understanding between the writer and the audience.

Stop and reflect

Equal opportunities need to be considered when creating texts. How can writers avoid discrimination or stereotyping? What other factors, related to equal opportunities and inclusivity, should writers take into consideration when creating texts?

Many writers use non-gender-specific terms such as 'you', 'trainees' or 'learners', for example. Some texts make use of an oblique (/) to give the reader different options: 'he/she' or 'and/or'. Other writers use brackets – (s)he – to show that they are being inclusive in their writing. These options can interrupt the flow of the text or be too confusing, so many writers now use the third person plural pronoun – they – rather than the singular form because it is not gender specific. Grammatically, this is incorrect but conventions are changing because of usage. Some publishers choose to write one chapter using a female pronoun and another chapter using to the male pronoun in order to maintain a balance. It is important to check images and content as well as language. For example, many old texts use pictures and case studies that do not reflect the diversity of our country today.

Language variety

Language variety is the term used to cover everything from accent and dialect to the use of jargon or technical terms within a specialised area. There is more about language variety in Chapter 8. Some uses of language are easily assigned to a variety. In other cases it is not so obvious what sort of language is being dealt with.

Stop and reflect

What language and stylistic features does an academic essay contain?

Academic essays are a specialised form of writing which can seem intimidating if it has been a while since you studied because they require the writer to think not only about the content but also about a logical sequence of presentation, precise vocabulary and more formal style and language. One of the criteria of an academic essay is that the writer should use the third person with no reference to 'I'. This affects the way in which sentences can be written. Instead of being direct and using active verbs a more impersonal structure can be required that uses passive verb forms. The most important thing to remember though is that paragraphs should follow a logical sequence with an introduction and a conclusion. The whole essay reflects the fact that the writer has sifted their evidence and drawn it together into a coherent argument making use of citations, quotations and references following the Harvard referencing system. If a writer makes a point, that point should be supported by examples and illustrations which are then explained. An academic essay also makes use of specialist terms and a sophisticated vocabulary to ensure that the writer makes their meaning as clear as possible. Reading academic papers and texts can help provide models of academic writing. The more an academic style of writing is practised the easier it becomes.

Task

Select a topic currently being covered by both a broadsheet and a tabloid newspaper. Go through two different articles. Consider the ways in which the two articles approach layout, structure, content and language. Discuss your findings with a group of peers.

Stop and reflect

Reflect upon the ways in which your language awareness has changed as a consequence of your reading and from carrying out the investigation. Consider how language variety impacts upon learners achieving their learning goals within your subject or vocational area.

The writing process

A text can be viewed as a product. This means that the emphasis is placed on the end product. The assumption is made that learners know how to create the text. The problem for learners is that they may not know or feel confident about the processes required to produce the final product. Learners may also feel intimidated by the volume of work required to produce an assignment and may feel so overwhelmed that they have no idea of where to start.

There are different theories about the way in which we create texts. The fact is, though, that it is a highly complex process and, needless to say, there are a variety of models for the ways in which texts can be created.

● The product approach

This strategy uses a model to copy layout, structure, content and even language. This has its benefits if the writing must be for a specific purpose and the writer is unfamiliar with the format. The benefit is that the writer has to identify textual features. This means that as a reading exercise the would-be writer interacts with the model text to identify specific features. The disadvantage is that writers can limit themselves if they rely on a specific model or formula. The writer is not thinking about the process, the language or the reasons behind format and style. The writer will not understand the principles behind the writing even if it is a relatively simple process to produce a parallel text to the one presented by the model. The learning that takes place here is specific – it is surface learning – so the learner develops little understanding of principles which can then be generalised.

● The process model

This model requires writers to identify the different elements of writing, carry them out, draft a text and ask questions of the text. A simple process model sees writers following through a sequence of steps from the start to the finish of the writing process. The recursive process model is where writers follow through a sequence of tasks and activities but may revisit different stages along the way.

In a **linear** process model the advantages are that there is a straightforward sequence of steps to follow to show learners how to plan and draft their own writing. The disadvantage is that this process does not encourage the writer to review and evaluate the writing during each step of the journey.

With a **recursive** process model the writer is encouraged to think about the processes involved, review and reflect on their writing at each stage of the process, which means that they may need to move backwards and forwards between the different processes in order to polish their text. The writer becomes independent. The disadvantage is that this is a time-consuming process. Ideally learners should have an opportunity to develop both strategies in order to progress.

Flower and Hayes (1981) identified the processes and knowledge required to create a text and recorded them in diagrammatic form as shown in the figure opposite.

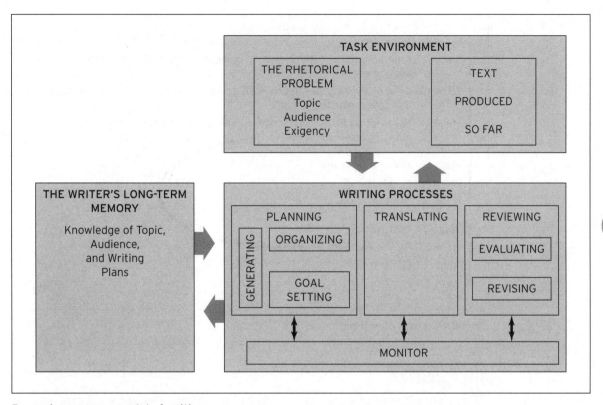

Recursive process model of writing

Source: Flower, L. and Hayes, J. R. (1981) 'A cognitive process theory of writing', *College Composition and Communication*, 32: 365–87, p. 370. Copyright 1981 by the National Council of Teachers in English. Reprinted and used with permission.

A much simplified version of the model could be given to learners before the writing process begins or after the process has been modelled by the tutor and the different stages discussed by the learners. The main stages in the process are shown in the diagram overleaf.

Many learners see this process as a linear model. In fact the model is recursive. Experienced writers return to each of the different stages as many times as necessary in order to refine and polish their text. This diagram shows two possible recursive processes. The first, shorter arrow shows a writer reviewing then redrafting the text. On some occasions writers draft their text, then having reviewed it re-plan their writing. The second arrow shows a writer reviewing their text and then revisiting their research. This in turn will lead to a modification of the plan and a redraft.

The process of composing, transcribing and reviewing a piece of writing for a specific purpose could be built into a scheme of work and successive session plans to model the process. Learners could identify the stages in the process for themselves in groups as part of a plenary activity. This could take the form of discussion, or, if learners were given a set of key words relating to the writing process on cards, it could be turned into a sorting and ordering activity. Learners could create their own process flow charts to compare with the one that the tutor provides at the end of the session. The one thing that these different approaches share is the fact that the learners discuss the process; **metacognition** takes place. There is also a framework available for the next time a writing activity occurs.

Metacognition
Thinking about what is involved in a task or process.

47

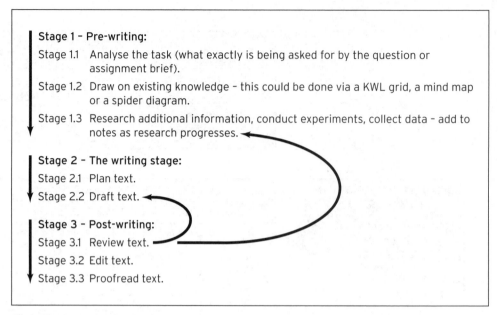

Stage 1 – Pre-writing:

Stage 1.1   Analyse the task (what exactly is being asked for by the question or assignment brief).

Stage 1.2   Draw on existing knowledge – this could be done via a KWL grid, a mind map or a spider diagram.

Stage 1.3   Research additional information, conduct experiments, collect data – add to notes as research progresses.

Stage 2 – The writing stage:

Stage 2.1   Plan text.

Stage 2.2   Draft text.

Stage 3 – Post-writing:

Stage 3.1   Review text.

Stage 3.2   Edit text.

Stage 3.3   Proofread text.

Simplified model of writing

Group task

Discuss how this information could be used to support learners in a vocational or academic programme area to develop their own writing skills.

Paragraphing skills

Generally, a paragraph is a cohesive unit of information. It will be structured so that the first sentence explains the topic of the paragraph, the mid-section of the paragraph provides examples or develops the point and the final sentence draws the topic to a conclusion or leads forward to the next point. There are different strategies that can be used for remembering how to structure a paragraph.

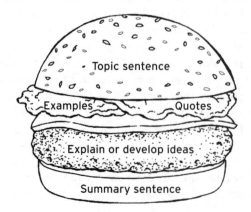

Think of a paragraph as being rather like a cheeseburger. The first sentence, the topic sentence, and the last sentence are rather like the two halves of the burger bun holding the meat, salad and cheese together. The meat and salad within a paragraph are the examples, points and further explanation related to the topic sentence.

There are two mnemonic devices to help remember the possible structures of a paragraph:

- **PEE** This stands for **p**oint, **e**xample, and **e**xplanation.
- **PQD** These letters stand for **p**oint, **q**uote, and **d**evelopment.

Alternatively it could be visualised as a flow chart with key words to act as prompts.

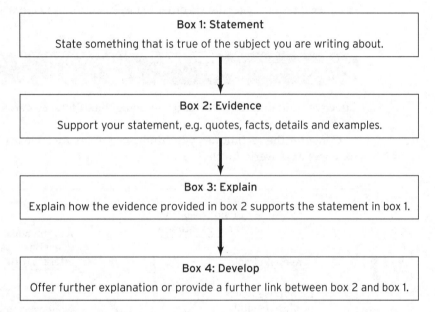

Source: Adapted from Cowley (2004: 71)

It may help to give an example that learners can use as a model alongside the flow chart. Alternatively, if learners are more independent, provide them with a model then ask them to deconstruct it, possibly in groups, and then create their own flow charts which can be compared to the tutor's flow chart during plenary feedback and discussion.

Proofreading

Proofreading for errors is an important part of the writing process. It is easy to become caught up in the flow of ideas when writing a text. Proofreading requires writers to look closely at the mechanisms they have used to express themselves. Is the material spelt correctly? Is the punctuation in the right place? Have the conventions of grammar been adhered to? Is the text cohesive? Does it make sense?

Some writers rely on spell-check facilities to answer these questions. This is not always a good idea as a spell-check facility will not identify a contextually incorrect word if it is spelt correctly. A checking facility may offer a grammar check but it will not check whether the argument is logical or whether a sentence makes sense or not so long as it has all the correct elements in place.

Often people do not perceive errors when they are writing because they are concentrating on the content. Perception is also important; the 'brain actively selects, organises and interprets stimuli' (Gration, 1989). This means that it is not always possible to see errors such as simple duplication of the word 'the' or omission of words like 'a' and 'an' because the reader knows that these grammatical presentations are unlikely, so discounts them. As a consequence of seeing what they expect to see and reading what they expect to read when they first complete a text, some writers find that they need to return to a completed text at a later date in order to identify errors and areas for improvement.

Professional writing

Effective written communication can make the difference between a good and a poor session.

Consider the techniques you might use to create a clear OHT (overhead transparency) or PowerPoint slide.

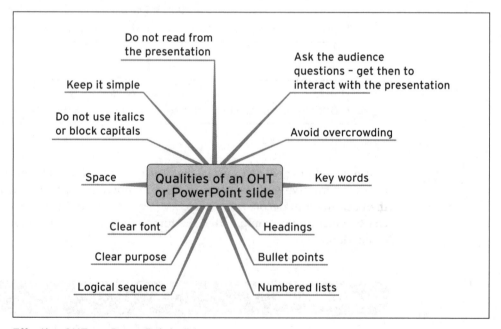

Do not read from the presentation

Ask the audience questions – get then to interact with the presentation

Keep it simple

Do not use italics or block capitals

Avoid overcrowding

Space

Qualities of an OHT or PowerPoint slide

Key words

Clear font

Headings

Clear purpose

Bullet points

Logical sequence

Numbered lists

Effective OHTs or PowerPoint slides

Stop and reflect

What factors do you consider when you create a worksheet e.g. *the level that the learners are working at*?

Audience and purpose are the key factors to be considered when any text is created. The audience of a worksheet are the learners who are going to use it. Vocational and academic tutors consider the level that their learners are working at and how much the learners already know about the topic covered in the worksheet. There is no point in creating worksheets just to keep learners occupied. Many learners are able to complete worksheets quickly and accurately but are unable to transfer the knowledge or skill from the worksheet into the context of their vocation or academic programme of study. Each worksheet used in a particular session or programme of study should have a specific purpose such as introducing specialist words and terminology; new concepts or processes; rehearsing skills or knowledge; using new skills or knowledge in a specific context; taking existing skills and knowledge and applying understanding in a more generalised setting; fostering independent learning.

Use the information provided in the mind map on page 50 to help you create a worksheet or activity for learners in your academic or vocational area.

4

The layout, content and language of a worksheet are important if the worksheet is to be effective.

Supporting learners

Vocational and academic subjects require learners to use the writing process for a variety of different purposes and audiences. Tutors can use a variety of visual, auditory and kinaesthetic approaches to support learners as they develop their own writing skills. It is also important that learners understand the purpose and audience for a particular piece of writing.

Stop and reflect

Do learners understand the marking criteria that will be applied to their work? Are learners given clear information about how to break down a task and how to present their information?

● Help kick-start the process

There's nothing worse than a blank page. It has to be filled. Many would-be writers find their minds going blank as soon as they pick up their pens. Beard (1987) identifies the fact that 'finding content' can be difficult. Tutors need to be able to help learners access their own knowledge of a particular topic and also to access the resources held in books, journals and the Internet. Individuals have many strategies available to them to access the information stored in their long-term memory. Personally I like to go for a walk to order my ideas. This is, of course, unlikely to be possible in a teaching and learning environment. Strategies such as mind mapping, snowballing exercises, summary and paraphrasing activities and discussion take the place of an invigorating walk to help ideas to flow.

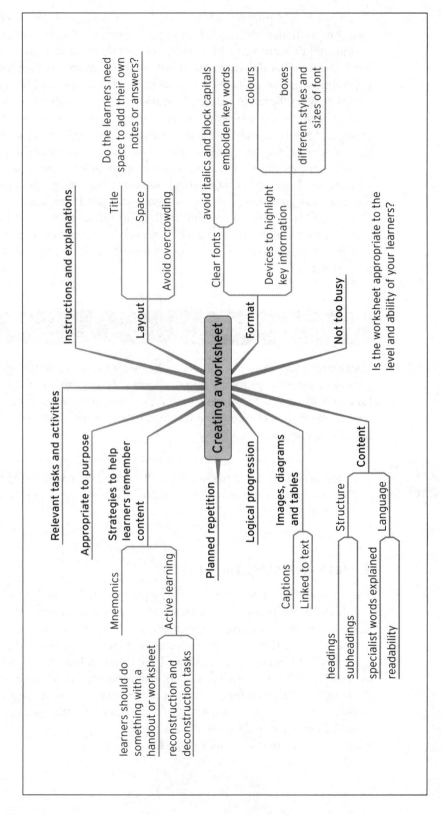

Creating a worksheet

Examples

In addition to explaining, written outcomes offer learners the opportunity to see and deconstruct exemplar material. Use DARTs-related reading activities to undertake analysis and reconstruction to ensure that learners engage with the material and develop additional subject or vocational knowledge. The use of examples offers models for learners to help shape their own writing.

Demonstration

This is another form of modelling. Guide learners through the writing process by modelling the different stages involved. Used as part of a structured session, this gives learners the opportunity to discuss different aspects of the writing process. It is important to remember though that learners need to be involved in decision making so that they are actively involved in the process rather than watching from the sidelines.

4

Take a metacognitive approach

Give learners an opportunity to talk through the writing task and decide how it should be accomplished. The use of exemplar material and the metacognitive approach means that tutors help learners to develop textual analysis skills using authentic materials. Once learners have identified how writers use layout, structure and language for a particular audience and purpose they can apply these techniques to their own writing.

Staged writing

Writing can be a lonely process but there is no reason why the whole process should be a solitary affair. Model strategies for interpreting the meaning of questions and essay titles; discuss exactly what is asked of the learners. Complete some of the planning stages of the cycle such as mind mapping as a group so that learners are confident of the context and content of their writing. Offer learners an opportunity to proofread one another's work having set ground rules for constructive feedback, which could include spelling, punctuation and grammar. It could also include the opportunity to suggest changes or additions to the content of a piece of writing.

Using writing frames

A writing frame offers an outline or a support mechanism for writers to scaffold their writing upon: it is a series of prompts. The number of prompts provided will depend on the level or skill of the writer. A writing frame can provide key words or phrases in an order most appropriate to the genre that the framework supports. They are a 'visual reminder of the characteristics of a particular genre and offer prompts' (HMIe, 2005).

The following prompts within a writing frame may be useful methods of supporting learners to develop their writing depending on the purpose and genre of the text to be created: key words or phrases, starters, connectives, and sequencing words, an outline for the structure of paragraphs and the order in which information should be placed in the text.

● Other strategies

- Offer shared writing opportunities for learners to activate their knowledge and develop their skills.

- Consider conferencing or paired work, giving learners the opportunity to evaluate and discuss one another's work as part of the drafting process.

- Provide learners with a checklist of key questions that they should ask themselves having completed their writing e.g. Does each paragraph start with a topic sentence? Examples of pro formas for peer or self-assessment can be found in HMIe (2005) *Developing Writing Through Reading Talking and Listening.*

- Give constructive feedback and build in formative assessment opportunities to support learners develop their writing skills.

Best practice

Even though this report is about the 11–16 age range the advice remains valid for vocational and academic tutors in the lifelong learning sector:

The 1998 report identified poor standards in writing in just over one school in five at Key Stage 3 and one in ten at Key Stage 4. The main problem was the failure of many pupils to continue to develop their basic skills. The report judged that too few pupils were taught the essential skills of spelling, grammar and punctuation. A great deal of emphasis has been placed on the teaching of writing in recent years and some of these criticisms no longer apply. The English programme invariably covers a range of genres and pupils are taught to identify the features of different text types. The most effective teachers make very good use of their own writing, sometimes based on pupils' ideas, to demonstrate or 'model' the process of writing.

Extract from the Annual Report of Her Majesty's Chief Inspector of Schools 2004/05 (Ofsted, 2006)
http://live.ofsted.gov.uk/publications/annualreport0405/4.2.5.html

---

Summary

- Writing requires consideration of audience, purpose and context.
- Writers make informed choices about the type of text that they create.
- Layout, content and language influence the style of a piece of writing.
- Writing has a register reflecting its degree of formality.
- There are several different models for the process of writing.
- Good practice requires tutors to model these processes and support learners as they develop their writing skills.
- Vocational and academic tutors should consider audience and purpose when creating resources to use with their own learners.

Test your knowledge

4.1* Identify the intended audience for each of the following types of text.

    a. A leaflet summarising the content of the Disability Discrimination Act (DDA) and the impact of SENDA (Special Educational Needs and Disability Act).

    b. A handout about paragraphing encapsulating the mnemonic device PEE which stands for point, example, explanation.

    c. A session plan.

4.2* Identify textual features that might reasonably be expected in the types of text identified below. Consider layout, content and language. It may be useful to discuss this question with a colleague or a group of peers.

    a. An informative leaflet about a specialist subject intended for general audience.

    b. A handout designed for your own learners. The skill identified should be acquired by the time learners achieve a level 2 qualification but many learners working towards a higher level qualification may still require a reminder about the best way to structure a paragraph.

    c. A session plan.

4.3 Complete the chart:

Text	Audience	Purpose	Textual features
a. A fire notice			
b. A report of learning styles			
c. An email to a group of colleagues letting them know about an end-of-year awards evening			
d. A quality questionnaire sent to all learners to find out about support services.			

4.4* Identify these text types.

XXXXXX

To: Date:
From: Time:

Subject:

Main body of text or message written or typed here.

---

a.

From:

Date:

To:

Subject:

Main body of text or message typed here.

---

b.

XXXXXX

Date:
To:

Apologies:

• Minutes from previous meeting.
• Business to be covered.
• AOB

---

c.

4.5* **a.** What type of text is this?

```
                                                          XXXXXXX
                                                          XXXXXXX
                                                          XXXXXXX
                                                          XXXXXXX

XXXXXXX XXXXXX
XX XXXXXX XXXXXX XXXXX XXXXXXXXX

XXXXXXXXXXXXXXXXXXXXXXXXXXXXXXXXXXXXXXXXXXXXXXXXXXXXXXXXXXXXXXXXXXXXXXXXXX
XXXXXXXXXXXXXXXXXXXXXXXXXXXXXXXXXXXXXXXXXXXXXXXXXXXXXXXXXXXXXXXXXXXXXXXXXX
XXXXXXXXXXXXXXXXXXXXXXXXXXXXXXXXXXXXXXXXXXXXXXXXXXXXXXXXXXXXXXXXXXXXXXXXXX
XXXXXXXXXXXXXXXXXXXXXXXXXXXXXXXXXXXXXXXXXXXXXXXXXXXXXXXXXXXXXXXXXXXXXXXXXX

XXXXXXXXXXXXXXX
XXXXXXXX
```

b. Identify the different features that you would expect to find in this type of text.

c. There are two possible endings to this text. What are they and what factor affects the choice of ending?

4.6* Look at these three expressions. Place them where you think they belong on the scale of register.

a. 'Shut up!'

b. 'I should be grateful if you would make less noise.'

c. 'Please be quiet.'

4.7 Session plan outlines are essentially writing frames.

a. Identify some of the key words and phrases that signpost the content and sequence of a session plan.

b. Sketch an outline for a session plan. Place the key words and phrases in the correct sequence.

c. Now check your session plan outline with the one provided by your organisation, training plan provider or plan provided by a text such as Reece and Walker (2000). Have you omitted anything that they have included or vice versa? Discuss the outcomes of this exercise with a group of peers and then amend your session plan outline to include all the information that you require.

d. Use your amended session plan outline to write a session plan, embedding the writing process into your vocational or academic area.

e. Discuss the reasons why a framework makes the writing process easier to complete.

4.8 **a.** Identify some of the features that could be included in a writing frame.

b. Identify an assessment that requires your own learners to produce a text. Create a writing frame at an appropriate level to support this process.

Where next?

Texts

Behrens, L. and Rosen, L. (2006) *A Sequence for Academic Writing*, Harlow: Pearson

Buzan, T. (1995) *The Mind Map Book: Radiant Thinking*, London: BBC Publications

DfES (2001) *Adult Literacy Core Curriculum*, London: DfES

Spencer, C. and Arbon, B. (1996) *Foundations of Writing*, Lincolnwood, IL: National Textbook Company

White, R. and Arndt, V. (1991) *Process Writing*, London: Longman

5 Grammar

Tutors are not expected to teach grammar within vocational and academic settings but it is important for practitioners to have an understanding of grammar as part of their own language awareness to be able to write effectively and also to be able to support learners as they develop their own writing skills. A grasp of grammar can help practitioners to make effective analysis of learner error e.g. subject-verb agreement; to improve the clarity and effectiveness of learners' speech and writing; to extend learners' control of style. This chapter is not intended to provide a comprehensive guide to grammar, but rather a basis upon which individual practitioners can build.

Minimum core element

Part B Personal Language Skills

- Understand and use the conventions of grammar (the forms and structures of words, phrases, clauses, sentences and texts) consistently when producing written text.

Grammar overview

Best practice

'. . . it is important that terms are introduced as they are needed, in order to focus attention on important distinctions or similarities. Their meaning will be apparent because they relate to an immediate context.'
(Cox, 1991: 44)

Cox is talking about the role of English teachers supporting their learners develop an understanding of language and context; it is up to individual vocational and academic tutors whether or not they use specific grammatical terms.

Describing language and the functions of different words within a sentence can be complex. This is one of the reasons why there seem to be so many grammar-specific words describing features and functions words within sentences. These words are often described as **jargon** but they are also useful specialist terms that can be used to describe the forms and functions of the different parts of language exactly and

Jargon
Specialist/technical vocabulary used by small groups of people.

59

without ambiguity. There is even a word to describe the language that is used to describe language: metalanguage.

● A definition

There are a number of different views about what grammar might be.

Stop and reflect

What do we mean by *grammar*?

Syntax
Order in which words are arranged in order to have meaning.

Morphology
Study of the structure of words.

Parse
Analyse sentence, identifying different units/features of language within it.

Most people regard grammar as the set of rules by which written, and spoken, language should be constructed. The definition you have written may have included word order (**syntax**) and the way in which word endings (suffixes) change tense and person (**morphology**). This is prescriptive grammar that lays down rules that must be followed. Prescriptive grammar sees languages as unchanging because any move away from the prescriptive rules is wrong. Until the 1950s the accepted method for teaching grammar was to identify and label the different parts of sentences. Learners were required to **parse** sentences. This lacked creativity. The Kingman and Cox reports (DES, 1998, 1989) identified the importance of knowing about language within its spoken or written contexts. A more modern approach to grammar is to use it to describe the way people are currently using language. This is descriptive grammar; it is non-judgemental. Grammar can also be used to generate new sentences following identified patterns. This is called generative grammar and is much more creative in its approach than a traditional prescriptive view of grammar.

● A brief history

Grammar and *grimoire* (a book of magic) are related words, as is the Scots word *glamour* meaning a magic spell (McArthur, 1992). Given that for thousands of years writing was limited to a small proportion of the population, it is perhaps not surprising that the word 'grammar' should be linked to mystery and magic.

Dionysius Thrax wrote *The Art of Letters* in about 100 BC. Greek grammarians were interested in the relationships and principles that lay behind the construction of phrases, clauses, sentences and texts. Thrax identified grammar as technical knowledge of the written word.

By the medieval period Latin was the dominant literacy of the western world. It was the language of religion, the state and education. The principles and practices that could be observed in Latin were gradually codified and applied to the English language. The advent of the printing press saw this process speed up but with an emphasis upon material influenced by the dominant written literacy of the time (Latin) rather than the marginalised literacy of the peasants (English).

Grammarians of the seventeenth and eighteenth centuries who did concentrate on English used Latin as their model not only because of the precedent set in earlier centuries but also because the Age of Reason drew on the classical past as a role model: consider architecture and fashion during this period. No wonder then that 'it was taken entirely for granted that classical languages *must* serve as models' (Bryson,

1991). Bryson also identifies some of the prescriptive rules that men such as the Reverend Robert Lowth set out for correct usage. It was Lowth's *A Short Introduction to English Grammar* (1762) that suggested that sentences should not conclude with a preposition and that writing that something was 'different to' something else rather than 'different from' was wrong.

By the nineteenth century it was realised that traditional grammar was inadequate to describe or make effective analysis of the English language. Descriptive grammar was established to set out in a systematic way, 'the rules that appear to govern how language is used' (QCA, 1998), the principal difference being that rather than prescribing how language should be used a descriptive grammar evolves rules based on a description of the way language is being used.

Between the 1950s and 1970s grammar ceased to be taught explicitly through rules and exercises such as parsing because research from the period questioned the validity of the technique. It became more important for learners to develop an authentic understanding of language through a range of different texts and through their own work. Grammar became contextualised rather than taught explicitly. However, further research established the importance of teaching some aspects of grammar through direct teaching. It was increasingly recognised that some studies of grammar had defined grammar too narrowly. Modern approaches reflect the broadening scope of grammar and recognise the importance of understanding language rather than rote learning.

The building blocks of grammar

Think of English as being made up from a series of building blocks that are joined together to make words, phrases, clauses and sentences. Crystal (1995) outlines a hierarchy – starting with the smallest building block and building level by level. This is systematic approach to grammar.

Affix
Additions to the beginning or ends of words.

The smallest building blocks that have any meaning are **affixes**. Affixes have no meaning on their own. They are added onto words to change the meaning of a word or change the word class. An affix like -s changes a word from a singular to a plural e.g. *boy* becomes *boys*. Adding the affix *-ly* to the adjective *easy* turns it into the adverb *easily*. Affixes can either be added to the beginning of words (prefixes) or they can be added to the end of words (suffixes).

Words can be used as building blocks to make new words. This kind of word is called a compound word e.g.

> *green + house = greenhouse*

Words are put together in clauses, phrases and sentences so that they produce meaningful communication. One word on its own is not always necessarily very useful: consider the way in which people who use a foreign language on holiday often have to rely on mime and gesturing alongside their vocabulary to get what they want. The channel of communication is very limited. There are eight groups or classes of words. Words may belong to different classes depending upon the syntax (order in the sentence) and morphology (addition of an affix).

A phrase is a group of words that do not make sense on their own but which can be used as a building block to the next level. There are often noun phrases in sentences. A noun phrase is a string of words that are all dependent upon the noun in some way e.g.

the very heavy plastic portfolio was delivered this morning.

The important thing to remember about phrases is that there is no main verb in the group of words.

A clause is a group of words that has a subject and a verb. If the clause makes sense on its own we tend to think of it as a simple sentence. There are two kinds of clause. There are main clauses and subordinate clauses. Here is an example:

When the learners arrived they identified their SMART targets.

This sentence contains a main clause and a subordinate clause. A main clause contains a finite verb and could stand on its own as a sentence:

They identified their SMART targets.

A subordinate clause depends on the main clause to have meaning. It cannot stand alone even though it has a verb of its own – _When the learners arrived_ is incomplete; there needs to be more information in order for it to make complete sense. There can be more than one subordinate clause in a sentence.

A sentence, the largest building block, is a group of words that makes complete sense on its own. Sentences can have different purposes: they can make statements, ask questions, give commands and they can be exclamations. Sentences can have different structures. They can be simple, compound or complex. For a more detailed explanation of sentences refer to page 71 in this chapter. A sentence can change meaning depending upon the order in which words, phrases and clauses are placed in it. This can be another factor that contributes to **ambiguity** e.g. _This means that when sentences are written down some learners do not always recognise that they are incomplete._ It is unclear in this sentence whether it is the learners or the sentences that are incomplete.

Ambiguity
Where there is more than one meaning to a sentence.

An understanding of grammar, whether implicit or explicit, aids writing and reading. Fluent readers may not be able to use the correct metalanguage to describe the process but use word order (syntax), word class and word endings (morphology) to help predict meaning.

Word classes

There are eight word classes or parts of speech that can be joined together to form meaningful sentences. Words can be categorised into the different word classes depending upon the role that they fulfil within sentences. Some word classes can be put together to form phrases – these include nouns, adjectives and pronouns. Other word classes can be added if a clause is to be formed e.g. verbs and adverbs. All of them can be joined together with conjunctions and prepositions to form sentences. Some of the word classes like verbs and nouns have lexical meaning. Other groups of words, usually the 'little words' like *a, an* and *the* are function words that 'glue' (Aitchison, 1999) words into meaningful sentences. The different word classes are rather like the ingredients for a cake in this respect. There have to be some basic ingredients to make a basic cake just as there have to be nouns or pronouns (the subject or the inferred subject of the sentence) and verbs to form a sentence. Extra ingredients can be added to the cake to make a cake that tastes better or to create a different type of cake. The same is true of sentences – other words from other word classes can be added to the basic components to make more interesting or different sentences. The way in which language is used will depend on audience, purpose and context.

In some languages word endings called inflections show grammatical functions such as word class. Modern English has very few inflected endings in comparison with Old English. The most commonly used inflectional endings in modern English are related to changing the tense of verbs and showing number rather than showing the word class of individual words within a sentence.

● Adjectives

Adjectives are often called 'describing words'. They are words which modify a noun or pronoun. They add to understanding of the noun and make material more interesting. Adjectives can convey attitudes and bias e.g. *the <u>vile</u> tutor or the <u>inspirational</u> tutor*.

There are three main groups of adjective; they can be placed before or after the noun they describe, e.g.: *The blue pen* or *The pen was blue.*

Most people think of adjectives as coming before the noun which they are describing e.g. *a <u>complex</u> diagram*. However, it does not always need to be next to the noun or pronoun e.g. *The learner was <u>cold</u>*.

● Adverbs

Adverbs modify or describe the action of a verb. An adverb describes how, when, why or where an action is performed e.g. *The lesson passed <u>slowly</u>*. Adverbs can also be comparative e.g. *I walked <u>more slowly</u> than my friend*. Many adverbs can be created by the addition of the suffix -ly e.g. the adjective *careful* becomes the adverb *carefully*.

● Conjunctions

Conjunctions are words used for joining different elements together – words, phrases, clauses and sentences e.g. *and, but, or, because.*

Pairs of conjunctions Some conjunctions work in pairs to join similar elements together e.g. *neither . . . nor, either . . . or, whether . . . or*. As might be expected there is a technical term for these kinds of conjunctions. They are called correlative conjunctions. It is unlikely that you would use this term with learners.

Coordinating conjunctions These join words, phrases, clauses and sentences so that both parts of the new form have equal importance. The conjunction 'and' is an example of a coordinating conjunction e.g. *vocational and academic.*

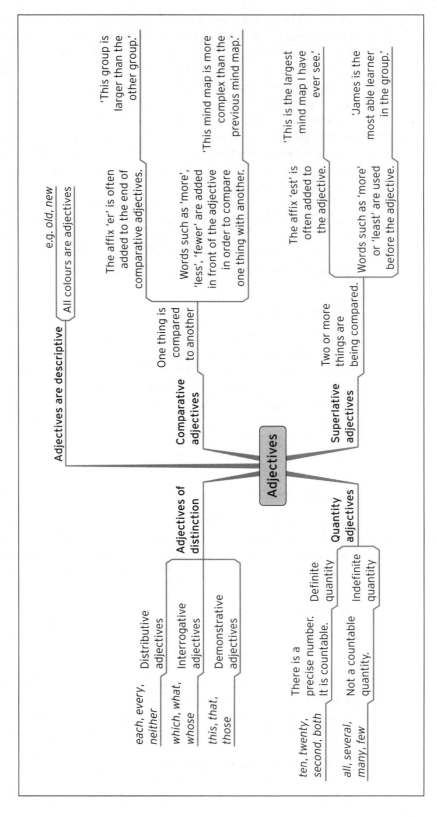

All colours are adjectives

e.g. *old, new*

Adjectives are descriptive

The affix 'er' is often added to the end of comparative adjectives.

'This group is larger than the other group.'

One thing is compared to another

Words such as 'more', 'less', 'fewer' are added in front of the adjective in order to compare one thing with another.

'This mind map is more complex than the previous mind map.'

Comparative adjectives

Adjectives

Superlative adjectives

Two or more things are being compared.

The affix 'est' is often added to the adjective.

'This is the largest mind map I have ever see.'

Words such as 'more' or 'least' are used before the adjective.

'James is the most able learner in the group.'

Adjectives of distinction

Distributive adjectives

each, every, neither

Interrogative adjectives

which, what, whose

Demonstrative adjectives

this, that, those

Quantity adjectives

Definite quantity

There is a precise number. It is countable.

ten, twenty, second, both

Indefinite quantity

Not a countable quantity.

all, several, many, few

Adjectives

Subordinating conjunctions These join words, phrases, clauses and sentences so that one part of the new form is more important than the other e.g.

Classes are unlikely to run unless there is a sufficient cohort of learners.

The first part of the sentence can stand on its own because it makes sense (*Classes are unlikely to run*). However, unless *there is a sufficient cohort of learners* does not make sense on its own; the subordinating conjunction means that it is dependent on the other part of the sentence to have complete meaning.

Fluent users of the English language are able to use the conjunction that offers the clearest meaning of what they wish to communicate and also has greatest impact. Less fluent users of the English language tend to rely on conjunctions such as *and*, *but* and *because*.

● Exclamations/interjections

Exclamations or interjections are words that express strong emotions. Interjection comes from the Latin word 'to throw into' and that's exactly what happens to an interjection. It is a word, or words, thrown into a sentence to express the emotion or opinion of the writer. Interjections can stand on their own e.g. *Impossible!* or they can be placed within sentences.

● Nouns

Nouns are commonly called 'naming words'. There are four different groups of nouns:

Abstract nouns these are naming words for concepts, ideas and emotions such as *happiness*, *humanism* and *bravery*.

Concrete nouns are the names for things that have a physical presence. These nouns are divided into a further three groups:

- **Proper nouns** e.g. the names of specific people, places and days of the week
- **Common nouns** e.g. *table, chair, dog, cat*
- **Group nouns** e.g. *army, cohort, flock, herd*.

Nouns can be masculine, feminine or neuter. This is called gender. 'Actor' is a masculine noun, 'actress' is a feminine noun but 'tutor' could refer to either a male or a female tutor.

● Prepositions

Prepositions are single words or groups of words that show the relation between one thing and another. Prepositions can show time (before, up to), position (under, with, beside), direction (towards, out of) and cause (with regard to).

Generally speaking, standard English suggests that it is important not to end sentences with prepositions.

● Pronouns

Pronouns are used to replace nouns. Writers who lack fluency will always refer to the noun; this sounds repetitive and breaks the flow of a text e.g.

The tutor saw the learner. The tutor talked to the learner. The tutor assessed the learner.

The use of a pronoun makes writing more fluent but also raises problems of ambiguity and correct **usage** e.g.

Usage
Way in which language is currently used.

The tutor saw the learner. He spoke to her.

In this example the reader has no idea who initiated the conversation because it is unclear who the pronouns refer to.

There are six groups of pronouns: **personal**, **reflexive**, **relative**, **interrogative**, **demonstrative** and **indefinite**. Three groups are covered in this chapter.

Demonstrative pronouns are the written equivalent of pointing: *this*, *that*, *those*.

Personal pronouns are most commonly used to replace nouns.

Personal pronoun	Singular 1st person 2nd person 3rd person	Plural 1st person 2nd person 3rd person
Personal pronouns used to replace the noun when it is the subject of the sentence. E.g. *The learners handed in their work* changes to *They handed in their work.*	*I* *you* *he, she, it*	*we* *you* *they*
Personal pronouns used to replace the noun when it is the **object** of the sentence. E.g. *The tutor had the book* changes to *The tutor had it.*	*me* *you* *him, her, it*	*us* *you* *them*
Personal pronouns used to show possession.	*mine* *yours* *his, hers, its*	*ours* *yours* *theirs*

Object
In a sentence, person/thing on the receiving end of the action.

There are three areas of difficulty associated with personal pronouns: the use of 'I' or 'me', number of person agreement and agreement with the verb.

> **Stop and reflect**
>
> Which of these two statements is the grammatically correct standard English form?
>
> *My learners and I are going on a field trip to Wales.*
>
> *My learners and me are going on a field trip to Wales.*

The easiest way, apart from knowing that 'I' is correct where the pronoun replaces the noun when it is the subject of the sentence, is to split the sentence into two parts e.g.

My learners are going on a field trip to Wales. I am going on a field trip to Wales.

Therefore the correct sentence is:

My learners and I are going on a field trip to Wales.

Stop and reflect

Which of these two statements is the grammatically correct standard English form?

The assignment was completed by my friend and I.

The assignment was completed by my friend and me.

Simple, it should be 'me' because it is the object of the sentence.

The second problem concerns number and person agreement. Nouns can show gender and number. The pronoun selected to replace it should show a similar person and number.

Jane studied animal care through a day release scheme.

This sentence becomes:

She studied animal care through a day release scheme.

Task

Sometimes it is important to read a sentence through to find out how it sounds. Decide which of these statements is best.

a. The athlete won the race. The athlete claimed that the athlete's diet was a deciding factor.

b. The athlete won the race. He claimed that his diet was the deciding factor.

c. The athlete won the race. He claimed that her diet was the deciding factor.

d. The athlete won the race. S/he claimed that her/his diet was the deciding factor.

e. The athlete won the race claiming that their diet was the deciding factor.

Some of the sentences are clumsy because the structure of the sentence breaks the flow of the text. Sentences *a, c* and *d* are clumsy. A sentence such as *b* is fluent but is not very inclusive. 'They' is a neuter pronoun so it is often used in place of 'he' or 'she'. This means that sentence *e* is inclusive but the number described by the pronoun does not agree with the number of the noun. Sentence *e* demonstrates the way in which grammar can change through usage as it is now acceptable to use the plural pronoun 'they' with a singular noun. There are other strategies that can be used to promote inclusivity. Some publishers use masculine pronouns for one chapter and then use feminine pronouns in the next chapter of a text. They continue to alternate between masculine and feminine from chapter to chapter.

It is important that the language we use should be as inclusive as possible. We talk and write about firefighters rather than firemen. A 'chair' rather than a 'chairman' is responsible for running meetings. The problem comes from replacing neuter nouns with an appropriate third person singular pronoun.

Finally, there is the difficulty of agreement with the verb. Verbs also show **number**. It is important to check that the number shown by the verb agrees with the number shown by the pronoun.

> ✗ *They was walking to work.*
> ✓ *They were walking to work.*

Possessive pronouns show ownership e.g. *my class, your book, their ideas*. Possessive pronouns take one form if they stand in front of the noun and another if they come after the noun.

1st person singular	2nd person singular	3rd person singular	1st person plural	2nd person plural	3rd person plural
my	your	her, his, its	our	your	their
mine	yours	hers, his, its	ours	yours	theirs

The most common problem with possessive pronouns occurs when people try to add an apostrophe to *yours, hers, theirs, ours* and *its*. Possessive pronouns do not need apostrophes. There is a full explanation in the next chapter on page 86.

● Verbs

Verbs are the words that express actions, feelings or states. They are often called 'doing words'. Verbs are a complex word class. There are lots of specialist terms used to describe different kinds of verb and different ways in which verbs can be constructed.

Most mistakes come from forming the verb incorrectly or using the wrong tense.

The form that the verb takes depends on the person (first person, second person or third person) and the number (singular or plural).

Person	Singular	Plural
First person	I	we
Second person	you	you
Third person	he/she/it	they

The infinitive This is the name of the base part of the verb from which all other parts are formed e.g. *to learn, to teach, to do*. Prescriptive grammar dictates that the infinitive should not be split. The most famous example of the split infinitive is the phrase 'to boldly go'. The adverb has been inserted between the two parts of the infinitive. The correct phrase should be 'to go boldly'. The only problem is that it does not sound so dramatic. The other factor to consider is that the prescriptive forms of grammar used Latin as their model – in Latin the infinitive is one word so cannot be split – English forms the infinitive in two parts so can be split. It is also an example of changing usage. Fewer people in the twenty-first century worry about split infinitives than previously.

Tense Verbs provide information about when an action occurred. There are three main tenses: present, past and future. The form that the verb takes shows person, number and tense e.g. *I teach, we worked, they taught.*

Tenses can be simple or continuous.

Present simple	I teach	Present continuous	I am teaching
Past simple	We worked	Past continuous	We were working
Future simple	They will work	Future continuous	They will be working

The easiest way to understand the difference between the simple and continuous tense is by looking at the past tense:

> *They worked.* This is the simple past. The event is completed.
> *They were working.* This is the continuous past. The action was ongoing.

Active and passive verbs If the subject of the sentence carries out the action, then the verb is active e.g. *The learner saw the tutor.*

If the subject is acted upon by the object, then the verb is passive. *The learner was seen by the tutor* uses a passive verb. Less fluent readers find sentences with passive verbs harder to follow. However, the passive form is less personal than the active form and tends to be used in more academic or formal writing.

Auxiliary verbs and participles Some verbs require a helping or auxiliary verb to form a tense and indicate number.

I teach makes sense on its own but *I teaching* does not make sense because it has no tense or number. The verb needs an auxiliary to help make complete sense e.g. *I am teaching* or *I was teaching.*

Of course, it would be impossible to refer to *teach* as the 'other verb' so it has to have a name too. The second verb which shows the action or state is called the 'participle'. The participle is the principal verb that gives the action, state or feeling.

> **Auxiliary verb + present participle**   *am + teaching*
> **Auxiliary verb + past participle**   *was + teaching*

Examples of auxiliary verbs include *to be, to have* and *to do.*

Imperatives Verbs can command. The imperative form of a verb gives order and can stand on its own e.g. *Sit down, turn left, go!* Imperatives are most likely to be found in instructions.

Regular and irregular verbs Some verbs are regular, others are irregular. The way to find out if a verb is irregular or not is to look at the way its past tense and past participle are formed. Regular verbs end in -ed e.g. *to talk, you talked, you have talked.* There are about 200 irregular verbs e.g. *to know, I knew, I have known.*

69

The problem with verbs is that they need to do a lot of work, so there are many different forms. This is where confusion arises.

It is important to make sure that the subject and the verb agree in terms of person and number:

✓ *She was sitting*
✗ *She were sitting*

Sometimes there is confusion between number and the kind of participle to use.

✗ *They was stood*
✓ *They stood*   ✓ *They were standing*

The phrases marked with a cross are considered quite acceptable by dialect speakers in specific regions but are unacceptable standard English forms.

Sometimes words from different classes become confused e.g. *passed* and *past*, *affect* and *effect*, *practise* and *practice*. One of the reasons for this is that they often sound the same. It can be useful to see what class a word belongs to in order to help remember which word to use where.

- *Passed* and *Past*

  Passed is a verb, e.g. *They passed their examinations.*

  Past can be a noun, e.g. *In the past they undertook the course as part of their BTEC.*

  Past can be an adjective, e.g. *They have been late for the past week.*

  Past can be a preposition, e.g. *She went past the staffroom.*

- *Affect* and *Effect*

  Affect is a verb which means 'to influence' something or someone.

  Effect is a noun meaning 'the result of something'. Although, just to make life difficult it can be used as a verb in the phrase 'to effect a change'.

- *Practise* and *Practice*

  Practise is a verb, e.g. *Fatima was practising the piano.* This refers to the act of rehearsing skills or knowledge.

  Practice is a noun, e.g. *A doctor's practice* or *Fatima enjoys her daily piano practice.* Just to confuse matters, American English spells both the verb and the noun as practice. Ensure that spell check facilities are tuned to UK English.

● Determiners

Determiners are function words that convey information about nouns. Articles are examples of determiners. 'The learner' and 'a learner' mean two different things. The first refers to a particular individual whilst the latter could mean any learner.

- *The* is the definite article.
- *A* and *an* are indefinite articles. *An* is used alongside words beginning with vowels or in some cases with words beginning with the letter *h*; usage of the indefinite article *an* is changing. Fewer and fewer people are using *an* in front of nouns beginning with *h*.

Determiners and prepositions can cause difficulties for learners who use British Sign Language (BSL) as their first language. The reason for this is that BSL signs the lexical words – i.e. the words that have meaning. It does not sign the function words like articles and prepositions. They are also the words that people skim over when they are speaking so that they are difficult to lip-read.

Sentences

A sentence is a group of words which makes complete sense on its own. In the written form it is bounded by a capital letter at the start and a full stop, question mark or exclamation mark at the end. There are four major sentence types: commands, statements, questions and exclamations.

Subject
In a sentence, person/thing carrying out the action.

Sentences can also be grouped by their structure. There are three structural groups: simple sentences, compound sentences and complex sentences. Simple sentences must contain a **subject** and a verb. They must make complete sense. Some sentence types such as commands do not always identify the subject explicitly, e.g. *Go away!* The imperative form of the verb identifies the subject – you – implicitly through its formation.

Sentences can be broken down into their constituent parts. The size of these constituent parts will depend on what the person looking at the sentence wants to analyse.

Morpheme
The smallest unit which has meaning.

- Sentences can be broken into **morphemes**, like this:

$$\boxed{Sentence}\; \boxed{s}\; \boxed{can}\; \boxed{be}\; \boxed{brok}\; \boxed{en}\; \boxed{in}\; \boxed{to}\; \boxed{morpheme}\; \boxed{s}$$

- Sentences can be broken down into words and word classes e.g. *prepositions, verbs, nouns* etc.

- Sentences can be broken into elements describing the different jobs that words perform within the sentence. The subject of the sentence is one element and the verb is another element. The subject is the person or thing that carries out the action of the verb.

- Sentences can be broken into the subject and the predicate. The predicate is everything apart from the subject, like this:

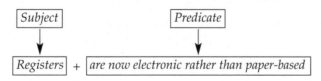

● Elements

The following elements can be used alongside the subject and verb: object, complement and adverbial. The elements can be used in different combinations. There are only a limited number of patterns that can be created.

Sentences must have a subject and a verb to provide a sense of time.

The subject of the sentence is who or what the sentence is about.

The verb expresses an action, feeling or state. It also provides the time in which the action occurred, occurs or will occur, e.g.

> *The learner spoke.*

The subject of the example sentence is 'the learner'. The verb expresses an action that took place in the past. In this sentence the verb can be described as intransitive because there is no object but the sentence still makes sense.

Sentences can be expanded in length by adding extra elements.

The object of the sentence is the person or thing to which the action is done. This can be expressed by the formula: **subject + verb + object**, e.g.

> *The learner + spoke + to the tutor.*

In this sentence the verb is transitive because there is an object in the sentence – an action is carried from the subject of the sentence to the object. Some verbs only make sense if there is an object; others can be either transitive or intransitive depending on the kind of sentence they are placed in. The main thing is that the sentence makes complete sense.

The complement comes after the verb to ensure the sentence has complete meaning by providing extra information about the subject element of the sentence. It can be expressed by the formula: **subject + verb + complement**, e,g.

> *He + was + happy.*

The adverbial describes the way in which the action was completed. This could be expressed by the formula: **subject + verb+ adverbial**, e.g.

> *The learner + wrote + slowly.*

Sentences can also be constructed using multiples of a particular element – although there must be only one main verb (or auxiliary and participle): **subject + verb + object + object**, e.g.

> *The tutor + gave + the learner + a handout.*

These formulae for sentence structure are generative. It is possible to create new sentences simply by adding words from the different element groups to form new sentences.

● Sentence types

There are three types of sentence: simple, compound and complex.

Simple sentences contain one main idea or clause and make sense. Apart from ensuring that the subject and the verb agree in person and number, the problem with simple sentences stems from the fact that we do not always speak in complete sentences. Meaning in spoken language is derived from other features such as context, tone, pitch and gesture. This means that when sentences are written down some learners do not always recognise that they are incomplete.

Compound sentences are made from two or more simple sentences that have been joined together using a connective or an appropriate form of punctuation. Here is an example: **simple sentence + conjunction + simple sentence**, e.g.

> *The tutor asked closed questions and the learners answered correctly.*

Commas are also used to link two or more simple sentences to form a compound sentence. This is one of the reasons why some people feel that a comma should never be used alongside *and* or *but* because they feel it is the equivalent of doubling the link joining the two simple sentences. This is a matter of usage and personal preference.

Complex sentences are constructed from a main clause and subordinate clauses. This means that only one part of the sentence will make sense if it stands alone.

> <u>*The learners cannot complete their practical assignment*</u> *unless they are supervised.*

The underlined part of the sentence makes sense on its own. This is the main clause. The last part of the sentence does not make sense unless it is alongside the main clause.

The subordinate clause can often be identified because it follows a relative pronoun or subordinating conjunction such as *after, because, although, if, until* or *unless.*

Writers use different sentence structures depending upon audience and purpose. Variety is one of the keys to interesting writing that flows smoothly, as is cohesion. Cohesion means that there are links between sentences e.g. *The book was very interesting. It provided the trainee with colourful anecdotes.* The pronoun 'it' refers back to the subject –'the book' – in the previous sentence.

Supporting your learners as they develop their grammar skills

Group task

Discuss the kinds of grammatical errors commonly made by your own learners in their written work and identify strategies that you could use to support them as they develop their grammatical awareness.

- Model good practice by ensuring board work, handouts and other resources are grammatically correct.
- Avoid overstressing errors and ignoring the positive features of each learner's writing.
- Avoid treating dialect features as errors – rather, encourage learners to consider their appropriateness for audience and purpose by discussing the degree of formality that readers might expect of different types of text.

● Provide a model answer and ask learners to identify a prescribed number of grammatical errors, then discuss how the grammatical errors reduce clarity of meaning or impact on the vocational/academic content.

Summary

Semantics
Study of how language communicates meaning.

● Grammar is a large area of language. It includes morphology, syntax and **semantics**.
● Grammar can be studied and interpreted in different ways.
● Knowledge about language including grammar should be grounded in authentic materials.
● It is important for learners to use appropriate grammar in the context of their vocational or academic subject to enhance the clarity and meaning of their work.

Test your knowledge

5.1* **a.** Sort these conjunctions into their correct category.

but, until, and, while, or, as well as, since, therefore, although

Coordinating conjunction: _____

Subordinating conjunction: _____

b. Conjunctions can have different effects on speech and writing. Some conjunctions can contrast items and place an emphasis on a particular point. Subordinating conjunctions have four main effects. Look at the table and decide what the heading for each column should be.

i. _____	*ii.* _____	*iii.* _____	*iv.* _____
when	*if*	*although*	*because*
after	*only if*	*whereas*	
before		*while*	

5.2* Here is a list of verbs that you might use as outcome verbs in the objectives section of a session plan. Some of them are regular verbs, others take an irregular form.

account, build, categorise, choose, contrast, describe, devise, discuss, extend, find, organise, outline, produce, rate, recognise, select, summarise, teach, tell, write.

Identify how the past tense is formed for the irregular verbs; you will need to look at the morphology to find patterns.

5.3* Identify the different elements in this sentence.

The learner wrote the essay slowly.

5.4* Some of these sentences are complete, others are incomplete. Identify the complete sentences and the essential elements missing from the sentence fragments.

a. *I am going.*

b. *The learners' different reading strategies.*

c. *Go!*

d. *at the end of the corridor on the second floor.*

e. *more vocabulary than others.*

f. *It is important to adapt language to the audience.*

g. *Entry-level learners only classes.*

Where next?

Crystal, D. (1996) *Discover Grammar*, Harlow: Longman

Crystal, D. (2003) (3rd edn) *Rediscover Grammar*, Harlow: Longman

Trask, R. L. (2001) *Mind the Gaffe: The Penguin Guide to Common Errors in English*, London: Penguin

6 Punctuation

As a trainee working towards QTLS and also as a professional working in a teaching and learning environment it is important to punctuate work correctly. Tutors are expected to be able to support their learners as they develop the essential communication skills that they will require to succeed in their own learning. Your subject specialism may not be English but if your learners need to put pen to paper you will need to be able to: assess that they have used **punctuation** to make their meaning clear; support learners who have gaps in their knowledge of punctuation; work with specialist staff to support learners who have punctuation needs identified on their individual learning plans. These expectations mean that you need a clear understanding of the basics of punctuation.

Punctuation
The signposting device for the written word.

Minimum core elements

A2
- Knowledge of how textual features support reading.
- Developing spelling and punctuation skills.

Part B Personal Language Skills
- Use spelling and punctuation accurately in order to make meaning clear.

Overview

Clause
Group of words that has a subject and a verb.

Phrase
Group of words that do not make sense on their own.

Punctuation is the device by which words are divided into groups that have meaning either by separating words into sentences or by linking words, **clauses** and **phrases** together. Ideas will be better understood if the punctuation is effective. Commas, semi-colons, colons, full stops, question marks and exclamation marks change the rhythm, pace and tone of spoken words as well as separate words, phrases, clauses and sentences on paper. Punctuation gives written words the structure and meaning that pitch, tone, pace and facial expression give to speech. Put simply, punctuation places strings of words into meaningful groups. Fluent readers skim across sentences to identify the punctuation marks to find out how a sentence should be read. In some countries such as Spain the signposting is even more apparent because punctuation marks such as question and exclamation marks, which are important to the way words are read, are located at the start of a sentence as well as at the end.

This chapter contains three tables identifying some punctuation marks, their uses and some hints on how and when to use them. Essential punctuation includes the use of capital letters, full stops, exclamation marks, question marks, commas and apostrophes to indicate ownership and omission – this group is summarised in Table 6.1. You may need to support your own learners as they develop an understanding of the accepted conventions of these punctuation marks. If you feel confident of your grasp of the first table of punctuation or are looking at the subject from a higher level of understanding, you should ensure that you are comfortable with the use of the punctuation marks contained in Tables 6.2 and 6.3. It is unlikely that learners working at level 2 or lower will require an understanding of colons or semi-colons which are summarised in the third table: an understanding of these punctuation marks will increase the fluency of your own writing.

Stop and reflect

Consider your punctuation habits. Discuss the way in which you use punctuation.

6

Some forms of punctuation mark are more common than others. You may have identified some of the following: comma, semi-colon, colon, full stop, question mark, exclamation mark, apostrophe of omission, apostrophe showing ownership, capital letter, dash, hyphen, single quotation mark, double quotation marks, rounded brackets, square brackets and ellipsis (. . .). You may also have identified paragraphing as part of the system that is used to divide chunks of words into units which have meaning.

The most frequently used form of punctuation, according to the International Corpus of English (ICE-GB), is the comma, followed by the full stop. People differ in their use of punctuation according to personal preference and the required style of writing. Some writers use heavy punctuation; others prefer light punctuation. Publishers often produce house guides for their preferred punctuation practice to ensure continuity. It is important to adhere to conventions and to remember that formal academic writing requires use of a wider range of punctuation marks whereas more informal writing styles are more likely to be lightly punctuated.

Snippet

The best writers may not be the best guides to the rules of punctuation. As Truss points out, Samuel Beckett and John Updike use commas in ways that would make a GCSE examiner flinch. But then, as Alexander Pope put it: 'Great Wits sometimes may gloriously offend'. You have to know the rules to escape them.

John Mullan, 'Comma chameleon', *The Guardian*, 16 December 2006

Although the Ancient Greeks invented the paragraph by leaving a line between units of text, consistent punctuation forms were not devised until much later. In fact, writers of Ancient Greece and Rome often left no space between words when they wrote. Punctuation only really developed with the advent of printing; initially marks were a matter of the printer's personal preference. Aldus Manutius the elder and his grandson, Aldus Manutius (presumably, the younger), designed an italic typeface at the end of the fifthteenth century that included a number of punctuation forms that would be recognised today; the semi-colon was born (Truss, 2003.) Even so, matters relating to the way in which the different forms of punctuation should be used had not been resolved by the middle of the sixteenth century. Shakespeare's First Folio exhibited interchangeable use of exclamation marks and question marks as well as editorial difficulties with colons, semicolons, commas and full stops at the end of lines (Crystal, 2004). It was also apparent that, up until this time, rather than signposting and clarifying meaning of written texts, that the purpose of punctuation was to show how the words should be spoken. Writers were beginning to recognise that punctuation could add to the meaning of the written word; Francis Bacon and Ben Jonson were amongst the first people to use a modern approach to punctuation.

Stop and reflect

Consider your views on the use of punctuation.

Today, Lynne Truss is well known for her 'zero tolerance approach to punctuation'. The novelist Chekhov was even moved to write a story about a man haunted by different punctuation marks. Other writers such as George Bernard Shaw take a more cavalier approach to punctuation although none more so than Timothy Dexter who in his text *A Pickle for the Knowing Ones or Plain Truth in a Homespun Dress* (1802) used no punctuation at all. The punctuation for the second edition of the book is included on a page at the back of the book with the instruction that readers should 'peper and solt it as they please.'

Punctuation to break text into sentences

● Capital letters

There are eight different types of occasions when a capital must be used (Burt, 1983). The one that most people remember is that a capital letter should be used to start a sentence. Fluent readers scan forward from a capital letter at the start of a sentence to the full stop at the end of the sentence to get a sense of the idea contained within the signposting punctuation. Text without capital letters is readable but requires more concentration because the capitals are not in place to signpost sentences.

Capitals should also be used for:

1. The pronoun 'I'.
2. Deities (gods) – God, Allah, Buddha. Pronouns referring to deities also have capital letters, as do religions (e.g. Islam, Catholicism) and related nouns or adjectives (e.g. Hindu, Christian, Sikh, Jewish).
3. The titles of books, newspapers, plays, films and poems.

4. The beginning of each line of traditional verse.

5. The beginning of direct speech.

6. The first word after a salutation e.g. Dear Sir/Madam.

Proper noun
Name of specific person, place and time of year.

7. **Proper nouns** – specific people, places and events. This last group is the biggest group and can cause most confusion.

  a. Days of the week, months of the year and some specific days, holidays and festivals such as Easter, Red Nose Day, Remembrance Sunday and Diwali. Neither the word 'holiday' nor the seasons of the year require capitalisation.

  b. People, companies and specific organisations. If the word university referred to any 'university' it would not require a capital letter because it would be describing a concept rather than an actual organisation. Here is another example: 'college' could describe any college but 'Chesterfield College' is a specific organisation. The same would apply, for example, to hospitals, libraries and armed forces.

  c. Anything derived from a proper noun requires a capital letter e.g. Shakespearian.

  d. Parts of the address such as buildings, roads, counties and countries. The names of rivers and mountains are also capitalised. Points of the compass do not have capitals unless they are used in the context of a specific area or place so 'the west' is not capitalised if it is a direction but is capitalised if it refers to a geographical location as in 'the Wild West'.

  e. Languages – English, Italian, Chinese.

  f. Subjects require capitalisation if they are part of a qualification title such as BTEC Art and Design but they do not need a capital if they are just the subject that is being taught e.g. 'I'm delivering two sessions of art on Thursday.' Of course, if the subject is a language it will need a capital letter.

  g. Some abbreviations use capital letters if the abbreviation comes from capitalised words e.g. BBC is an abbreviation of British Broadcasting Corporation which is a specific organisation. NVQ is an abbreviation of National Vocational Qualification. Interestingly, member of parliament is not capitalised but when it is abbreviated to MP it is.

This list demonstrates that capitalisation is not always as straightforward as it first appears. There are always exceptions – 'learndirect' is the name of an organisation. Convention dictates that it should start with a capital letter – it does not. If in doubt, check.

Punctuation to end sentences

The full stop (.), exclamation mark (!) and question mark (?) are used to show when a sentence has ended. They separate one sentence from another. Fluent readers scan ahead when they are reading to find the full stop so that when they read they can 'pick up' a complete sentence rather than individual words. These essential punctuation marks and checkpoints appear in Table 6.1.

Table 6.1: Essential punctuation

Full stop .	• Used at the end of all sentences that are not exclamations or questions. • When using a full stop, two spaces are sometimes left after the punctuation mark. • Sometimes used after initial letters and abbreviations.	**Checkpoints** It is important to be consistent with the use of full stops after initial letters and abbreviations. If you have shortened a word at the end of a sentence or address, you do not need to use a full stop to show abbreviation and another to show the end of the sentence; one is sufficient. You do not need full stops for lists and labels.
Exclamation mark !	• Used to emphasise the content of a sentence, phrase or word. It is commonly found after an exclamation of strong emotion or a command. Interjections can also be signposted by an exclamation mark. • Used within direct speech to show that a word or sentence has been shouted or said suddenly.	**Checkpoints** Do not use more than one exclamation mark at a time; pepper your work with them or use one in brackets to make your own comment on something (!).
Question mark ?	• Used instead of a full stop at the end of a sentence asking a direct question. This includes rhetorical questions.	**Checkpoints** Indirect questions do not need question marks. Sentences beginning: *why, who, how, when* or *what* are not always questions.
Comma ,	Used to mark a short pause, separating words, phrases or clauses. It is the weakest of the pauses indicated by a punctuation mark. • It can separate items in a list. The last item on the list is indicated by the connective *and*: *You will need a scheme of work, session plans and materials.* • It is also used as part of the punctuation to show direct speech: *Zahra said, 'This is starting to make sense.'* • Commas can be used like brackets, before and after a phrase or idea, to add information to a sentence and which could be removed without destroying the sentence. Look at the way the commas are used in the previous sentence for an example. • Refer to the spider diagram on page 83	**Checkpoints** Avoid placing a comma before a connective. Check to make sure that you have not used a comma to join two separate sentences. Commas are often used to separate modifiers (e.g. moreover) or words used to add emphasis (without doubt) from the main sentence. Check to see whether writing contains too many inessential words and phrases and remove them.
Apostrophe '	Used to show possession. • If the owner is singular, add the apostrophe at the end of the word and follow it with an *s*: *Jane's book. The girl's book.* • If the word is singular but ends in *s*, you still need to add an apostrophe and another *s*: *James's book.* • If the owner is plural just add the apostrophe: *The girls' book.* • However, if the plural does not end in *s* you will need to add an apostrophe and an *s*: *The men's book.* Used to identify contractions. • You use an apostrophe when you want to leave out one or more letters. The apostrophe goes where the missing letters should have been. *We have* becomes *we've.*	**Checkpoints** There are no apostrophes with possessive pronouns (*its, hers, his, ours, yours*). Do not confuse *it's* and *its*. *Its* is the possessive pronoun. *It's* indicates the contraction for *it is* or *it has*. Do not confuse *who's* and *whose*. *Who's* coming out? (Who is coming out?) *Whose* book is that? To whom does that book belong?

● Full stops

A full stop is used to mark the end of a sentence and, traditionally, to show abbreviations. The words *ante meridian* are usually shortened to *am*. In the past full stops would have often been placed after each letter to indicate an abbreviation. Modern usage has discarded the full stops so that it is more common to see *am* rather than *a.m.* The same evolution has occurred to the abbreviation *eg.* The use of full stops to indicate abbreviation should be consistent and follow the preferred house rules of the institution or organisation. If in doubt, check. Full stops have one other function. Three of them together (. . .) become an ellipsis. These three dots indicate that something has been omitted from a lengthy quotation or in more informal writing the writer has trailed off leaving the rest of the explanation or the resolution of an event up to the reader.

● Exclamation marks

Prosody features
Sounds created alongside words in speech.

An exclamation mark is used at the end of a sentence when the writer wishes to emphasise something. It can also show strong emotion, a command or an order. Exclamation marks echo **prosody features** of spoken language. An exclamation mark shows the reader how the words should be said. Academic writing should avoid exclamation marks, exclamation marks in brackets in the middle of a sentence (!) to indicate that the writer is startled or shocked, and multiple exclamation marks (!!!) to indicate that the writer is very shocked or emphasising something extremely important.

● Question marks

A question mark traditionally appears at the end of a sentence that asks a direct question. A direct question requires an answer. An indirect question does not ask the question but tells the reader what the question was. The following sentence illustrate this:

> *What initial assessment techniques do you use?*
> *The trainer asked which initial assessment techniques you used.*

Rhetorical question
The speaker or writer asks a question but does not expect an answer. The question is a device that signposts the topic addressed by the speaker or writer.

Tag question
Short question following a statement.

Did you know that sometimes questions are rhetorical? This means that the writer asks a question and then answers it. **Rhetorical questions** are stylistic devices, often used in persuasive pieces of writing to involve the reader, but they are also direct questions so must have a question mark. Question marks can also be used in more informal writing to suggest that the writer is uncertain about something. In spoken language a statement can be turned into a question by changing the way it is spoken; a piece of informal writing can use a question mark to the same effect e.g. *The staff meeting is on Tuesday?* Another method of changing a statement into a question is by the addition of a **tag question** at the end of the statement, like this: *The staff meeting is on Tuesday, isn't it?* Again, this is the kind of question that is more likely to be used in speech, so is only likely to be seen in dialogue or informal writing.

Punctuation within sentences

● Commas

Commas are the most widely used form of punctuation and they are usually described as indicating a brief pause in spoken language. They fulfil a clarifying function. They do this in two ways: firstly by separating words, phrases or clauses and, secondly, by marking insertions into the basic sentence. An insertion is an additional piece of information that the writer wishes to provide but which is not necessary for the sentence to have meaning. Look at the third sentence in this paragraph for an example of an insertion. The word 'secondly' is unnecessary to the overall meaning of the sentence. By placing a pair of commas around the word it is as if it has been bracketed. The comma is also the mark most likely to be misused because of its varied usage. It is important to be clear about why you are using the comma. If you are unsure about the use of commas, begin by using commas to separate words in lists and progress from there.

There are different uses of commas; the easiest use is the listing comma. A good way of checking whether or not you have used the comma correctly in a list is to see whether it can be replaced with the word *and* or even *or*. Commas are also often used to link dependent sentences. Be careful with this one though; independent sentences should be separated by a semi-colon or full stop or else the resulting sentence will be very long and difficult to follow.

The presence or lack of a comma causes a difference in meaning of a sentence.

Task

Look at these pairs of sentences. Decide what is the difference in meaning of each of the pairs.

a. *They are pretty lively trainees.*
They are pretty, lively trainees.

b. *They sat in groups naturally.*
They sat in groups, naturally.

c. *You sent Philip our best support tutor.*
You sent Philip, our best support tutor.

The first sentence of the first pair links the words *pretty* and *lively* whereas the second sentence separates the two words. The first sentence identifies the behaviour of the trainees whereas the second sentence lists two characteristics of the trainees; they are pretty and lively. In sentence pair *b* the first sentence suggests that it is normal behaviour for the groups to gather but the second sentence suggests that the writer would not expect them to do anything else. Sentence pair *c* demonstrates how a lack of comma can cause **ambiguity**, or lack of clarity. The first sentence actually says that Philip received the support tutor, implying that he needed the support. However, many people may read the sentence to mean that Philip is the support

Ambiguity
Where there is more than one meaning to a sentence.

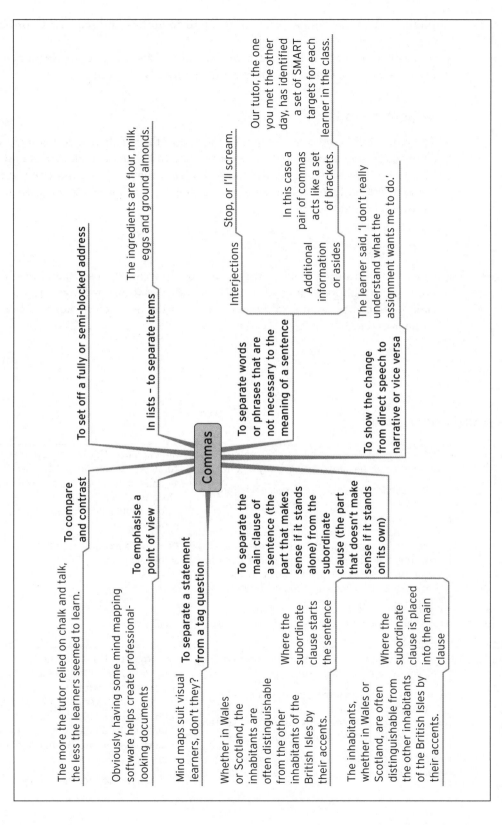

The different uses of commas

tutor. Only the second sentence of this pair identifies Philip as the tutor because a comma has signposted meaning.

Commas are used to help make the meaning of a sentence clear. Reread work carefully to ensure that there are no ambiguities caused by their use.

● Semi-colons

The pause following a semi-colon (;) is longer than the pause following a comma. Semi-colons are used to create a list of phrases rather than single words and to combine two ideas in one sentence. The first idea leads to the second one but they are both important. Think of the semi-colon as the pivot point on a set of scales balancing two roughly equal weights.

● Colons

Colons (:) are stronger than semi-colons but are weaker pauses than full stops. They are used to signpost lists and to introduce explanations or longer quotations that cannot be incorporated into the main body of the text. Semi-colons and colons are summarised in Table 6.2.

Table 6.2: Advanced punctuation

| Semi-colon ; | The separation indicated by a semi-colon is stronger than the pause indicated by a comma.

• It is used to break up lists when each item on the list is a clause and a comma would be confusing.
• It is used to indicate separate clauses within sentences. David Crystal (2003) describes it as the punctuation equivalent of the word *and*. This means that it can link two separate sentences into one compound sentence.

It is important to check your punctuation; use the grammar check with the punctuation option turned on. | **Checkpoints** Not sure whether to use a colon or a semi-colon? If the two clauses seem equally balanced, use a semi-colon. The best check for this is whether each clause could stand on its own as a short sentence.

Do not use a capital letter after a semi-colon. |
| Colon : | It is stronger than a semi-colon but has less pausing power than a full stop.

• It can be used to introduce an example, quotation or a list.
• It can also be used to link a series of separate clauses in the second part of a sentence.

Poorly punctuated work creates an impression: a bad one. | **Checkpoints** Not sure whether to use a colon or a semi-colon? If the first part of the sentence leads to the information contained in the second part of the sentence, use a colon. The second clause should not be able to stand on its own as a short sentence if you choose to use a colon.

Do not use a capital letter after a colon. |

● Apostrophes

An apostrophe (') has two uses.

- It shows omission (where letters have been missed out from a word or words have been missed from a phrase). *Can't* is short for *cannot*. *Would've* is the shortened form of *would have*. Many learners with literacy difficulties write this contracted or shortened form exactly as they hear it spoken so that it becomes two separate words – would of – this is incorrect. Shortened forms are suitable for informal writing as they reflect the way we speak. More formal writing should avoid contracted forms of words.

- It shows ownership. *The lecturer's pen* means that the pen belongs to the lecturer. The use of the apostrophe to show ownership is more fully explained in Table 6.1 on page 80. The correct name for an apostrophe that shows ownership is the possessive apostrophe.

Snippet

> **The little apostrophe deserves our protection.**
> **It is indeed a threatened species!**
> John Richards, Chairman of the Apostrophe Protection Society

6

Apostrophes can cause problems. There is even a name to describe one type of wrongly placed apostrophe. The greengrocer's apostrophe is the name given to apostrophes that are placed in a position that shows ownership where no apostrophe is actually needed.

Knowing where to put the apostrophe to show ownership Look at the following examples.

The tutor's board The positioning of the apostrophe between the noun and the *s* means that the board belongs to one tutor.

The tutors' board The positioning of the apostrophe after the *s* means that there is more than one tutor – but still only one board.

So far so good but there are four more points to remember.

Group noun
Name given to a specified group of people/things.

- ✓ *The group's presentation* The word group is a **group noun** but despite the fact that there is more than one person in a group the apostrophe is placed between the noun and the *s*.

- ✓ *The women's education* Plural nouns that are irregular such as *men, women, children* and *mice* place the apostrophe between the noun and the *s* as well.

- ✓ *James's portfolio* Nouns ending in s if it is someone's name need an extra *s* to show ownership.

- ✓ *Ladies' class* However, if the owner is plural and already ends in an *s* there is no need to put an extra *s* after the word but before the apostrophe (think how difficult it would be to say).

- ✗ Do not put the apostrophe over the *s* if you are not sure where it goes.

Knowing where to put the apostrophe that shows omission It is usually very straightforward. The apostrophe goes in place of the missing letters.

> ✓ *I'd* is short for *I had* or *I should*. The apostrophe goes where the missing letters were.

> ✓ *can't* is short for *cannot*. The apostrophe goes where the missing letters should be.

> ✗ *ca'nt* The apostrophe has not replaced anything and the missing letters are not indicated at all.

Of course, there are some contractions that do not fit the rule. They just have to be learnt: *shall not* becomes *shan't*, *will not* becomes *won't*.

Knowing whether a word needs an apostrophe or not

> ✗ *book's, pen's* and *pencil's*

These are examples of the so-called greengrocer's apostrophe. There is no need for an apostrophe in any of these words. The *s* is in place to show that there is more than one of each thing. No letters have been missed out and none of the books, pens or pencils own anything. There should be no apostrophes present.

Pronoun
Word used to
replace a noun.

Understanding possessive pronouns The possessive **pronouns** *his, hers, its, ours, yours* and *theirs* do not need an apostrophe. The most common mistake is made with the possessive pronoun *its*. Sometimes it is worth remembering possessive pronouns as a group. Very few people would try to add an apostrophe to the pronoun *his*.

> ✓ *It's started to rain.* Here the apostrophe is used to show a grammatical contraction. The sentence should say: *It has started to rain.*

> ✓ *The email is on its way.* This sentence does not need an apostrophe. There is no contraction. Its does not stand for it is or it has in this sentence, so it does not need an apostrophe.

> ✗ *The assignment is well on it's way.* The word is the possessive pronoun. The form shows ownership without an apostrophe. Nothing has been removed. There is no need for an apostrophe.

Using the correct punctuation mark Occasionally a comma can be spotted in place of an apostrophe. Always use the correct punctuation mark. The comma separates things so that a fluent reader will take it as a cue for a slight pause.

> ✗ *The trainee,s certificate* should read, *the trainee's certificate*.

> ### Task
>
> **a.** Select an article from a newspaper. Scan through it, highlighting the apostrophes. Decide why the writer has used the apostrophe in each case.
>
> **b.** Proofread a piece of your writing, checking that you have used apostrophes accurately. Scan the work looking for apostrophes. In each case explain to yourself why the apostrophe is present. This involves rehearsing your knowledge of apostrophes.

Check through texts carefully to make sure that you are using the apostrophe correctly. Refer to examples that you know to be appropriately punctuated if you are unsure of whether you have used an apostrophe correctly or not. Then scan the text again, this time searching for words ending in *s*. Ask the question, should any of these words have an apostrophe or not? People tend not to miss the *s* from words that are possessive because they can hear it, either as an *s* or even a *z*, when they speak. Say the phrases *Bert's breakfast* and *dog's dinner* to hear it for yourself. Unfortunately, there's no aural reminder of the apostrophe's existence – it is a piece of punctuation that helps give meaning and clarification to a text.

● Parenthesis

A parenthesis is an extra piece of information included in a sentence. If the additional information is removed the sentence still makes sense. The additional information is separated from the main part of the sentence by punctuation:

1. A pair of brackets – the opening (( ) and ( )) closing brackets are the strongest way to signpost parenthesis. Brackets are often used when the writer wants to give directions and also when the additional information is virtually a sentence in its own right – it may well have a verb.

2. A pair of commas – these are used when the additional information is closely linked to the content of the sentence.

3. A pair of dashes – this indicator of parenthesis is quite informal. It signposts an interruption.

There are no hard and fast rules as to which method you must choose to show parenthesis. The different kinds of punctuation marks used for parenthesis are summarised in Table 6.3.

Table 6.3: Hyphens, dashes and brackets

Hyphen -	• The hyphen is most commonly used to show words that belong together. This is part of the compound-word formation process: *Short-sighted, colour-blind, three-quarters* • Used to compound words in order to avoid vagueness or confusion within a sentence: *The session was half-empty.* • It can be used to add prefixes to words: *co-opt* • It is used to join broken words at the end of one line of writing leading to the next line.	**Checkpoints** Check whether a word is fully compounded (requiring no hyphen), is at the hyphenated stage or consists of two words placed next to one another. *Three quarters* or *three-quarters* are both acceptable. Be consistent. Try to avoid breaking a word at the end of a line.
Dash —	• The dash is used to interrupt a sentence with a phrase that doesn't fit grammatically with the rest of the sentence. It identifies a secondary thought or additional information. It is quite informal. *Learners used mind maps and flow charts – the session leant itself to the needs of learners with a visual learning preference.*	**Checkpoints** Where the interruption takes the form of a separate closely linked clause, commas should be used rather than a dash.

Brackets ( )	• Brackets are used in a similar fashion to the dash but are a stronger indicator of the presence of additional information. *The session lent itself to learners with a visual learning preference (my own learning preference is kinaesthetic).* Many writers use a pair of commas rather than brackets to show additional information within a sentence if the parenthesis is closely related to the main part of the sentence.	**Checkpoints** The correct phrase to describe something written inside brackets is 'in parentheses'. Make sure that if you use brackets at the end of a sentence the full stop is outside the brackets.

● Quotation marks

There are two types of quotation mark – single (' ') and double (" "). The other name for these marks is 'inverted commas'. Whenever a piece of text quotes what someone else has said or written, their words should be in quotation marks, either single or double, 'which to use depends on personal preference' (Cullup, 1999).

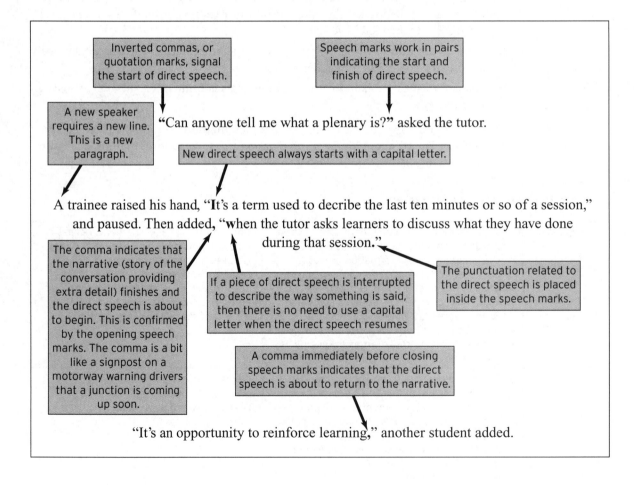

Direct speech records what someone says as if they were speaking. The words they use are clearly signposted by the punctuation that surrounds their words so that the speech is separate from the narrative that describes who said what, where, when and how.

Indirect or reported speech This is where the writer reports, using their own words, what a speaker has said. Reported speech does not need quotation marks. *Their senior manager told the assembled tutors that they had worked extremely hard in preparation for the new course.*

Quoting someone else's actual words in a piece of academic writing If a writer quotes someone else's words it is important that the reader knows that the words do not belong to the writer. Quotation marks provide the reader with this information. This is called a citation. A citation should be correctly referenced. There is an explanation for this process in Chapter 3 on page 33, e.g.

> *Semi-colons fulfil an important function though as Burt (1983) says they are 'never essential but often very desirable'.*

Longer quotations do not need quotation marks. This is because writers must use a layout that shows that they have moved from their own words and ideas to the thoughts and words of someone else. There should be a new paragraph and the quotation should be indented to set it apart from the rest of the text. The quotation should also be acknowledged by providing essential information about the source, e.g.

> The advent of the minimum core reflects the evidence that many learners did not receive sufficient support to acquire the necessary literacy skills in order to achieve their vocational or academic programme of study:
>
> > . . . there are constraints: there are too few specialist teachers; too many vocational tutors lack the skills needed to teach literacy and numeracy; and there is too much unsatisfactory teaching.
>
> Ofsted (2005) p. 22

The colon following the word 'study' is used to indicate a quotation will follow. This is supported by the layout of the material. There is a change of paragraph and the quotation is indented to set it apart from the rest of the text. This shows that the writer is now using someone else's words. There is no confusion about who has written which part of the paragraph.

An ellipsis (. . .) is used to show that the quotation is a continuation of something longer. The reader knows that the writer of the quotation said something related to the topic. However, the writer of the paragraph you have now read either felt that the whole quotation was too long or else that the content was not relevant to the paragraph writer's purpose.

● Other punctuation

The hyphen (-) is used to join words that have been split because the end of the line has been reached. This should be avoided wherever possible. However, if it is necessary to break a word at the end of a line ensure that it is split at the end of a syllable e.g. cog-nitive. The hyphen can also be used to link words that would not ordinarily go together e.g. *do-it-yourself*. Its final use is to link affixes to words that look awkward e.g. *co-opt*. Usage of the hyphen changes as a word or linked word becomes more familiar to a larger and larger group of people.

The dash (– or ~) has a bracketing function, as already described in the section on parenthesis, and is also used in informal writing to show dramatic pause or a hesitation.

URL
Another name for a
website address

The oblique (/) is now more commonly recognised as a forward slash from email addresses and **URLs**. In ordinary written format the oblique separates alternatives e.g. *Dear Sir/Madam* and is also used in a conventional format for the presentation of the date e.g. *13/05/1972*.

Layout

Spacing is related to punctuation. Space separates words whereas a new paragraph creates a larger space. Paragraphing is a way of organising a piece of writing so that related sentences are grouped together. The content of a paragraph will deal with the same topic, idea or theme. A new paragraph should be started whenever you change topic. There are two methods of showing a new paragraph:

1. Typewritten work – leave a line between one paragraph and the next. There is no indentation.
2. Handwritten work – indent the first line of the new paragraph. This means leave white space between the margin and the opening capital letter of the first sentence of the new paragraph: 2 cm is sufficient (apply a rule of thumb if need be – measure the distance from the tip of your thumb to the thumb joint).

Use one method or the other, not both.

Strategies to improve your own punctuation

- Spell-checking facilities should have the grammar and punctuation options enabled so that you can make an informed choice about the structure of your sentence and the type of punctuation you are using. Use the 'explain option' to rehearse understanding of punctuation and make decisions.
- Invest in a definitive guide to punctuation that you find easy to understand.
- If in doubt, check.

> **Task**
>
> Collect examples of the different uses of punctuation. Consider why the writer has used a particular type of punctuation and what the effect on the sentence might be. Use examples of good practice as models for your own punctuation.

Supporting your learners as they develop their punctuation skills

- Model good practice by ensuring board work, handouts and other resources are correctly punctuated.
- Construct a model answer complete with punctuation errors at a level appropriate to your learners' abilities. Ask them to proofread the text for a specific number of punctuation errors.
- Provide students with questions that must be turned into statements and vice versa (DfES, 2001a).
- Ask learners to generate questions and answers on a specific topic. The questions should be correctly punctuated.
- Glossary activities can help with spelling and with technical terms that require capital letters.
- Ask learners to swap work with one another to proofread for punctuation errors (DfES, 2001a).
- Negotiate with learners for an aspect of punctuation they wish to improve – focus on this in marking and offering support strategies rather than attempting to correct everything.

6

Summary

- Punctuation and layout add meaning and clarity to texts.
- Punctuation works with grammar.
- Fluent readers use punctuation to signpost their reading.
- The conventions of punctuation are gradually changing.
- Punctuation is a matter of personal preference, in-house practice and text type.
- It is important to be consistent.
- If in doubt, check.

Test your knowledge

6.1 Create a mind map identifying the different groups of words that require capital letters. Provide some examples from your own vocational or academic area as well as examples that learners should be familiar with in a wider ranging context.

6.2 **a.** There are four different types of noun: abstract nouns, common nouns, proper nouns and group nouns. Place these nouns under the correct heading.

> *class*   *learner*   *whiteboard*   *session plan*   *textbook*
> *cohort*   *college*   *behaviourism*   *intelligence*   *David Crystal*

b.* Decide which of these words or phrases that you might use during your studies towards QTLS are not correctly capitalised.

> *Kolb,*   *Learning Cycle,*   *abstract conceptualisation,*   *anadragogy,*
> *unesco,*   *Education,*   *Self-Actualisation,*   *disability discrimination*
> *act,*   *sir Claus Moser,*   *english,*   *literacy,*   *dfes*

6.3* Are these statements True or False?

a. Commands end in a full stop unless the writer wants to express strong force or emotion. *True/False*

b. All abbreviations need full stops to indicate the fact that the letters are an abbreviated form. *True/False*

c. Question marks and exclamation marks not only separate sentences but are also used by writers to convey meaning. *True/False*

6.4* Look at this list of sentences. How is the comma used in each sentence?

a. A good session needs clear learning outcomes, differentiation, a range of resources and learning activities to meet the needs of different learning styles.

b. 'Good morning, Mrs Watson.'

c. The tutor provided flipchart paper, markers, glue and images from magazines.

d. The learning cycle, initially developed by Kolb, offers a simple overview of the learning process.

e. 'Class, it's time to recap on everything we've covered during the last hour.'

f. 'I'm a bit nervous about the observation,' she said.

g. 'Don't worry,' I replied, 'I'm there to support you constructively.'

h. This is straightforward, isn't it?

i. The learners paused, searching through their memories for the best answer to the question.

j. In retrospect, it would have been best to use a snowballing or small group activity to give them some time to develop their responses.

k. Although he had never taught before, he instinctively recognised the need to set SMART targets.

l. Of course, it is important to use accurate punctuation to model good practice.

m. Please place relevant materials in your teaching portfolio, schemes of work, teaching and learning activities, resources and handouts, but not your reflective journal.

6.5* Here are some sentences taken from a self-assessment report compiled by Top Trainees, a private ICT training organisation. Add the punctuation required to complete these sentences:

a. how well do learners achieve

b. learners at top trainees continue to achieve excellent success rates

c. attendances continue to improve with 92 per cent of learners on daytime courses attending 100 per cent of sessions

d. the organisation consistently achieved excellent overall success rates

6.6* Replace the missing punctuation from this newsletter article about advice days. There is one semi-colon in the extract.

the advice day which was held at the end of October provided a chance for year 11 pupils to sample the course available to them in the lifelong learning sector

for most of the visitors it was their first visit to a college and an ideal opportunity for them to find out about which courses they wanted to study lecturers were available to speak to and provide guidance throughout the day each department produced displays and presentations potential students were shown around the college as well

courtney jones said that the day was a positive vehicle for adverting the diverse range of courses and facilities that the college had to offer

6.7* This job advert has been punctuated wrongly. Make corrections.

Programme: Manager salary £2,0000 pa -plus expenses and pension contribution).
Work with, young people 14-19 years delivering exciting enterprise, learning programmes; widening participation is an essential component of the job.

Enterprise. Intiative has an opportunity for an exceptional candidate to be responsible for organising the delivery, of business and enterprise programmes, to young people in the lifelong learning sector across the county. The role will encompass all: aspects of successful programme delivery including coordination and presentation on the day. plus supporting work such as training volunteers and teachers, as well as pre event preparation.

The successful applicant will work with business volunteers', teacher's and young people to ensure that all benefit from the successful delivery of Enterprise Initatives education programme's.

Where next?

Texts

Cullen, K. (ed) (1999) *Chambers Guide to Punctuation*, London: Chambers

Davidson, G. (2005) *Improve Your Punctuation*, London: Penguin

Gee, R. and Watson, C. (1983) *The Usborne Book of Better English*, London: Usborne Publishing

King, G. (2004) *Good Punctuation*, Glasgow: Collins

Todd, L. (1995) *Cassell's Guide to Punctuation*, London: Cassell

Trask, R. L. (1997) *The Penguin Guide to Punctuation*, London: Penguin

Websites

www.apostrophe.fsnet.co.uk The Apostrophe Protection Society

www.bbc.co.uk/skillswise

www.standards.dfes.gov.uk/primary/profdev/literacy leads to DfES standards site and the National Primary Strategy. For a basic introduction and self-study package select 'grammatical knowledge for teachers'. There are five self-study modules including one on punctuation.

7 Spelling

Crystal (1995) estimates that there are approximately 400 words with irregular spelling patterns amongst the most frequently used words in the language. Despite this, spelling is about 75 per cent regular. This chapter identifies some of the factors that affect English spelling and investigates a range of strategies to improve and check spelling as well as the limitations of the different checking mechanisms that spellers have available to them. Most learners need to adopt a range of strategies to improve their spelling. An interest in words, investigation and pattern recognition, effective memorising techniques and the modelling of good practice are procedures that vocational and subject tutors can implement to support their learners.

Minimum core elements

A2
● Developing spelling and punctuation skills.

Part B Personal Language Skills
● Use spelling and punctuation accurately in order to make meaning clear.

The development of English spelling and formation of words

● A brief overview of the history of English language

The Romans, Vikings, Anglo-Saxons and the Normans have all made their contribution to English. The Vikings, for example, are responsible for the difficult spelling of Wednesday – originally it was Wodnesdaeg (the day of Woden). Over time, Norse and Anglo-Saxon languages grew closer as the different groups of people communicated with one another. This resulted in a simplification of the **inflectional** system that had given meaning to word classes rather than the order of words as they were spoken or written (syntax). Interestingly many of the conjunctions, prepositions and basic words that we use today are derived from Old English. In fact, most of the first hundred most

Inflection
Use of word endings to vary the word class.

95

Derivation
Original source of a
particular word.

commonly used words are Old English in origin; Bragg (2003) lists them and identifies the paucity of Old Norse and words **derived** from the French language.

The Normans introduced the Norman-French language alongside the Old English dialects that had evolved from the Viking and Anglo-Saxon languages; they ate mutton and pork whereas the peasants farmed sheep and swine. They were the lords of the land and gave English words that reflected this such as *court*, *sovereign*, *author-ity*, *parliament*, *property* and *rent*. Students of law still have a specialist vocabulary that has many words derived from French as a consequence. The Normans also wrote English using their own spelling system including *qu* for *cw* (Crystal, 1995) and changed *hw* to *wh*; they also added the digraph *ch*. They were trying to create an ordered system of spelling. The only problem was that they added an *h* to some words that started with *w* (Brown and Brown, 1992) so errors in the spelling system were introduced because of lack of understanding.

As time passed, new words were introduced into the language and pronunciation and grammar changed. Unfortunately it did not evolve consistently from writer to writer. In fact, as Bryson (1991) observes it is possible to guess where early writers came from because of the spelling patterns that they used that reflected their individual dialects. This was not a problem whilst few people were literate and books were a rare resource. However, the advent of the printing press meant that books could be produced more easily. Words began to be fossilised. Once they were set down in print it was less likely that their spelling would change as rapidly.

From the sixteenth century onwards the impact of classical languages began to be more marked beyond Church and State roles as scholars demonstrated their learning and their belief that English should be modelled on the classical languages. Think about words such as *curriculum*, *education* and *experiment*. More recent classically derived additions include *pedagogy* and *andragogy*. They are based on Latin and Greek words that have been anglicised. Having some knowledge of prefixes and suffixes can help break these types of word into manageable chunks. Other words such as *stimulus* retain their Latin form and this can have an impact on the way that plurals or other word classes are formed e.g. *stimuli* (takes the Latin form for the plural) or *stimulation* (the root word is taken so that the suffix can be added without problem).

As merchants and adventurers travelled the world, new words borrowed from other languages made their way into English. Some subjects and specialist areas may have more of these loan words than others, for example music terminology borrows heavily from the Italian language whilst some areas of mathematics draw on words derived from Arabic such as *algebra* and *algorithm*. The journeys that words go on can be fascinating. The Italian words *cappuccino* and *espresso* have travelled from Italy, to America and then into the UK as part of the country's growing café culture.

In some ways English is like a piece of software that has evolved over time. Lots of programmers have contributed to the software. They have all brought something new to English making it rich, diverse and interesting. They have also introduced odd glitches and bugs. These glitches and bugs are inconvenient but they don't stop the software from working!

The spelling of specialist words can be supported in some subject and vocational areas by looking at the derivation of words to support subject specific knowledge.

Task

This activity was originally a jigsaw-matching or cut-and-match exercise to be carried out by small groups. The jigsaw edges could be smooth or shaped depending on the level of the learners involved. A task of this type is appropriate for learners who need an understanding of plant names such as florists or horticulturalists. This activity led on to a discussion about the way plants are named and the current system for naming plants.

Match the correct modern plant name to the correct original name and meaning.

Plant name and word journey	Original name	Meaning
Dandelion Middle English via Old French	Orkhis	Turban
Garlic Old English	Cuslyppe	Thought
Orchid Originally Greek borrowed by Latin; used by 17th century botanists	Lupinum	Lion's Tooth
Tulip Originally a Persian word borrowed by the Turks, then Latinised and used in 16th century England via the Lowlands	Garleac	Wolf-like
Cowslip Old English	Pensee	Spear leek
Daisy Old English	Dent-de-lion	Cow's slimy dropping
Lupin Latin	Doegseage	Testicle
Pansy A loan word from France in the 16th century; modern spelling evolved in the 18th century	Dulband	Day's eye

Words and definitions selected from Flavell and Flavell (2000). The correct answers to this task can be found in the Answers to Test your knowledge on page 204.

7

Consider your own subject or vocationally specific vocabulary: is there some interesting **etymology** in your curriculum area that would help your learners to understand the vocabulary and improve their spelling?

Etymology
Study of the derivation or history of words.

If there are some interesting words and phrases that learners need to know and to be able to spell, consider short active learning exercises, a mini research activity or a version of *Call My Bluff* as strategies.

● Words

Task

Write a definition of the word 'word'.

Words have several different functions. They can have a **lexical meaning**. This means that they have a denoted meaning. The word 'dog' for example has no hint of dogginess about it whereas some languages, such as Chinese, use logographic symbols that have closer links to the thing that the symbol represents. Words also have **syntactic meaning**; they have a grammatical function.

The linguistic term for a word is a **morpheme**. Morphemes are the smallest unit within the language framework that make sense. There are two kinds of morpheme.

- **Unbound morphemes** make sense on their own. They are usually referred to as words e.g. *pen*. The word 'pen' has a denoted lexical and syntactical meaning.

- **Bound morphemes** do not make sense on their own. They need to be tied to other morphemes in order to make sense. They are usually referred to as prefixes and suffixes e.g. *un-*, *dis-*, *-ing*.

Word formation

English is a living language. It is constantly changing. Grammar, punctuation and vocabulary change as they are used over time. The study of word formation and function is called morphology.

Vocabulary develops and changes in two ways:

- Older words are given new meanings. Over time, pronunciation, spelling and meaning can change.

- New words or neologisms are introduced. Neologisms are formed in many different ways and they appear in areas where there is a need for vocabulary or lexis to expand.

●Forming new words

Words (unbound morphemes) can be deliberately created in a variety of ways.

Compounding Compound words are two words that are joined together to form one new word. The meanings of the two separate words are merged in some way: the first word usually modifies the second word in some way.

The writing convention for creating compound words is fluid. They can move through three stages.

1. Open: There are two separate words that are written alongside one another e.g. *global warming* or *World Wide Web*.

2. Hyphenated: This form is most usually a clarifying strategy or a bridging strategy when the writer is not sure if the compound is one word or two e.g. *warm-up* or *warm up*.

3. Solid: The two words are joined as one word e.g. *blackboard, whiteboard, software, icebreaker* and *copyright*.

Affixing When speakers or writers add an affix to a word (the root word) they change either the lexical meaning of the word or the word class to which the modified word originally belonged. The ability to break a word down into its root and its affixes is a helpful strategy for both spelling and reading individual words. Teaching about affixes usually begins with the concept of root words as unbound morphemes that make sense on their own but which can be changed by the addition of affixes. More advanced readers and spellers realise that affixes can be added to root words that are bound morphemes.

Prefixes are added to the front of words to modify meaning e.g. *re + test = retest* or *dis + miss = dismiss*. The majority of prefixes come from Old English, Latin or Greek. This means that sometimes prefixes can duplicate meaning. Prefixes rarely change spelling although sometimes they will be hyphenated where the prefix is unusual, ends in a vowel and is placed in front of a root word beginning with a vowel e.g. *co-opt*.

Here are the meanings of some prefixes.

Old English prefixes	Latin prefixes	Greek prefixes
be (to make) e.g. *befriend*	**ab** (away from) e.g. *abstract*	**anti** (against) e.g. *antisocial*
mis (wrong) e.g. *mistake*	**ad** (to) e.g. *advance*	**auto** (self) e.g. *autobiography*
out (beyond) e.g. *outreach* (as in outreach centre)	**ante** (before) e.g. *antenatal*	**biblio** (book) e.g. *bibliography*
over (over) e.g. *overhead*	**de** (down or away) e.g. *decommission*	**homo** (same) e.g. *homogenous*
un (not or reverse) e.g. *undecided, undo*	**dis** (negative) e.g. *disappear*	**photo** (light) e.g. *photograph*
	re (again) e.g. *reassess*	**tele** (from afar) e.g. *telescope*
	trans (across) e.g. *transfer*	

There are many other common prefixes. The ones included in the table are a small selection.

Suffixes are added to the end of words e.g. *assess + ing = assessing*. The addition of a suffix to a root word is likely to change the root word's number or its word class in some way e.g. the addition of the suffix *-able* to the end of verbs changes the verb into an adjective: *enjoy* becomes *enjoyable*.

Many dictionaries such as The *Shorter Oxford English Dictionary* (OED) (Brown, 2002) provide definitions of prefixes and suffixes and the way in which they change word meaning and word class. If the dictionary is based on historical principles, it may also provide an overview of the way in which the use of the affix has developed over time. Here are two examples from the OED.

---

a–, *prefix*. 1. OE away, on, up, out, as in arise.
–able, *suffix*. Adjectival suffix originally only found in words from French or Latin as in *separable*, but subsequently used to form many adjectives. By analogy directly from the stem of English verbs, as in *appreciable* from *appreciate*. Later freely used to form adjectives from verbs of all types (*bearable*, *reliable*).

There are a number of patterns that can be identified as prefixes and suffixes are added to root words:

> *prefix + root word*
> *root word + suffix*
> *prefix + root word + suffix*

Or, in the case of one of the English language's longer words:

> *antidisestablishmentarianism* (**prefix + prefix + root word + suffix + suffix + suffix**)

Understanding of affixes can help spellers to construct words and spell them correctly. There is more information about the role of suffixes in spelling in the section on spelling rules. Readers use affixes to break down difficult words into manageable chunks and work out meaning.

Back formation This is where words from one word class such as nouns are shortened to form a word that belongs to another class such as verbs e.g. *edit*: the verb comes from *editor* the noun.

Clipping Clippings are also called curtailed words. It simply means that the original word is abbreviated.

- The beginning is clipped leaving us with words like *phone* from *telephone* or *bus* from *omnibus*.
- The end may be clipped leaving words like *pub* from *public house*.
- The beginning and the end can be clipped so that the word becomes *flu* rather than *influenza*.

Acronyms A new word is formed from the initial letters of other words e.g. *AIDS* is a recognised word but it stands for *Acquired Immune Deficiency Syndrome*. Some of these words retain both the acronym and the phrase, others are remembered only for the new word. It is important to remember that an acronym is only an acronym if the letters are sounded as a word. If the individual letters are said e.g. HRT then it is not an acronym.

Eponyms People give their name to a noun or an activity. The Earl of Sandwich famously gave his name to the sandwich. The Duke of Wellington provided a name for a type of boot.

Portmanteau words Portmanteau words are two words that are merged together to form a new one. Lewis Carroll's poem *Jabberwocky* (Carroll, 2003) contains many examples such as the word *chortle* (*chuckle* + *snort*). A more modern example is the word *emoticon* (*emotion* + *icon*).

Borrowing Many words in the English language are derived from words borrowed from another language. Another term related to borrowing is 'loan word'. Examples of these kinds of words include *commando* (from Afrikaans); *cipher, lemon* and *sofa* (from Arabic); *bungalow* and *shampoo* (from Hindi/Urdu). Some borrowings remain true to their original pronunciation and spelling e.g. *fiancé* (from French). Others retain their original spelling but their pronunciation changes from the original e.g. *chauffeur* and *souvenir* (from French). Other borrowed words become completely assimilated over time e.g. *guerrilla* (from Spanish) and *tomato* (the Americas via Spain). This can impact on spelling because the addition of suffixes does not always follow the predicted pattern and sounds are not always represented by the predicted letters. Borrowings mainly occur where there is no name to describe a thing, state or event so the noun is borrowed from the original language.

Words are needed to be able to describe, name and narrate events and experiences. New words are created to meet the needs of the situation. They may remain current for a few years and then drop from common usage e.g. *yomping* to describe walking long distances was in common usage during the 1980s following the Falklands War but is now used infrequently. Other new words remain as an established part of the language and their meaning may evolve e.g. *blitz* which came into common usage during the air-raids of the Second World War as a shortened form of *blitzkrieg* (German meaning *lightning war*). It was originally used as a verb to describe the bombing raids; it then became a proper noun to describe the period and has evolved into modern colloquial language as a verb for doing something quickly e.g. *Let's blitz the paperwork*. Warfare (e.g. *kamikaze*), exploration (e.g. *chimpanzee*), science and technology (e.g. *robot* and *laser*), social phenomena (e.g. *alcopop, docusoap* and *decluttering*) and politics (e.g. *cold war, Thatcherism* or *Blairite*) are often the stimuli for an upsurge of new words.

One area where vocabulary has developed rapidly in recent years is alongside new technology and innovation. The language of computing, the Internet and mobile phone technology is increasingly familiar to us. Language from this lexical field provides many examples of vocabulary changing or being created, all of which may well be familiar unless you are a *newbie* (a newcomer to the Internet) e.g. *boot up, chatroom, hard drive, memory stick, laptop, surfing, blogging, hacking, flaming, spam, texts, messaging, wap*.

Stop and reflect

Consider whether or not there are any recent neologisms (new words) in your subject or vocational area. The more innovative and developmental your area of work the more likely it is that there will be an expanding vocabulary.

Confusing words

Given the variety of sources that English is derived from and its lengthy evolution it is hardly surprising that some words have duplicated either their sound or their spelling but have different derivations and meanings.

● Homophones

These are words that sound alike but which are spelt differently and have different meanings e.g. *weather* and *whether* or *your* and *you're*. In speech the meaning of the homophone is worked out from context. Spellers need to make sure they make the appropriate choice of spelling for the context in which the word is being used.

Syntax
Order in which words are placed in a sentence.

- Many homophones come from different word classes so this is one way of helping to remember which word to choose e.g. *new* is an adjective because it describes a state whereas *knew* is a verb and changes its form according to person and tense. The **syntax** of a sentence can help spellers decide which word to use.

- If there is a pair of words that frequently get confused it may help to use a memory strategy as a checking system e.g. *If the sun shines **we are at her*** (weather).

- It can be confusing to learn homophones together. If there is a particular group of words that cause difficulty, learn them in their separate groups rather than together because this is where the memorable patterns are likely to be found e.g. *they're*, *their* and *there*:

  - *They're* belongs to the group: *I'm* (I am), *you're* (you are) and *they're* (they are). It is formed from a pronoun and a verb.

  - *There* belongs with the place group: *where*, *here* and *there*. There is a clear pattern to help spellers use the correct *there* for place.

  - *Their* belongs to a possessive pronoun group: *my*, *your*, *his/her*, *their*. It shows belonging.

It is then simply a case of checking that the correct version of the word has been chosen based on a personal checking mechanism of abbreviation, place or belonging.

● Homonyms

These are words that are spelt the same but have different meanings. They may also have different pronunciations e.g. *sow* and *sow*. The meaning of each word and its pronunciation is gained from the context in which it is used e.g.

I sow the seeds.
The sow produced ten piglets.

Analysing errors

Tutors should be able to identify their own spelling errors and the spelling errors of their learners. It is even more helpful to understand what kinds of spelling errors are being made because spelling errors often fit into recognisable patterns. It is more useful to develop a strategy that can be applied to a pattern of errors than to identify individual words because the learner will then be able to approach the problem from the perspective of an underlying principle. They can then apply this principle to a range of situations rather than having to commit single words to long-term memory.

The following types of errors can result in poor spelling:

- Using the wrong homophone e.g. *It's to late* rather than *it's too late*.
- Leaving out letters e.g. *Febrary* rather than *February*.
- Shortening or lengthening words by omitting or adding syllables e.g. *rember* rather than *remember*.
- Putting letters in the wrong order (transposing) e.g. *attepmt* rather than *attempt*.
- Doubling where a second letter is not required e.g. *neccessary* rather than *necessary*.
- Not knowing the rule for a particular spelling pattern. (More about spelling rules on page 106.)

7

Grapheme
Letter.

- Mixing up sounds or not knowing the **grapheme–phoneme** links (letter–sound links).

Phoneme
Smallest unit of sound.

- Reliance on spelling a word as it sounds.
- Reliance on spell-check facilities which do not pick out homophone errors, additions or omissions if a 'correct' word is produced.

 Snippet

> Spelling Bees are a popular pastime in the USA. Nine million children between the ages of 12 and 14 compete for a place in the national competition. The finalists spell words like *tmesis* (putting a word in another one), *izzat* (honour) and *kundalini* (life force in your spine), *poiesis* (the act of making) and *koine* (common language). There's even an award-winning documentary about the spelling contest called *Spellbound*.

Spelling strategies and their implications

Good spellers use a range of different strategies to ensure they have increased the probability of selecting the correct letters to represent the different sounds within a word (the grapheme–phoneme links).

● Spelling phonetically

This strategy is usually described as spelling a word the way that it sounds. It is a useful strategy but there are limitations. There are approximately 44 different phonemes but there are only 26 graphemes. This means that letters have to be paired up to form some of the sounds. Pairs of letters that form a single sound such as *ch* are called digraphs. Some sounds such as *tch* are formed from three letters called trigraphs. Other sounds can be blended together so that each sound can be still be heard but they are frequently used patterns of sound such as *pl* as in plunge or *cl* as in *clear*. Spelling phonetically requires knowledge of the different links between graphemes and phonemes. It also requires an understanding of the fact that because English has developed over a period of at least two thousand years, many sounds have more than one possible spelling choice.

There are twenty-one consonants. Some of them, such as the sound /*b*/ as in hu**b,** offer limited links between the phonemes and their written representation. Other sounds such as /*k*/ as in **cat** are more problematic because there are more choices e.g. **k**ite, la**ck**, **ech**o or even pla**que**. Often the choice of written or graphemic form to represent a particular sound depends on the position of the sound within a word. George Bernard Shaw once demonstrated the complexity of grapheme–phoneme links by writing the word GHOTI. The word is actually FISH but he selected alternative graphemic representations:

gh = f   as in cou**gh** or tou**gh** but it could just as easily have been *ph* as in *phone*.
o = i   as in w**o**men
ti = sh   as in na**ti**on or atten**ti**on but it could have been *ch* as in *cache*.

Some of the most varied graphemic representations occur in the representation of the vowel sounds. The complexity of the relationship between graphemes and phonemes is one of the reasons why spelling can sometimes be quite difficult.

There are five vowels: *a, e, i, o* and *u*. The letter *y* can sometimes act as a vowel (e.g. *crypt*). Vowels have two forms: a short form and a long form. The long form is the name of the letter in the alphabet.

Vowel	a	e	i	o	u
Short vowel sound	as in *cat*	as in *bet*	as in *lip*	as in *top*	as in *hut*
Long vowel sound	as in *mate*	as in *bee*	as in *I*	as in *no*	as in *tune*

Vowel sounds can be combined to form sounds such as *ow* in *flower*. These merged sounds or glides are called diphthongs. These complicate spelling still further. The same *ow* sound in *flower* is also present in the word *cloud* for instance.

One of the reasons that people make spelling mistakes when they spell **phonetically** is that they make the wrong choice of letters to represent the sound that they can hear. Another reason is that we often hear the sounds or the word that we expect to hear but people use pitch, rhyme and tone when they are speaking. Depending on where a speaker comes from and what effect they wish to give their utterances, such

Phonetics
Symbols used to represent the sounds of a language.

as surprise or to ask a question, sentences rise and fall. This means that words are often unstressed or unclear – either in the middle of the word or at the end because the speaker is hurrying on to the next word. Problems with words ending *-able* and *-ible* can stem from this lack of clarity. Words ending in *-able* are more common though. When people speak they run words together (assimilation) and drop letters (elision) during the flow of conversation: sometimes speakers do both. These factors can have a negative impact on spelling if there is a dependence on phonetic spelling.

The other difficulty with relying on spelling phonetically is the number of silent letters in English. Some of the silent letters have been fossilised. This means that they were once pronounced e.g. *knife*, *what*, *gnome*. Other silent letters were deliberately added by writers during the seventeenth and eighteenth centuries to make words look more like the classical languages they were derived from e.g. *pneumonia* and *mnemonic*. Some silent letters are the result of mistakes. The silent letter *h* in *ghost* is a result of William Caxton mimicking the typesetting he saw in Holland where it was used to represent a specific hard *g* sound (Brown and Brown, 1992).

Task

Identify words from your vocational or subject area that contain silent letters.

7

Learners may need support remembering these words. The words in your list will depend on your curriculum area but you may have identified words such as *weigh* and *weight*, *psychology*, *island* and *listen*.

There are some groups of letters that do not look right together. This is because English allows only certain combinations of letters e.g. *clunch* looks as though it may be a real word but most spellers will know that it is unlikely that *wvix* is correctly spelt.

● Chunking

Breaking a word into smaller chunks makes it easier to spell. Words can be broken down in a variety of ways including affixation and syllabification.

A syllable is often described as a beat. A syllable is the smallest part of a word that is spoken at one time. One way of identifying a syllable is to rest an elbow on a table and the hand from the same arm under your chin. Try saying 'remit' aloud. You should feel your jaw move twice. There are two syllables in the word *remit*.

- Each syllable must have at least one vowel. It could be the vowel on its own. Remember that the letter *y* can sometimes take the place of a vowel e.g. *crypt*.
- Prefixes and suffixes are usually a syllable long.

By breaking these words down into syllables the danger spots for misspelling them are often separated so cannot be ignored. It can also be helpful to use syllables to decide whether there are double letters or not as they tend to be sounded in separate syllables e.g. us-u-al-ly, nec-es-sary or suf-fix.

● Using spelling rules

It is not the intention of this chapter to provide a guide to all the spelling rules that English spelling draws on. Rather, its aim is to encourage individuals to investigate groups of words in order to identify patterns and formulate some rules for themselves. A word of caution though: there are always exceptions to the rules. It is also important to remember the whole rule, e.g. most people remember the rule: **i** before **e** except after **c**. However, there is more to it than that. The rule is actually:

i before e except after c where the sound is ee

There are a number of useful spelling rules; some of them are related to phoneme–grapheme links, others to syllables and some to suffixes. Here is a selection of useful rules to know:

- The flossy word rule. One-syllable words ending in *f, l* or *s* need a double letter after a short vowel e.g. *staff, fill, kiss*.
- Rules for forming plurals, including knowing when to change a *y* to an *i*.
- The silent or magic *e* rule. Words requiring a final long vowel sound followed by a consonant may be formed by the addition of a silent *e* at the end of the word e.g. plate. This applies to single-syllable words and multi-syllable words where the stress is on the final syllable e.g. *invite*. There is a defined pattern of letters: consonant, vowel, consonant + final *e*. The best way to see the rule in action is to compare words with a short vowel sound with words that have the long vowel sound e.g. *kit* and *kite*, *fat* and *fate*, *sit* and *site*, *mut* and *mute*, *pet* and *Pete*, *cod* and *code*. Of course, other letter patterns can form the long vowel sound so there are a number of caveats on the rule that most people understand implicitly. The rule itself provides a useful base for adding suffixes that begin with a vowel. It also forms the basis for the rules relating to dropping final vowels when adding suffixes beginning with a vowel.
- Doubling the final consonant when adding suffixes beginning with a vowel e.g. *run* has a short vowel sound but if the suffix *-ing* is added the vowel has the effect of changing the short *u* sound to a long *u* sound. This is prevented by doubling the final consonant e.g. *running*. There is more to this rule based on syllables and letter patterns.

Spelling rules are based on patterns. It is possible to work out a spelling rule by investigating patterns. One of the most common uses of a suffix is to change a noun from its singular form to its plural form. The most common way of doing this is to add the suffix *-s* to the noun.

Task A

Identify some words from your professional practice that are turned into their plural form just by adding *-s*.

Words you might have thought of include *books, texts, handouts, worksheets, learners, students, tutors, lecturers, teachers, assistants, tables, desks, assessments, assignments.*

However, not all words are turned into their plural form so easily.

Task B

Look at these pairs of words. Sort them out according to the pattern they follow and then express the three rules for creating plurals.

*address addresses   box boxes   lady ladies   bully bullies   reply replies
display displays   identity identities   activity activities   essay essays
dictionary dictionaries   opportunity opportunities   holiday holidays
activity activities   buzz buzzes   fox foxes   church churches   flash flashes
watch watches   match matches*

- Words ending in *tch* and *ch* where the sound is *tch, sh, ss, x* or *z* add *es.*
- Words ending in a vowel + *y* add *s.*
- Words ending in a consonant + *y*, change the *y* to an *i* then add *es.*

There are some words that retain the inflectional ending *-en* from Old English e.g. *child children, man men, woman women, brother brethren, ox oxen. Mouse* turns into *mice* and *louse* turns into *lice*. If the rule was consistent *house* should turn into *hice* rather than *houses*! Other words retain the inflectional ending that identifies their derivation from Latin e.g. *criterion criteria, fungus fungi, formula formulae, syllabus syllabi* although *syllabuses* is gradually turning into the accepted form of the plural. Some words do not change from their single form to their plural and meaning is worked out through context e.g. *sheep.*

7

Task

Identify the pattern for spelling the plural form of words ending in *ff, fe* or *f* from these statements.

Cuff becomes *cuffs.*	*Cliffs* becomes *cliffs.*
Wolf becomes *wolves.*	*Belief* becomes *beliefs.*
Wife becomes *wives.*	*Knife* becomes *knives.*
Scarf becomes *scarves.*	*Handkerchief* becomes *handkerchiefs.*
Roof becomes *roofs.*	

- Words ending in *-ff* can be pluralised by the addition of the suffix *-s.*
- Words ending in *-fe* are turned into plurals by changing the last *f* of the root word into a *v* and then adding the suffix *-s.*

- Words ending in *-f* can be pluralised by changing the *f* into *v* and adding the suffix *-es* where the sound is /*v*/.
- If the sound remains as an /*f*/ then the suffix *-s* can be added.

It is an important strategy to be able to compare similar words and work out patterns.

● Does it look right?

Have you ever written a word down and then looked at it and suddenly doubted that it is spelt correctly? The best way to deal with this is to write down some different ways of spelling the word in question. Often whole-word recognition reading will help identify the correct spelling. Also if a number of different spellings have been committed to paper it makes it easier for the speller to use a dictionary or glossary to locate the correct spelling.

● Dictionaries and glossaries

A glossary is a list of words or terms and their meanings. The words can often have a specialist meaning. Glossaries are found at the back of many documents including this text. Dictionaries provide more information than glossaries. Words in dictionaries and glossaries are in alphabetical order.

Here are some further useful points to note when using a dictionary.

- The top left corner of each page has a word printed in a bold font. This tells the reader the first word on the page.
- The top right corner of each page has a word printed in a bold font. This tells the reader the last word that appears on that page.
- Each word is followed by additional information including: its different meanings; what part of speech it is; different ways of using the word; compounds; pronunciation.

The problem with dictionaries is that spellers need to be able to use alphabetical order effectively. They also need to have a reasonable idea of how the beginning of the word should be spelt. Silent letters can cause difficulties as can unusual grapheme–phoneme links. For example, the word phoneme sounds as if it starts with an /*f*/ rather than an /*p*/.

Snippet

When I took the first survey of my undertaking, I found our speech copious without order, and energetick without rules: wherever I turned my view, there was perplexity to be disentangled, and confusion to be regulated; choice was to be made out of boundless variety, without any established principle of selection; adulterations were to be detected, without a settled test of purity; and modes of expression to be rejected or received, without the suffrages of any writers of classical reputation or acknowledged authority.

Samuel Johnson (1755) Preface to *A Dictionary of the English Language*

Task

Glossaries are a useful way of introducing specialist words and terms. Using the words within their correct context is an important strategy for committing them to long-term memory. Identify some other strategies that vocational and academic tutors could use to develop a knowledge of specialist vocabulary e.g. crosswords.

Incorporating short word-games into the routine of delivered sessions can be a useful strategy to improve reading skills as well as spelling. Strategies include word searches, DARTs-related activities such as cloze procedures, games including hangman and pelmanism. (Refer to Chapter 3 for a full explanation of DARTs.) The latter involves two sets of cards – one set could be words, the other set could be definitions. The cards are shuffled and spread out, face down. Learners then turn the cards two at a time. If they match a word and definition they keep the pair; if not, the cards are turned face down and the next learner takes their turn. The game also develops memory skills. Other activities could include jigsaw words where words are split into different parts and must then be joined up.

Proofreading

Good spellers also proofread their words once they have finished writing to ensure that they have removed any errors that may have occurred during the writing process. Some spelling errors are typographic errors. This means they have occurred as part of the mechanical process of creating the text. Other errors occur because the writer is concentrating on what they want to communicate rather than on correct spelling. The proofreading stage of the process involves looking carefully at a piece of text to identify spelling, punctuation and grammar mistakes.

Strategies to remember how to spell words

There are various strategies that can be used to remember how to spell words. Remember that 75 per cent of spelling follows regular patterns. This means that an understanding of spelling rules and recognition of the different patterns such as syllables and affixing will help develop accurate spelling. In addition, it is important to develop strategies to remember and check irregular spellings and spellings for words that cause individual problems.

● Look/say/cover/write/check

Multi-sensory learning activities are proven to be more effective for moving information from the short-term to the long-term memory. The look/say/cover/write/check method activates visual, aural and kinaesthetic strategies. It also incorporates rehearsal of knowledge.

Look Look at the correctly spelt word carefully e.g. *committed*. What is noticeable about it? It has a double *m* and a double *t*. Look at the shape of the letters – words with ascenders (b, d, f, h, k, l, t) and descenders (g, j, p, q) are more recognisable because they make a more distinct shape.

Say Say the word. Break it into chunks or emphasise the part that you have difficulty with e.g. *com-mit-ted*.

Cover Cover the word that you have memorised.

Write Write the word from memory. Can you see it in your mind? Can you hear it in your mind?

Check Match the word you have written to the original. Do this at least three times or until the word is correct. It is important to then use the word in context.

● Mnemonic devices

A mnemonic is a sentence or a phrase that helps you to remember something. A mnemonic to remember the vowels is: **a**ngry **e**lephants **i**n **o**range **u**nderpants. The initial letter of each word in the phrase identifies each of the vowels.

Here are a couple of examples of the way mnemonics can be used to remember specific words.

> *There is land in an is**land**.*
> *There is a para in se**para**te.*
> *Watch out for the bus in **bus**iness.*
> *Con**science** is a science.*
> *Necessary has one collar and two socks.*

In all five cases the mnemonic focuses on the part of the word that causes spelling difficulties. There is no point developing a mnemonic to help remember the part of the word that you can already spell correctly.

Task

Create mnemonics for these words: *miscellaneous, personnel, environment*.

● Auditory memory

Sound the word out as it is spelt rather than as it is pronounced e.g. *p-neumonia, Wednes-day, sc-issors, kin-a-e-s-thetic*.

● Visual memory

Take note of ascenders and descenders of letters to see the shape that the word makes, or create an image in your mind that focuses on the difficult area of a particular spelling e.g. *necessary*.

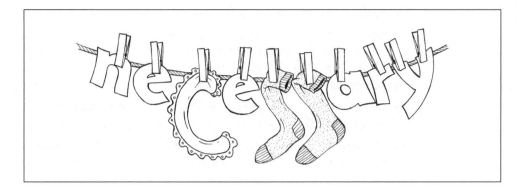

The image is entirely up to the person who has difficulty with the spelling. Take, for example, the word *knowledge*: there are two possible areas that could be difficult and fortunately they form two separate words *owl* and *edge*. So I envisage an owl on the edge of a cliff about to fall off. This works as a strategy for me but it might not work for you! The key is to create your own picture in your mind so long as it focuses on the area of spelling that causes problems. Some people find it more confusing to break words down this way. So it is important to remember that what works for you will not necessarily work for all your learners and vice versa.

Try to focus on the area that causes problems. *Always* is a word that can cause some difficulty. Lee (2002) suggests:

This makes use of a mnemonic as well as a visual prompt.

The act of looking at the word and manipulating it helps the memorisation process. This is one of the reasons why the process should be as individual as possible. If the process of identifying shapes, words within words, and images is a passive experience then it is unlikely to be as effective as if learners create the memory strategies themselves. The process can be modelled and prompts can be offered but the strategy must belong to the person who needs to remember the word.

Summary

- Spelling can be supported through a raised interest and awareness in words.
- Words are created in a variety of ways.
- Words can change meaning over time. Words can also have a common meaning and specialist meanings which may be different from those in common usage.

- Focus on patterns by grouping similar words together.
- Use spelling rules, knowledge of grapheme–phoneme links, chunking devices (syllabification and knowledge of roots and affixes), serial probability and dictionaries to spell words correctly.
- Proofread work for spelling mistakes once a piece of writing is complete.
- Do not rely on spell-checking facilities in computer software.
- Support learners by offering them multi-sensory strategies for learning how to spell.
- strategies include look/say/cover/write/check, mnemonics, rules and chunking either by syllable or by affixes and root words.

Test your knowledge

7.1* How many morphemes are there in this sentence?

Many spelling rules are linked to adding suffixes to words.

7.2* Work out what the prefixes in these words might mean:

a. **inter**active, **inter**cede, **inter**ruption, **inter**cept.

b. **extra**ordinary, **extra**terrestrial, **extra**vert.

7.3* Look at each of the groups of words. Decide what role the suffix plays – either the way that it changes word class or the way the suffix adds to the meaning of the word.

a. *professional, tutorial, individual, visual, aural, formal*

b. *taxonomy, economy, astronomy, autonomy.*

7.4* a. Break these words down into prefixes, roots and suffixes: *review, multicultural, developmental, multisensory, inflexible, assessment, reassessed.*

b. Decide how breaking words down like this might help with spelling.

c. Can you identify a possible spelling rule from the pattern that develops?

7.5* The homophones *to*, *too* and *two* can cause learners problems. Identify the correct word class for each word and suggest some strategies for checking whether the correct word is being used.

7.6* Select the correct homophone from the body of this memo that has been sent to all staff.

All staff are reminded that *new/knew* registers must have a course code. Staff who do not *no/know* the relevant code should contact *they're/their/there* line manager for clarification.

It is *our/hour* policy that students cannot be enrolled until a course code is provided. They will not be *allowed/aloud* to remove materials from the resource centre and will not *be/bee* certificated *wear/where* they have *passed/past* portfolio *based/baste* courses.

7.7* How many syllables are there in these words: probably, remember, experience, professional, achievement, sufficient, conclusion, candidate, participant?

7.8 **a.** Use a range of the strategies described in this chapter to learn words that are key to your professional practice and which cause you difficulty.

b. Identify appropriate strategies to support your learners as they develop their own spelling skills.

Where next?

Texts

Abell, S. (2000) *Helping Adults to Spell*, London: Basic Skills Agency

Crystal, D. (2002) *The English Language*, London: Penguin

Crystal, D. (2004) *The Stories of English*, London: Penguin

Pratley, R. (1988) *Spelling it Out*, London: BBC Books

Websites

www.askoxford.com

www.bbc.co.uk/skillswise/words/spelling/

www.class.uidaho.edu/luschnig/EWO/18.htm

www.literacytrust.org.uk/Database/Primary/spelling.html

7

Speaking and listening

We encode and decode spoken communication all the time. Research suggests that some people can spend up to 75 per cent of their time either speaking or listening (Burley-Allen, 1995). Practitioners in the lifelong learning sector need to encode information (speak) so that their learners can decode it successfully (listen and understand). They also need to actively support learners as they develop effective encoding and decoding skills.

Minimum core elements

A2

- Making appropriate choices in oral communication episodes.
- Having a knowledge of fluency, accuracy and competence for ESOL learners.
- Using spoken English effectively.
- Listening effectively.

Part B Personal Language Skills

- Expressing yourself clearly, using communication techniques to help convey meaning and to enhance the delivery and accessibility of the message.
- Showing the ability to use language, style and tone in ways that suit the intended purpose and audience, and to recognise their use by others.
- Using appropriate techniques to reinforce oral communication, check how well the information is received and support the understanding of those listening.
- Listen attentively and respond sensitively to contributions made by others.

Varieties of language

Varieties of language
Language form distinct from other forms of the language.

We all speak slightly differently. American English is a **language variety** as is legal English. The second form is closer to a style or register of the language but both types of language describe a group of people who share common traits or geographical factors. Adult learners are expected to develop their language skills so that they can choose which variety of language to use that best fits the audience and purpose of their speech or writing: this includes the use of standard English (there is more information about standard English on page 116 of this chapter).

● Accent

Accent
The way we sound when we speak.

Accent describes the way in which people pronounce words, using different stress, pitch and rhythm. Accent can be derived from geographical or social location. There are only 44 individual phonemes (sounds) in the English language but we may individually pronounce the same sound slightly differently depending upon our background. If you come from the north of the country you might say 'path' with a short /a/ sound as in the word 'cat' but if you come from the south you might say it more like /ar/ as in the word 'cart'. It is the same letter but two speakers from different geographical locations represent the sound differently. Some regional accents are stronger than others. People may also find some regional accents more attractive than others.

● Dialect

Dialect
Words, phrases and grammatical constructions peculiar to a geographical region, social stratum or occupation.

Lexical features
Vocabulary that is not standard English.

Syntactical features
Way in which a speaker/writer uses grammar.

A **dialect** is a regional, social or even occupational form of language which has characteristics of the parent language but which differs in other respects. It will have some vocabulary or **lexical features** which will not be found in the standard form and will not be fully understood outside the region, society or occupation where the dialect is spoken. For example, in parts of Nottinghamshire and Derbyshire a pavement is a 'causey'; a small alleyway is a 'gennel' and someone who is sulking is described as being 'mardy'. Dialect varieties of the language also use non-standard grammar or **syntactical features** e.g. *I were late* instead of *I was late*. In the past, regional dialects were considered socially inferior to the standard form of the language. This was emphasised by the standard form that BBC English took. However, there are a growing number of presenters who have a regional accent and there is an increased recognition of the importance of language variety.

The phrases 'formative assessment' and 'summative assessment' are examples of occupational dialect or a variety of language that exists within the lifelong learning sector. These specialist terms allow teachers, tutors and lecturers to identify the exact purpose of an assessment but people from outside the profession may struggle with the meaning of the vocabulary. The other term often associated with occupational dialect is **jargon**. Specialist vocabulary can be important within a profession because professionals can use one or two words rather than a lengthy explanation. It can be precise and meaningful. For example, beauticians are familiar with the words *depilation, desquamation, effleurage, epidermis* and *hydrotherapy*. It is easier for a beautician to talk about 'effleurage' than to refer to 'stroking massage movements'. Other beauticians will be familiar with the lexis or vocabulary. Other people may know some of the words or may be able to work out their meaning but will not find the specialist vocabulary so straightforward. This leads to the negative connotations of the word 'jargon' which suggest that someone uses words and acronyms to sound knowledgeable and that the jargon is designed to confuse the people trying to decode the message, especially if the audience comes from outside the profession familiar with the jargon. Examples of negative jargon include meaningless buzzwords and phrases such as 'blue sky thinking'; elaborate constructions such as 'learning resource centre' rather than library; and euphemisms that are used to disguise what is actually being said.

Jargon
Specialist/technical vocabulary used by small groups of people.

8

Stop and reflect

Discuss the extent to which practitioners need to use specialist vocabulary to describe the various mechanisms involved in teaching and learning processes.

The language people use to encode a message should be clear and without ambiguity. It can be argued that specialist terms enable people to communicate effectively about complex ideas and concepts. The same is true of any language variety. *Introducing the Grammar of Talk* (QCA, 2004) identifies that speakers who use dialect forms make use of non-standard grammar but, as Cox identifies, 'it is important to understand that dialect forms are grammatical and rule-governed . . . but the rules are different from those of Standard English' (Cox, 1991: 29). Writing something such as 'he done it' is not acceptable in a written format but for spoken discourse, excepting formal situations, its meaning is clear.

Snippet

> Some people think that flowery language and complicated writing is a sign of intellectual strength. They are wrong. Some of our greatest communicators were – and are – passionate believers in the simplicity of the written word. As Winston Churchill described a particularly tortured piece of 'officialese': 'This is the sort of English up with which I will not put.'
> Baroness Thatcher speaking for the Plain English Campaign

● Standard English

Standard English is another variety of English, originally a dialect from the south-east of England, that is now widely regarded as a 'good' or 'proper' use of English because people regard its use of language and grammar to be correct. Trudgehill (2000) identifies it as a dialect. The Kingman Report (1988) attempted to define standard English as 'the written form used by all writers of English, no matter which dialect area they are from.'

● Received pronunciation (RP)

RP is a model for pronunciation that many people hold to be correct in the same way as standard English is held to be the correct written from of English. This form, or accent, is also known as BBC English or the Queen's English. Crystal (1987) describes it as a 'prestige' accent. Reasons for its use lie in educational history and the development of public broadcasting. RP is regarded by some as being a neutral accent. It is also the form of English most likely to be taught to second-language speakers in other countries. It is not necessary for native speakers to use RP. The Bullock Report (DES, 1975) and the Kingman Report (DES, 1988) both identified that accent is part of our identity. The only caveat to this is that people should be able to speak with sufficient clarity to be understood beyond their accent boundaries.

● Ideolect

Idiolect
A personal speech pattern.

Some people have very noticeable ways of pronouncing certain sounds. The TV presenter Jonathan Ross has a strong **ideolect** because his /r/ sounds a little like a /w/. We all have an idiolect that reflects the way that we pronounce individual sounds and are representative of our language experiences.

The important thing is that language is appropriate to the audience and for the purpose for which it is being used. The study of the choices and unwritten rules that influence the kind of language that people use when they speak (or write) is called **pragmatics**. Some people have more choice about the kind of language that they can use than others.

Pragmatics
The features of conversation that people take for granted.

● Elaborated and restricted codes

Register
Level of formality informality of a piece of writing.

Elaborated code
Ability to switch between different language forms to suit audience purpose.

Restricted code
Having only a limited variety of language to choose from.

Many speakers, and indeed writers, recognise that they must use an appropriate **register** and form depending upon the context in which they are communicating. These people have an **elaborated code** that allows them to communicate effectively depending on the situation in which the communication takes place. This means that they may use dialect words with their family and friends but they can switch to a more standard format when they communicate with people such as bank managers and teachers. They are able to access a standard variety of the language which is used for formal transactions within society.

Put simply, people who are only able to communicate effectively in their dialect and who cannot switch between formats are said to have a **restricted code**. The idea of elaborated and restricted codes was developed by Basil Bernstein in the 1960s (Bernstein, 1975). His research identified that some people in authority, teachers and employers for example, can unintentionally discriminate against users with restricted codes of language i.e. those who are dependent upon a variety other than the standard communication, because their use of language is more informal and their vocabulary can seem more limited.

Labov's (1972) research identified that it was too simplistic to say that people were limited to only one form of English but that the range of styles that people were able to adopt depended upon their experiences and their education. Tutors need to respect learner language choice but recognise that in certain situations it is better to speak and write in a more standardised form. Just as with the written form, spoken language needs to be selected or modified to meet the needs of audience and purpose.

Differences between spoken and written English

Spoken language and written language differ in structure and content e.g. people tend not to speak in complete sentences. One of the reasons for this is that spoken language is an immediate form of communication: in most circumstances it is not planned. Another reason is because both speaker and listener are using context as part of the communication process.

Identify some of the features that you might find in spoken language that you would not necessarily expect to find in written language.

There are many ways in which speech and writing differ:

Colloquial
Informal style of speaking.

Idiom
Phrases that do not mean literally what they say.

- Spoken language is usually less formal than written language. It is **colloquial** and uses **idioms** such as 'it's raining cats and dogs'.

- People use more slang in speech. Slang is very informal and changes with fashion and age. People often use slang to show that they belong to a particular group. It changes quickly.

- Speech relies on tone, volume and gesture for added meaning. Consider a transaction between a parent and child. The parent says the word 'bed.' This is neutral: it's a statement. However, the child does not want to go to bed. The tone of the word can be created by the addition of a question mark into the transcript: 'bed?' The remark, 'bed!' may include emphasis, increased volume and gesturing towards the stairs. This could be a 'shooing' motion with the hands or if the tone is more severe the accompanying gesture could be a pointed finger.

Substituting
Using non-verbal communication to replace verbalised message.

- Spoken transactions may **substitute** non-verbal communication such as gestures for verbal input. A shrug is a good example of where someone will substitute a gesture for words.

- Conversation can be repetitive. Speakers can come back to a topic, either using the same words or paraphrasing what they said earlier. Some speakers have phrases that they may use unconsciously.

- People will use fillers to cover silence or gaps for thought. These can be sounds like 'mmm' and 'er' or phrases such as 'you know'. Some of these fillers can have overtones of dialect. In Carlisle, for example, many speakers will finish a phrase with the sound 'eh' e.g. 'The weather's not good, eh'. This can either be a statement or a question depending upon the tone and pitch that the speaker uses.

- There can be false starts in speech, with people back-tracking to change how they want to say something.

- Speech uses phrases and words rather than sentences. Sentences are left incomplete either because their meaning is clear within the context or because there is shared knowledge. This is called ellipsis. An idea can also be completed by another speaker.

- People interrupt one another – this may lead to a change of conversation in mid-flow.

- Conversations can be disjointed by one person changing the direction of what they are saying e.g. *They know about assessments – how to categorise them.*

- Spoken language does not have punctuation as such; instead there will be pauses and discourse markers that are used to indicate a change of topic. There are heads used at the beginning of a conversation so that speakers can place themselves in the conversation e.g. *That homework, it was meant to be finished for today.* The first two words state what is coming next. There are also tails which finish a topic off or reinforce what has been said e.g. *I'm going to do the BTEC national, I am.*

- Spoken language can be vaguer than written language. Speakers use words that do not impact on the meaning of the spoken language but which are used to involve the other participants of the spoken communication e.g. *He'll go to university, or something* or *You need to take pens, pencils and stuff.*

Deixis
Expressions which cannot be understood unless context is known.

- **Deictic** expressions are used. These are one-word utterances that make sense only within the context in which they are used. This feature can be the spoken equivalent of pointing at something e.g. *this*, *that*, *those*. Deixis helps to orientate the speaker to what is being spoken about or when (temporal deixis) e.g. *now*. Deictics are often used when the communication is part of a shared activity and will be used alongside context and non-verbal communication.

Best practice

'All teachers display and make use of key words. Opportunities for speaking and listening are built into schemes of work, together with a wide range of writing and research.'
(Ofsted, 2006)

● Mode

Style
Way in which language structure content are organised.

Mode is simply another word that means the same as purpose e.g. *inform*, *instruct*, *explain* or *persuade*. The audience and purpose of a piece of text or speech will affect the **style** used by the writer or speaker. Remember, texts and spoken language can have more than one purpose; the primary purpose is the most important although there may be secondary purposes behind a piece of writing as well.

8

Speaking

Context
The situation in which spoken language is used.

Adjacency pairs
Turn-taking and expected patterns within transactions.

Effective spoken communication is an essential skill for practitioners in the lifelong learning sector. There are many different types of spoken English. The most basic distinction is that between monologue and dialogue. The first form of speech requires one person; a lecture is a monologue. The second form of spoken English requires more than one person and it requires interaction. Interaction produces patterns of conversation or exchange of ideas. Although spoken language is not structured in the same way as written language, there are still conventions such as, openings which may be an exchange of greetings, or **context** setting. Conversation follows a turn-taking pattern that requires speakers and listeners to be able to follow aspects of non-verbal communication and things like pauses as well as the utterance to decide who should speak and when someone can take a turn at speaking. Sometimes there are distinct patterns to turn-taking. A question from one person should be followed by an answer from someone else. These patterns are called **adjacency pairs**. Most of the time people follow the expected patterns.

It can be a useful strategy to break the pattern of the adjacency pair when a learner asks a question. The natural reaction is to answer the question. Consider the option of replying to the question with another question, or making a questioning response, to prompt or help the learner draw on their own knowledge and arrive at an answer for themself. The questioning response seeks additional information and can also be disguised information or advice that the receiver can use as a prompt to activating their own knowledge or arriving at a conclusion. This process helps learners to become independent; it also helps the tutor to facilitate the needs of the learner.

● Functions of spoken language

Spoken language can also serve a variety of functions and have specific constructions or discourse features depending on the kind of communication that is occurring. Language can be used to express ideas, thoughts and feelings.

- It can have an **expressive function**; we talk to ourselves, swear and say things like 'well I never', 'crikey' or use an expression familiar to a small group of people like family or friends such as 'Well, I'll go to the foot of our stairs.' Expressive language tells listeners how we feel about something or allows us to express our emotions: the verbal equivalent of stamping our feet, perhaps.

- Language also has a **transactional function** where people take turns to exchange information; it can mean recording facts, thinking or making a statement of identity. It can involve interacting on a professional level or a social level e.g. having a conversation. Interaction requires an explicit understanding of the words and language people use and it also requires an implicit understanding of when words should not be taken literally because of factors such as idiom, turn of phrase, sarcasm and irony.

● The rules of spoken language

Phatic language
A communication that has little literal meaning.

There are unwritten rules for all these different kinds of spoken language. For example, when people initiate conversations they will probably use **phatic language**. This is the language that we use to oil the social machinery such as when we meet and greet someone e.g.: *Terrible weather!* or *How are you today?* The responses required are almost formulaic. The speaker does not really want to know how the other person is; the question is simply a form of greeting and the required answer is *'Ok'*, *'Fine, thanks'* or something similar. This can be difficult for language users who are not aware of these discourse features in spoken language. Learners with the autistic spectrum disorder can have difficulty grasping phatic conversation as they can take statements at face value rather than recognising the social interaction behind the words.

Accommodation
When speaker changes way of speech to match the listener's.

Paralanguage
Speakers add meaning to their words by the way they speak.

People change the way that they speak depending on context, audience and purpose. We often **accommodate** successful communication by trying to change spoken features and **paralanguage** to match the perceived needs of the listener. A stereotype of accommodation is when a native speaker slows down and speaks more loudly to a non-native speaker in an attempt to facilitate understanding. Neither of these are necessarily successful strategies for effective communication but both serve to illustrate the more subtle ways in which we change what we say to meet the needs of our listeners.

- We might simplify language if we are explaining a concept or process to someone who is unfamiliar with them.

- We may emphasise key words, repeat ourselves or paraphrase what we have to say.
- We may even change our accent to sound more like the person with whom we are communicating.

Of course, the process also works in reverse. If someone wishes to emphasise the fact that they are different or if they do not want to accommodate the person with whom they are communicating because they do not like them or because they feel **Speech divergence** angry for example, they will show **speech divergence**.

Speech divergence
The opposite of accommodation.

Spoken communication tends to be immediate. This means that if there is confusion or ambiguity the listener can often ask for clarification and give verbal and non-verbal feedback. For example, if a practitioner in the lifelong learning sector wants people to work in groups on a particular topic they will explain the task; then if learners have blank expressions on their faces or look confused it is possible to clarify the task further. Some of the learners may ask questions or request further information about the task.

Models of communication

There are various models of communication, some more complicated than others. Shannon and Weaver's model of communication (Ellis and McClintock, 1991) identifies a sender who encodes information which can be sent by one or more channels of communication that is then decoded by the receiver.

Shannon and Weaver, who were electronic engineers, identified the fact that information could be blocked if:

- The sender and the receiver were not using compatible channels of communication e.g. language differences, cultural differences, specific learning difficulties and disabilities preventing interpretation of non-verbal communication or implicit content.
- Blockages or 'noise' blocking the channel of communication e.g. distractions.

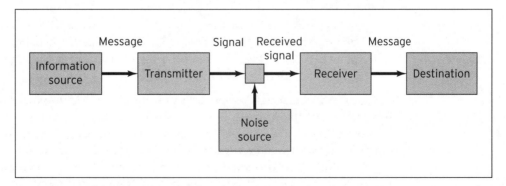

Shannon and Weaver's model of communication

Source: Cited in Ellis, R. and McClintock, A. (1991) *If You Take My Meaning: Theory into Practice in Human Communication*, London: Hodder & Stoughton (p. 72). Originally Shannon, C. E. and Weaver, W. (1949) *The Mathematical Theory of Communication*, Urbana: University of Illinois Press. Reproduced by permission of Hodder & Stoughton Ltd.

Shannon and Weaver's 1949 model does not perfectly describe the complexities of the communication process but it is a starting point for practitioners to consider factors impacting on clear encoding, transmission and decoding of spoken language. One of the most significant weaknesses of Shannon and Weaver's model is the fact that it is linear. There is failure to include a feedback loop that enables receivers and senders to check whether or not transmission of a particular message has been successful. Later models of communication recognise the need for feedback. Despite this, it is a useful starting point to consider some of the issues that affect clear communication.

Some factors to consider when speaking in a classroom setting:

- Try not to speak too fast.

- Speak clearly and, if need be, project your voice. Consider volume, pitch and tone.

- Structure spoken communication so that the topic is clearly identified. This should allow listeners an opportunity to access prior knowledge. It can be useful to ask listeners to consider what they already know about a topic so that they can predict the content of what you have to say. This can be built into the structure of sessions and into the progression of teaching and learning activities.

- Use words and phrases to identify where one topic of conversation has finished and another is about to begin. These are called 'discourse markers' and can be words like 'right', 'ok' and 'moving on'.

- Use straightforward language and paraphrase yourself – explain terms in a different form to give learners a chance to interpret specialist terms and jargon.

- Signpost with sequencing words such as 'now', 'first of all', 'finally'.

- Scaffold active listening skills by explaining what you are going to be talking about, identify key words by writing them on the board, pause to ask questions to check that learners are listening so that you can rehearse information if need be and conclude by summarising what you have said.

- Select an appropriate level of formality. Fluent speakers who use the elaborated code know when to switch register and style. It can be useful to consider this as a process rather than assuming that learners know how to switch between varieties of language.

- Do not be afraid of silence. Many practitioners answer their own questions if learners do not offer immediate feedback. Remember that learners need an opportunity to frame their ideas before verbalising them. Try counting to ten to allow a pause to be long enough that a learner will fill it.

Clarification through supporting presentations, handouts and diagrams is an important part the process. If a tutor demonstrates something practical such as a beauty treatment, a welding technique or a flower arrangement, it can help if learners are provided with written support. This could take the form of a handout that needs to have information (from the demonstration) added into it; alternatively a supporting diagram may be an effective way of clarifying the communication.

This diagram was used to support a practical demonstration. It illustrates the way in which effective communication can effectively cut out noise which impedes meaning. The demonstration is supported by a diagram which illustrates the content of the demonstration. The diagram uses symbols standard to the tutor, and their meaning

Each flower is assigned a simple shape so that a diagram can be created to show arrangers how to place their flowers in their arrangements.

may be supplemented by the addition of a key where learners are unfamiliar with the symbols used. The diagram is an aide-mémoire for the learners who must then create their own flower arrangement.

Using questions

Questions are an important tool in a tutor's repertoire. It is important to ask the right kind of question so that learners are involved and challenged without feeling threatened or embarrassed because the question is too difficult.

Closed questions have limited right or wrong answers. They are used to check that learners have understood factual or knowledge based material but they do not engage the learner in evolving processes or concepts or in a developing discussion of ideas e.g. *When should you use a question mark?* Or, *Have you completed the assignment?*

Open questions do not have correct answer as such. An open question gives the learner a chance to express their own views and opinions and to shape their own hypothesis. Tutors may use open-ended questions as prompts to encourage learners to consider different options or to consider analysis. They may also be the kind of questions that require learners to justify responses. Open questions can be used at higher levels to encourage learners to transfer skills or knowledge into new situations or as part of a problem-solving process.

Rhetorical questions are used to signpost what a speaker is saying. No answer is expected because the speaker is going to provide it immediately after the question has been asked. The device is designed to draw listeners into what the speaker is saying so that they think about the material under consideration. This can be a difficult concept for some learners who do not recognise the rhetorical device and think they have been asked a question. They will then interrupt the speaker because they think they have been cued to do so by the question.

Tag questions are statements turned into questions by adding a question to the end of the statement e.g. *The weather is unusual for the time of year, don't you think?* Other tag questions include *isn't it, don't you, aren't they.*

Whatever kind of question is asked it should be relevant to the learners and the material they have been covering and it should be clearly expressed so that learners know exactly what is being asked of them.

Learners may need time to think about the answers to questions, so give them a chance to reflect on what they want to say. This may be done through pauses and silence or it can be done through more structured activities that give learners an opportunity to formulate their responses.

Best practice

'Some tutors are too ready to answer questions on behalf of their students, especially if the answers are not immediately forthcoming. Both tutor and student are content this way because progress appears to have been made. The good teacher, however, will give students time to search for an answer, judging the right time to offer a prompt or to re-phrase the question to elicit a response.'

(Ofsted, 2002)

Do not be afraid of direct questioning – draw learners into a discussion; ask them questions by name. However, this needs to be done carefully: do not ask a question of a learner if you do not think they will have an answer, and avoid asking questions in a regular pattern.

Confirm good answers by mirroring the response; write the key ideas or words on the board; use confirming body language. It is important never to reject an answer, but it may be that a learner will need to be prompted with hints and additional questions. If an answer trails off the point, draw the learner back e.g. *That was a good idea. Now what about . . .*

Stop and reflect

Discuss the different ways in which questions can be used as part of a session.

Questions can be used to check learner understanding as part of the formative assessment process. They could be used as part of the summative assessment process if the summative assessment is practical (think about driving tests). Questions can be used to scaffold learner interaction with the subject. They can be part of a teaching and learning activity, such as a KWL grid where learners generate their own questions. More information about KWL grids can be found on page 29. Learners can also work in pairs to generate questions and answers in a particular topic in the style of an interview.

Active listening

Hearing and listening are not the same thing. Research has shown that learners spend a lot of their time listening. Listening is not an easy task; it requires concentration and many learners need to develop effective listening skills for different purposes. There are many different barriers to effective listening. Some of the filters may be due to specific learning difficulties or disabilities, including attention deficit disorders. Other factors include how tired a listener is; whether they are interested or not (go on – be honest – how many times have you tuned out of the conversation during a large meeting or presentation because you did not perceive the content as relevant?); distractions; an emotional response to the topic under discussion; poor decoding or language skills; the listener hearing what they want to hear. Listeners often listen selectively and discard information they do not want to hear. Other listeners may add information or change the content of spoken communication to what they want to hear.

Stop and reflect

Consider some of the different purposes for listening e.g. for information about train cancellations or for information about a homework task within a learning environment.

It may help to create a spider diagram or mind map.

People listen for a variety of reasons: for information, for instruction, to be persuaded, to be entertained or for an explanation. The attention that someone gives to a speaker will depend upon the context in which they are listening. For example, listening to a lecture requires concentration whereas listening to a radio programme may be more superficial and the listener simply picks up the gist of what is being discussed. Just as people read in different ways for different purposes, so there are different listening strategies. If people are listening to instructions, such as directions, then they will probably listen to every word. If they are listening for specific information, then they will probably tune in to key words. We also listen empathically. This means that we pick up on the emotion of the person speaking rather than what they are actually saying.

Active listeners ensure that they engage with the speaker, in a face-to face scenario, and the material to which they are listening. This requires more than not interrupting the speaker and getting rid of distractions.

● Engaging with the speaker

- Non-verbal communication is an important part of the process. Listeners should try to look towards the speaker and use eye contact to show that they are paying attention to what the speaker has to say. Listeners may tilt their head to one side, smile in agreement sometimes, lean their chin on their hand, lean forward slightly towards the speaker, nod their head when they agree with the speaker and make sounds of agreement. A good listener does not look elsewhere, appear distracted or start to yawn.

- Use verbal feedback, which may be a sound such as 'mmm' or 'er' or a phrase such as 'I see.' This is called back channelling. The listener is supporting the speaker in what they say.

- Ask questions once the speaker has finished talking.

- Be constructive.

● Engaging with the material

- Activate prior knowledge, then try to predict what the speaker might say next.
- Do not jump to conclusions and interrupt.
- Be prepared to suspend judgement.
- Identify key words and phrases.
- Summarise and paraphrase what has been said. Mirror what the speaker has said. This is where the listener may repeat key words and ideas in the form of a confirming statement or question. This has the effect of clarifying information. A similar strategy can be used to reflect the emotions or feelings of a speaker. This may be done by non-verbal communication in the form of a sympathetic expression.
- Ask questions of what has been said. These can be clarifying closed questions or more general open questions.

Clear verbal communication

Task

This is a back-to-back communication activity to consider the different aspects of speaking and listening. You will need paper, pen/pencil and something on which to rest. This requires three participants, a sender, a receiver and an observer to record the way in which the other two perform.

- The sender – the person speaking – and the receiver – the person listening – should sit back-to-back.
- The observer should sit so that both the sender and the receiver can be observed.
- The sender must draw a simple image on a piece of paper. It should be more complex than a basic shape but it does not need to be a work of artistic merit.
- The sender must then describe the image to the receiver so that the receiver can replicate the image as closely as possible. The sender must not look at what the receiver is doing and the receiver must not ask questions.
- The observer should make a note of the conversation, the gestures and the other features of the transaction employed by both the sender and the receiver.

Discuss the activity afterwards to identify the difficulties of giving and receiving instructions where communication is limited.

Summary

- People speak with different accents, including received pronunciation.
- People may use different lexical features depending upon their geographical location, social level and profession.
- The way someone sounds and the words that they use are part of their identity.
- Standard English is a form of dialect used by important social institutions such as government and education.
- Learners need to be able to switch between different types of language depending upon the audience and purpose of their speech. It is important that learner language choice is respected but that learners are drawn towards recognising the necessity of an elaborated code permitting them a wider choice in their use of language.
- Spoken and written English differ in structure and content.
- Effective communication requires clarity of language, content and structure as well as opportunity for listeners to seek clarification.
- Clarification within a teaching and learning setting may include an opportunity for questioning and discussion or may be supported by handouts and board work.
- There are different kinds of questions. Closed questions are self-limiting whereas open questions give learners an opportunity to develop their own thoughts. Some learners have difficulty recognising when statements have been turned into questions or when the question is rhetorical and merely signposts content.
- Active listening requires the listener to interact with the content of the transaction and with the speaker.
- Effective teaching practitioners scaffold the listening process.

8

Test your knowledge

8.1 Explain what the following terms mean:

a. *Accent*.

b. *Dialect*.

c. *Standard English*.

d. *Received pronunciation*.

e. *Idiolect*.

8.2* Identify the grammatical errors that appear in these dialect forms:

a. *They was going to find out about it on the Internet.*

b. *I done the work yesterday.*

c. *It ain't right.*

d. *The information was in them books.*

e. *Me and her went to the resource centre but didn't find nothing.*

8.3 Create a table similar to the one shown here. Think about the four modes of language use. For each mode identify some of the parallels and differences that exist between written language and forms of speech.

Mode	Writing	Speech
Entertainment	Novels	Storytelling
Information	Newspapers	TV/Radio News
Persuasion	Posters	Preaching
Instruction/Advice	Manuals	Coaching

8.4 Identify some of the strategies that you might use to do the following:

a. Engage with the speaker.

b. Engage with the material that you are listening to.

8.5 Identify the strategies that you would use to confirm that you have listened to and understood:

a. directions to a given location

b. a learner who is concerned that they are falling behind with their work.

8.6* Consider the following:

a. Identify the steps and resources required within the process for explaining a topic to a group of learners.

b. How can vocational and academic tutors develop their learners' listening skills?

Where next?

Texts

Halliday, M. A. K. (1975) *Learning How to Mean: Explorations in the Development of Language*, New York: Elsevier

Keith, G. and Shuttleworth, J. (2006) *Living Language*, London: Hodder & Stoughton

Nelson-Jones, R. (1986) *Human Relationship Skills Training and Self-Help*, London: Cassell

QCA (2003) *New Perspectives on Spoken English in the Classroom*, London: QCA, downloadable from **www.qca.org.uk**

Websites

www.bbc.co.uk/skillswise

www.bl.uk The British Library houses a collection of British accents and dialects which can be found in the collections section of their website:
www.collectbritain.co.uk/collections/dialects/ (accessed 28 April 2007)

www.plainenglish.co.uk

8

9 Non-verbal communication

Spoken communication is affected by the ways in which speakers and listeners use non-verbal communication strategies. In fact there is evidence that a significant part of communication comes from non-verbal signals. Non-verbal communication can reinforce, complement or place emphasis on a speaker's words. It can also imply the opposite of what a speaker is saying. Listeners are much more likely to accept the non-verbal communication as the correct information rather than the spoken word, even though they may not be aware of the fact that they have interpreted unspoken signals. This chapter looks briefly at the range of non-verbal communication that tutors can use to support their spoken words; the ways in which non-verbal signals can be interpreted and also looks at the ways in which non-verbal signals can have different meanings, depending on where you come from.

Minimum core elements

A2

- Listening effectively

Part B Personal Language Skills

- Using appropriate techniques to reinforce oral communication, check how well the information is received and support the understanding of those listening.
- Using non-verbal communication to assist in conveying meaning and receiving information and recognising its use by others.

Channels of communication

Non-verbal communication refers to the non-verbal signals which accompany speech. Some of these signals are voluntary and are used to clarify meaning. This means that the sender is deliberately communicating using non-verbal signals. The speaker in this instance is effectively using two channels of communication, the verbal and the non-verbal, each confirming the content of the other. Sometimes, though, a speaker may communicate one message through the verbal channel but deliberately send the opposite message through the non-verbal channel e.g. winking after saying something to signal the opposite to be true (Forgas, 1989). Other elements of non-verbal communication are involuntary. This means that the sender is unaware that he or she is communicating feelings, emotions or a message that may be contradicting the spoken content of the communication.

Inexperienced tutors may sound calm and in control of a situation but they could be sending an involuntary contradictory message by the way they are standing in a hunched position; by holding their hands clasped in front of them or by fiddling with the collar of their jacket or shirt; or by remaining behind their desk the whole time (this may unconsciously be perceived as a 'safe place') (Neill, 1991). These involuntary messages are called **leakage**.

Leakage
Non-verbal communication that contradicts what the speaker is saying.

People often think of non-verbal communication as body language. However, non-verbal communication is much more than that.

Briefly note down some of the ways in which people can communicate non-verbally.

Gesture, posture, facial expression and eye contact are what most people think of when they consider non-verbal communication. Other aspects of non-verbal communication include **proximity**, what we wear, and the way in which we say something – so tone and stress are non-verbal communication techniques. These last two techniques are part of a **paralanguage** that we use alongside words. Other examples of paralanguage include volume, pace, emphasis, pauses and other sounds such as coughing. The final non-verbal communication strategy is appearance. People make judgements based on their understanding of what someone else is wearing – this could include clothing, make-up and ornamentation.

Proximity
Physical distance between people.

Paralanguage
Voiced communication devices that work alongside speech.

9

Clothes and communication

The way people dress tells others something about them. The most obvious example of dress communicating something is the uniforms that people wear. Uniforms are used by the armed forces to show what rank the wearers have and what job they do. Nurses wear distinctive uniforms, whilst the popular stereotype gives a hospital doctor a white coat and stethoscope. People do not have to wear a uniform for their clothes to communicate something about them.

Snippet

I wish I had invented blue jeans. They have expression, modesty, sex appeal, simplicity – all I hope for in my clothes.

Yves Saint Laurent

Task

Consider what message you would like your clothes to communicate about you.

It is important to maintain an image of professionalism combined with approachability. Many training providers and institutions have rules about what may or may not be worn during working hours.

Paralanguage

Paralanguage is the term used to describe the voiced elements of non-verbal communication. There's much more to words than just saying them. The way something is said will influence the listener's interpretation of the words. The following factors have an impact on what is said:

- Pace
- Tone
- Pitch
- Rhythm
- Volume
- Noises e.g. whistles, gasps, yawns, coughs or **fillers** such as 'um' and 'er'.
- Silence can be a form of paralanguage too.

Fillers
Form of paralanguage used to fill gaps between speech.

Meaning is gained depending upon whether the speaker's voice rises or falls. It also depends on which syllable the speaker emphasises. Listen to people around you to find out how they use paralanguage to add extra meaning to their words.

Body language

Kinesics
Study of body movements in non-verbal communication.

Orientation
The way people position themselves in relation to others.

Posture
The way someone stands or holds themself when they are sitting.

The term **kinesics** describes the scientific study of the way people use body language to communicate. According to Birdwhistle (1970) all body movements have a potential meaning. The way in which body movement is used to communicate depends on cultural codes and also upon individual behaviour. Proximity, **orientation**, facial expression, gesture, **posture**, head movement, eye contact and touch can all have meaning and can affect the way people interact. Chapter 8 identifies some of the ways in which non-verbal communication can encourage active listening. There are other aspects of body language that can be used effectively in a classroom, from gauging learner response to maintaining control.

● Expression

Most trainees, certainly in the secondary sector, are told at some point or other, either as a joke or in all seriousness, not to smile before Christmas! The reasoning behind this is that they need to stamp their authority on their classes – to show that they are in control. The fact is, though, that tutors need to be approachable and interested in what their learners have to say. It is also true to say that facial expression gives cues

Snippet

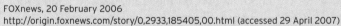

> **Scientists Train Soldiers in Non-Verbal Communication**
>
> A US computer program trains soldiers to communicate effectively. The program's residents react according to how well or poorly a soldier handles a situation. A single woman will turn away — and a nearby group of men bristle — if a soldier charges up to her. Young children will warm to a soldier who stoops to their level and removes his sunglasses before asking simple questions, Vilhjalmsson said in displaying the program.
>
> 'They are building an impression of you as you interact with them,' he said. Simple motions are important, such as placing a hand over the heart in greeting . . .
>
> 'Gesturing is not merely hand-waving. It conveys substantive information — thoughts that often are not conveyed in words,' said Susan Goldin-Meadow, a professor of psychology at the University of Chicago.
>
> FOXnews, 20 February 2006
> http://origin.foxnews.com/story/0,2933,185405,00.html (accessed 29 April 2007)

about emotions and feelings. There are very many different facial expressions and many different degrees of emotion or feeling. Sadness and interest, although it is not an emotion as such, along with anger, disgust, happiness and surprise are, according to Wainright (2003), the six most easily distinguished emotions.

9

● Eye contact

Eye contact is an important part of non-verbal communication. If someone maintains eye contact for too long or stares at another person this can be threatening or intimidating. If someone avoids eye contact they can seem very shy, embarrassed, nervous or downright untrustworthy.

If someone wishes to meet someone else they may make eye contact across a room. If someone is speaking they will make eye contact at different points in the communication: before they start to speak to signal that they have something to say; to check that the listener is following what is being said and also to encourage a response from the listener. If the speaker avoids eye contact with someone they are holding a conversation with, it could mean that they do not want a response or an interruption.

Eye contact is an active listening strategy. If someone does not maintain eye contact or at least watch the speaker, it usually signals boredom or that the listener is not paying attention.

Wainright identifies that people who are depressed avoid eye contact. In some cultures it is not polite to maintain eye contact when listening to someone speaking. Learners on the autistic spectrum may find it difficult to make and hold eye contact. Non-verbal communication is not necessarily straightforward.

● Gesture

Some gestures have an obvious meaning, others are much more subtle. Many cultures have a complicated system of gesticulation. Gestures do not have a common meaning around the world. In western society nodding confirms agreement. In some African cultures nodding indicates disagreement.

Gestures can tell tutors a lot about their learners. If a learner is feeling uncomfortable in a situation they could do one or more of the following:

- Cross their arms. There are degrees of arm-crossing, from folded arms with fists tightly clenched to holding one arm across the body holding the other arm that hangs straight down the side.
- Cross their legs.
- Lock one ankle behind the other.
- Engage in displacement activities, such as fiddling with a pen or scratching.
- Sit with both elbows on the table, head in hands, looking down to the table – this effectively shuts everybody out.

● Posture

Posture relates to the way someone stands or sits. An upright posture could mean confidence and assertiveness. Crossed arms and legs can suggest fear or nervousness.

Of course these gestures can be very subtle and can vary from person to person. The best way to find out about more about the gestures people use is to watch out for them. Next time you attend a meeting observe the gestures that people use to indicate they would like to make a point.

● Proximity

According to Edward Hall (1973), people use space and distance to communicate. There are different kinds of distance: intimate distance, personal distance, social distance and public distance. This is best illustrated with a diagram (see opposite).

There are a number of factors which affect the overall diameter of the different special zones and who is allowed into each of the zones. These factors include previous personal experience and cultural expectations. People from different cultures have different sized spatial zones. Conversation distance for western Europeans and North Americans tends to be between handshake distance and fingertip to fingertip (with arm outstretched) whereas Latin American people are more likely to stand much closer together to hold a conversation. Northern Europeans do not often touch one another when they are speaking whereas some Middle Eastern, Mediterranean and Asian cultures use casual contact as an accepted part of communication. It is best to be informed about specific cultures.

People try to keep their personal space intact even when they are part of a crowd.

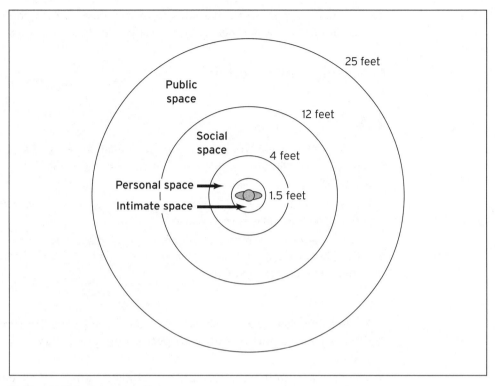

Hall's spatial awareness theory

Source: Hall, E. T. (1973) *The Silent Language*, New York: Anchor Press

Task

Consider these situations. Decide how people might try to maintain their personal space. The best way to find out is to observe the situation for real and note down the different strategies that people use.

a. A group of people sitting around a large meeting table.

b. In a queue.

● Orientation

The way someone sits or stands in relation to the person that they are communicating with will either enhance or impede the communication.

It is easier to communicate with someone face to face than it is to communicate with someone slightly to one side of you. Speakers will orientate themselves towards the listeners who seem to be listening most intently.

The layout of a classroom can impact on whether or not a learner is facing the tutor or has to twist round to one side to see the tutor. Layout can also impact on the dynamics of group interactions. If a group of four people are sitting in a row it is unlikely that any meaningful discussion will take place between the two people at opposite ends of the row. Note the way that people turn towards one another during discussions and pair work. It stands to reason then that if people cannot see one another or turn to one another easily, then effective communication will be limited.

● Putting it all together

> **Task**
>
> Consider the different types of non-verbal communication that teachers use. Feedback here will consider head movement, facial expression, eye contact, body movement.
>
> **a.** How can tutors show the following: agreement, reassurance, showing an interest, signalling that the learner is wrong?
>
> **b.** Some learners ignore ground rules during class discussion and seek to dominate the rest of the learners. Identify some of the non-verbal communication strategies that these learners might use.

a. There are various ways of showing all the above – consider your own strategies, discuss your responses with your peer group and observe what people around you do.

b. The obvious paralanguage features include volume and speed. These learners ignore the turn-taking signals made by others, interrupt and may also make forceful gestures this can include pointing, exaggerated shaking of the head and dismissive gestures with the hands.

Individuals who are on the autistic spectrum may not be able to interpret non-verbal cues. This means that they do not always follow the flow of a conversation because they do not see the non-verbal cues.

Summary

- Non-verbal communication includes body language and voiced communication such as tone and pitch.
- Non-verbal communication can be voluntary or involuntary.
- People are more likely to accept a leaked non-verbal message than the message from the spoken channel.
- Non-verbal communication can support or reinforce the verbal message.
- Non-verbal meaning can depend on gender and culture.
- Some learners may have difficulty interpreting non-verbal cues.

Test your knowledge

9.1 **a.*** Read this story. You may remember it from the previous chapter on speaking and listening:

> 'Bedtime,' said the parent.
>
> 'Bedtime?' asked the child.
>
> 'Bedtime!' repeated the parent.

Consider how one word may be said in three different ways. The punctuation provides a clue as to how the paralanguage should sound.

b. Consider how many different ways these simple words/phrases might be said:

(i) *Now.*   (ii) *Do you understand.*

9.2* Match these images to the moods or feelings which best describe them: *anger, disgust, fear, happiness, surprise*

a.   b.   c.   d.   e.

9.3* What might these non-verbal signals mean? Remember, some signals can mean more than one thing.

a. Shrugging

b. Rubbing hands together

c. Leaning back against the edge of a table, hands flat on the surface

d. Hands on hips

e. Steepling fingers together.

9.4* Look at these four diagrams: what does the orientation of the people involved suggest?

 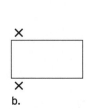 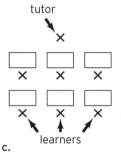 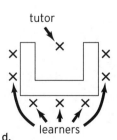

a.   b.   c.   d.

Source: Myers. G. E. and Myers, M. T. (1985) *The Dynamics of Human Communication – A Laboratory Approach*, New York: McGraw-Hill, (p. 237). Material is reproduced with permission of the McGraw-Hill Companies.

Where next?

Texts

Axtell, R. E. (1991) *Gestures: The Do's and Taboos of Body Language Around the World*, Chichester: John Wiley & Sons

Lambert, D. and The Diagram Group (1999) *Collins Gem Body Language*, Glasgow: HarperCollins

Pease, A. (1993) *Body Language*, London: Sheldon Press

10 Factors affecting the acquisition and development of language and literacy

The aim of this chapter is primarily to consider the different factors that influence the acquisition and development of language and literacy, barriers to learning and some strategies to overcome those barriers. Most educational research about language and literacy development is based on children. This chapter offers a brief overview of the key theories tied to child development, as they provide a useful starting point for a description and contrast with some of the available models of adult learning that can be drawn on by vocational and academic tutors. This chapter gives vocational and academic tutors an opportunity to reflect on the strategies that could be used to support learners as they develop their literacy skills within an embedded setting. It also provides an opportunity for tutors to reflect upon the rationale for embedding functional literacy skills into vocational and academic settings.

Minimum core elements

A1

- The different factors affecting the acquisition and development of language and literacy.
- The importance of English language and literacy in enabling users to participate in public life, society and the modern economy.
- Potential barriers that can hinder development of language skills.
- The main learning disabilities and learning difficulties relating to language learning and skill development.
- Awareness of issues related to varieties of English.
- The importance of context in language use and the influence of the communicative situation.

Personal language history

Everyone has a personal language history that accounts for the way they speak and the extent of their vocabulary range or lexis. Adults can identify external forces (people, locations, books, aspirations, etc.) that have influenced their acquisition of language and the way that they use language. It is possible for some adults to identify significant periods of their lives by the way that their use of English or varieties of English have changed and developed.

Task

Complete a mind map considering the influences on your acquisition of language and literacy skills e.g. parents, school and hobbies. The varieties of English you use may be situated in your interests, hobbies and your employment. Snowball this activity with a partner if possible.

The more we are exposed to language and the more we use it, the wider our repertoire of language becomes so that we can draw on it depending upon the situation and context (the domain) in which we are communicating: we have an **elaborated code** rather than a **restricted code**. Some of the language and processes we are familiar with are transferable from one situation to another. Other aspects of language and literacy are situated within specific domains.

Restricted code
Having only a limited variety of language to choose from.

Task

Consider these questions. They are prompts for reflection and discussion. They are designed to help you think about the way that you acquired and developed language and literacy. You do not have to answer all of the questions and you may generate others during your reflections. If possible discuss your answers with a group of peers. There may be some responses that are common to everyone but you may be surprised at the diversity of experience.

1. Which language(s) or dialect(s) did you hear first, do you think? From whom? E.g.

   English was the first language I heard spoken by my parents: one came from London, the other from Essex. Families and friends spoke with these accents although one Aunt had a strong Norfolk accent and another relation spoke with a Canadian accent. I still use expressions that my family used but which I now discover are not in common usage where I currently live – for example when I get lost or the traffic is diverted I go 'all round Will's mother's to reach my destination.

2. How many language(s) or dialect(s) were you using by the time you went to school? With whom? E.g.

   Some speakers speak in Urdu at home but speak in English at school. Elsewhere teachers may require an approximation of standard English in the classroom whereas the language of the playground may make more use of regional dialect vocabulary.

3. Think about the place(s) where you went to school. Where did you go to nursery or kindergarten; first/primary/middle school; secondary school? How did these places impact on the way you used language? E.g.

   When I moved to a new school I swiftly discovered that the way I spoke was different from the way the rest of the children spoke. They labelled my accent as posh and I quickly learnt to accommodate their use of language in order to avoid teasing. At home the process was reversed. I also discovered that some of the words I used at school were slang and I was not to repeat those words at home under any circumstances.

4. Which language did you learn to read and write in? Did this differ from your pre-school language experience?

5. Which language or dialect did the teachers or instructors use? Did this affect your own use of language? Why?

6. How have the jobs you have done, since school, affected your language use? E.g.

   Specialist vocabulary or language varieties associated with specific jobs: I have worked in education so I use specialist vocabulary related to teaching and learning.

7. Consider your hobbies and interests. How have these affected your language?

   Many hobbies and interests have specialist language and vocabulary. My hobbies include photography, family history, crochet, cross-stitch and gardening. All these areas of interest have specialist vocabulary including words like pixel, exposure, aperture, treble, half treble, Aida and evenweave, to name but a few. Most hobbies and interests have their own vocabulary. The linguistic term for vocabulary is lexis. Hobbies and interests have words that are associated with that particular area. An interest in military history would produce a vocabulary including war, militia, artillery, cavalry, corps, brigade, army, etc.

8. Think about speaking, listening, reading and writing. Do you still use all the languages and dialects you have learnt?

   *A manager in a further education institution uses standard forms of the language with a faint regional accent. During conversations with his siblings his accent becomes stronger and he makes use of dialect words and grammatical forms that are correct within the dialect variety. He **accommodates** his language to match theirs.*

Accommodation
When speaker changes way of speech to match the listener's.

10

Standard English
A prestige dialect used in formal situations.

Descriptive grammar
Used to describe the way people are currently using language.

You may have shared some common language experiences with your peers but language histories tend to be as individual as the people writing them. The diversity of individual linguistic experience is such that the 1988 Afro-Caribbean Language and Literacy Project revealed 173 varieties of language in use other than **standard English** in Inner London: the number has increased since then (Harris and Savitzky, 1988). Personal language histories are a strategy to help people value their own use of language and recognise standard English as yet another language variety that they can draw on. **Descriptive grammar** can then be utilised to identify the differences in structure that exist between different varieties of language without judging, stigmatising or belittling anyone's language identity.

Acquisition and development of language in children

Research identifies that there are a number of specific stages that babies and children pass through during their acquisition of language. Babies make sounds to show whether they are comfortable or not. Then they progress to cooing followed by babbling. By the time they reach eighteen months most babies are using single words to communicate. At two years they are linking the words into pairs followed by short sentences. As children grow, their vocabulary expands as does their understanding of grammar.

There are a number of theories relating to the way that language is acquired but, in general terms, it is accepted that language development is innate but must be developed through exposure to language. In effect this means that child language acquisition is governed by both nature and nurture.

Behaviourist learning was made popular by B. F. Skinner (1973) and is based on what can be seen and described. He suggested that children acquire language skills through imitation and reinforcement through positive confirmation by those around them. The main basis for this belief is that children who do not hear language spoken do not speak and that children who are exposed to language acquire language skills gradually. His theory was supported by an early experiment conducted by Akbar the Great in India during the sixteenth century. He placed newborn children in a speech-free environment. By the fourth year of the experiment the children were still without speech (Crystal, 1995). The problem with behaviourist theory is that, generally, children pass through similar stages of development regardless of how much they are exposed to language and positive reinforcement. They also go through a phase in their development when they may hear irregular verbs in use but form them in a regular pattern – e.g. *I runned* rather than *I ran*. If children learnt only through imitation they would be restricted to the language that they hear other people use.

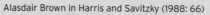 **Snippet**

It was my mother, not my father, who did the correcting of my speech, and I slowly built up a hazy picture of the nature of her expectations.
Alasdair Brown in Harris and Savitzky (1988: 66)

Cognitive theory or Piaget's Development Model (Tusting and Barton, 2003) suggests that there is a cognitive process at work in the acquisition of language. He suggested that language skills grow with a child's maturing intellectual abilities. The greater a child's cognitive skills the greater the child's corresponding linguistic ability. He outlined four distinct stages in the process. At stage one, babies come to recognise the difference between the outside world and themselves. By the time they reach the age of two, children will reach the second or pre-operational thought stage of their development. This is the single-word stage. The third stage of the process is the intuitive stage. This is the stage where children use regular rules but are likely to say things like 'I runned' rather than 'I ran'. The fourth stage is the concrete operation stage. This is where children learn to think logically. This stage should have been achieved by the time a child reaches the age of eleven. Piaget identified that the ability to conceptualise abstract ideas followed on from this. Piaget's theory identifies the features of cognitive development as taking place before adulthood and relies upon children to take an active part in the language acquisition process. They are not passive receivers – they are active processors of information and ideas.

Generative theory, developed in 1965 by Noam Chomsky and developed by Steven Pinker (1994), suggests that children have an innate capability to work out the rules that govern the language around them because they are born with a 'blueprint' for language that has been described as a universal grammar. The ability to extrapolate rules from what they hear around them has been called a language acquisition device (LAD). The problem with this theory is that there is other evidence available to suggest that children need interaction in order to develop their language skills.

Borwick and Townend (1993) identify the following factors as essential for the development and acquisition of language within children:

- Environmental stimulation
- Cognitive development
- The role of the primary caregiver in supporting stimulation and development of language skills.

Adults as learners

10

Adults are not blank canvases. They have characteristics that differ from children including:

- Sight and hearing that may not be as good as they used to be. The same can apply to memory and energy levels. Jarvis (1995) makes the point that physiological changes may lead adults to underestimate their capacity to learn resulting in a self-fulfilling prophecy that as we get older we are less able to acquire new skills and knowledge.
- Previous experiences of education. Adults may have barriers to learning created by their experiences of education many years ago.
- Wider knowledge and life experience.
- Established values, attitudes and habits.
- Expectations of the learning process.
- Motivation e.g. by desire to get work or gain a promotion.
- Coping strategies to disguise lack of functional literacy. Chapter 1 identifies the CBI's definition of functional literacy on page 4.
- Commitments and responsibilities that can impact on their ability to learn.
- A better idea of how they can learn and what their problems are.

> It was when I was on my way to give birth to my daughter that I realised I needed to get some learning. I was being wheeled under all these signs and I couldn't read them and I just panicked because, I thought, I can't read a bedtime story to my baby.
>
> Student explaining why she came to a literacy class.

Adult learners do not necessarily want to develop functional literacy in traditional 'English classes' (HM Treasury, 2006). They do not see the relevance of speaking, reading and writing skills in an isolated context. Unlike the learner in the snippet, many of them believe they already have sufficient knowledge. However, learners do need to develop literacy skills situated within their chosen academic or vocational area. Often learners do not recognise that they are developing these skills unless tutors outline the skills that learners are developing and reinforce the learning through discussion and generalisation.

Adult learning theories

Adult learning theories are wide-ranging and cover many different areas of study, including psychology and educational theory. It is not the intent of this chapter to investigate these theories in detail, simply to introduce the different concepts.

● Behaviourism

Pavlov's famous experimentation in the 1920s revealed that dogs which had been conditioned to associate the ringing of a bell with food would salivate when they heard the bell ring even when there was no food (Tusting and Barton, 2003). In the behaviourist model of learning the adult, as with the child, receives a reward as the result of exhibiting a specific desired behaviour. The theory of conditioning as a learning mechanism for humans was developed by Thorndike who suggested that when learners were given a stimulus the tutor's response could strengthen or weaken the learners' behaviour. This theory was developed further by Skinner (1973) who developed the idea of operant learning. Essentially tutors reward learners when they make a change in the right direction. In order for this to be successful complex theories and procedures must be broken down into small steps with clear objectives. This model also identifies the importance of repetition and reinforcement with rewards. Tusting and Barton (2003) note that operant learning is often associated with behaviour modification programmes, such as giving up smoking or losing weight.

- Success is measured by the way learner behaviour changes from the start to the finish of the programme.
- The emphasis on external measurement of changed behaviour means that no emphasis is given to developing understanding or independence.

However, vocational and academic lecturers can draw important information from this theory including:

- The importance of breaking tasks into manageable chunks with specific outcomes. Consider the way in which learners are presented with activities that involve literacy skills. In academic subjects learners may be required to write an essay or a report. For many learners this is not a manageable chunk. The tasks need to be broken down so that learners can move successfully through the different stages of understanding the task, researching their material, collecting evidence, planning their response, drafting, editing and finally proofreading their response to the task.

- The necessity of rewarding positive developments. This relates to the kind of feedback that tutors give learners. Written criticism should be constructive and should look for something that the learner has done well or partly achieved as well as discuss areas for improvement. Rewards during discussion or question-and-answer activities may take the form of confirming learner responses by writing key points on the board; repeating the learner's answer and using positive non-verbal communication.

Cognitivism

Piaget's model investigates the development of thought processes within children. His model stops short of the thought processes within adults. The important thing about his theory is the way in which learning and development occur because of changes that the learner makes in 'mental constructs and processes, the development and increasing sophistication of "mental maps" and "schemata" for representing the world' (Tusting and Barton, 2003). There are many different learning models associated with cognitivism.

Social learning theory Cognitive development within adults takes place in their workplace or social setting. Bandura (1977) identified that adults match their behaviour to the behaviour they see around them. Whilst this has links with behaviourism, Bandura's social learning theory makes the point that the observed behaviour modification process must be internally developed by adults changing their behaviour to match the attitudes and actions of their peers. Change relies on the learner noticing a behaviour or action, remembering it, copying it at a later date and, most importantly, being motivated to do so.

Social cognition Vygotsky and other researchers developed social learning theory further (Tusting and Barton, 2003). Not only do people develop within a workplace or social setting but they need to interact with one another in order to solve problems and thereby develop their cognition. Vygotsky made the point that this should be guided and he also found that having appropriate tools and activities enabled people to perform tasks that they could not perform without the tools or scaffolds in place.

Gagné's learning hierarchy Gagné developed a progressive learning model that recognised that there is a range of factors impacting on the learning process (Tusting and Barton, 2003). Some of these factors are external to the learner; other factors are internal and must build on what the learner already knows. One of the problems of this theory is that it is linear but adult learners do not always develop in a linear way. This is particularly noticeable in terms of their literacy. Learners can have spiky

10

profiles or strengths and weaknesses. Most tutors have come across a learner who performs well in spoken activities but whose written work does not reflect the same level of ability. Despite this, it is still a useful structure. There are nine stages to the learning hierarchy that Gagné identified.

1. The learner's attention needs to be gained. They need to be receptive to learning.

2. The learners need to know what the objectives and outcomes of the learning are. They need to know why they are doing something. There are different kinds of learning outcomes and tutors will offer different instruction depending upon the outcome but, generally speaking, stages 3–9 should then occur in sequence.

3. They need to be reminded of their prior learning. They must retrieve their existing knowledge.

4. They need to be presented with a stimulus e.g. they could be given a definition of a technical term associated with a specific vocational or academic area.

5. Tutors must then guide the learning process e.g. they could use a term correctly or model a process. The correct term for this stage is 'semantic encoding'.

6. The next stage is where the learners perform. They use the terms correctly or follow through the process. They may be asked to generate their own examples of something that the tutor has shown them.

7. The tutor gives feedback. This is the reinforcement stage of Gagné's hierarchy.

8. Assess learner performance.

9. The last stage is about generalisation. Learners are able to transfer their specific knowledge into wider contexts.

Situated cognition Gagné published his learning theory in 1977. Over time psychologists recognised that much of their research had taken place in controlled conditions. Lave developed a model of situated learning. He discovered that people performed differently in artificial situations compared with how they performed in their everyday lives. Further research reveals that artificial situations are limited because the problem is prescribed and there is usually only one solution. In real life people have to work out what the problem is and then set about solving it. There may be more than one solution.

Vocational and academic lecturers can draw important information from these cognitivist theories including:

- The importance of specific outcomes.
- Modelling can be an effective way of supporting learners to develop skills including literacy skills.
- Learners need to know why they are doing something.
- It is useful to build on existing knowledge.
- Learners should be able to work together in order to solve problems.
- It is important to scaffold the learning process.
- Authentic materials reflect real life.
- In real life, adults identify problems and solve them. There is more than one solution to a problem.

● Humanism

Carl Rogers is often associated with humanist theory for adult learning (Tusting and Barton, 2003). His premise is that the tutor actually facilitates learners who have an intrinsic desire to grow. Adults are driven, or motivated, by a desire to self-actualise – to achieve their potential. The learning process is initiated by the learner who identifies a need to develop within themself. It is then the tutor's responsibility to facilitate this process by providing the learner with stimuli, activities and resources to facilitate the development.

● Andragogy

Malcolm Knowles's text *The Adult Learner: A Neglected Species* (1990) set out four key principles about adult learning:

1. Self concept. Adults want to learn things that have an immediate relevance to their home life or their work. In other words the learning needs to be authentic. This impacts on teaching because it is important that they understand why they are being taught something.

2. Experience. Adult learners can draw on experience as a resource for their learning. This means that experiences, including mistakes, should provide the basis for learning.

3. Adults are self-directing. They need to be involved in the learning cycle, from planning to review.

4. Adult learning is problem-centred rather than content-orientated. Adults may be motivated to learn in the context of their wider lives rather than learning for the sake of learning.

Humansim and andragogy suggest the following aspects need to be taken into consideration when planning literacy for vocational and academic programmes:

- Learners need to be involved in the planning and development of the activities.
- There needs to be an effective assessment of learner requirements.
- Learners need to be able to progress towards their individual targets.
- Materials and resources should facilitate learner growth rather than learners being told how to do things.
- Learners should be involved in evaluation and review processes.

● Experiential learning

Kolb's learning cycle outlines a four-stage learning cycle to describe the adult learning process (Kolb, 1984).

In theory learners can access the learning cycle from any of the four stages. However, for the purposes of this introduction to experiential learning, let us assume that a learner starts at the concrete stage of the learning process. The learner does something, follows a set of instructions, writes a report, takes an order from a client or takes notes from a presentation. The next stage of the process requires them to

10

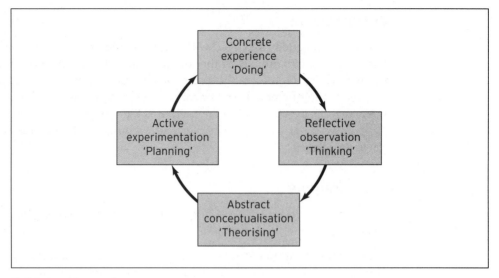

Kolb's learning cycle

Source: Kolb, D. A. (1984) *Experiential Learning: Experience as the Source of Learning and Development*, Englewood Cliffs, NJ: Prentice-Hall

think about what they have done; whether it was successful or not; what went well; what could have been done differently. This leads to the third stage in the cycle. Learners solve any problems that they have identified; they decide what they would do differently next time they have to carry out the activity. The fourth stage requires them to put their strategy for improvement into action.

Snippet

Tell me, and I will forget. Show me, and I may remember. Involve me, and I will understand.
Confucius

Learning styles

In addition to learning theories, there are other factors involved in the way in which adults acquire and develop literacy skills. People have different styles of learning and different preferences about where and how they learn, for example. There are different theories and models that have been created to explain them. The ones outlined here are a small selection of the most frequently used models. It is not the intent of this chapter to offer an in-depth critique of any of the models mentioned: rather, to identify the range from which tutors can draw strategies to support their learners.

- Honey and Mumford (1982) developed a learning styles survey based on Kolb that identifies people as having learning preferences based on whether they are activists, reflectors, theorists or pragmatists.

- Bandler and Grinder identify four modalities for learning (Tusting and Barton, 2003). Some learners have a visual learning preference which means, for example, that they like to see diagrams; others have an auditory learning style so they like verbal instructions; kinaesthetic learners prefer to be active; tactile learners like writing. The tactile modality is often dropped and tutors refer to VAK – visual, auditory and kinaesthetic.

- Dunn and Dunn list a wide range of factors that can impact on adult learning, including physical preferences, emotional factors such as motivation and determination, environmental factors such as seating, and sociological preferences including the way a learner relates to groups of different sizes (Dunn and Dunn, 1978; Carbo, Dunn and Dunn, 1986; Dunn, 2000).

- Brain dominance. Some learners exhibit right-brain learning preferences; others exhibit left-brain learning preferences. If a learner is right-brain dominant they are likely to be a global thinker who likes to see the whole picture. They are more likely to be experiential learners. Left-brain dominant learners are often described as analytical. In linguistic terms this means that a learner is likely to want to understand the separate parts and then put them together. This means that these learners are more likely to benefit from traditional methods of teaching languages.

- Gardner's multiple intelligences. In 1983 Howard Gardner, a cognitive psychologist, identified seven different kinds of intelligence, many of which are not developed in an educational setting (Gardner 1993, 1999). Since then he has identified a further two types of intelligence. The nine areas of intelligence are Visual/Spatial Intelligence, Musical Intelligence, Verbal/Linguistic Intelligence, Logical/Mathematical Intelligence, Interpersonal Intelligence, Intra-personal Intelligence, Bodily/Kinaesthetic Intelligence, Naturalist, Extistential.

10

Stop and reflect

Consider the ways in which learners in your vocational or academic subject area prefer to learn.

Task

Identify some strategies that you could use to help make literacy and language skills meaningful to your own learners within their vocational or academic context.

Barriers to language and literacy development

The National Adult Learning Surveys which occurred in 1997, 2001, 2002 and 2005 confirmed that there are many different barriers to learning which change little with the passage of time. Some of these barriers are concrete and readily identifiable, such as lack of childcare facilities or difficulties getting time off work for study, although their solutions may not be so straightforward. Other barriers are situated in personal psychology and emotion.

These barriers or blocks to learning can be categorised in different ways. Maxted (1999) describes them as 'cultural, structural and personal' whilst Harrison (1993) sorted them into 'situational, institutional and dispositional' groups. The three categories identified by the Skills and Education Network (2004) are physical (such as lack of mobility or childcare requirements), structural (transport, equipment and facilities) and attitudinal (prior negative experiences, lack of role models). Attitudinal barriers are often the most difficult to overcome.

Task

Rogers (2002: 239) identifies that learning is much more than a reasoning process and that we are all subject to emotional knowledge about our own capabilities. For example, I *know* that I can't knit because I tried twenty years ago and succeeded only in bending a perfectly good pair of knitting needles into right angles because I gripped them so tightly.

Identify a skill you *know* you cannot learn even though you may not have attempted this skill for many years or may not even have tried to acquire it. Consider whether your blocks to learning this skill come from pre-existing knowledge or self-perception. Think about the extent to which the two factors are intermingled.

Developing literacy skills and knowledge is subject to the same range of barriers that can impact on any learning. The Basic Skills Agency publication *Getting Better Basic Skills – What Motivates Adults* (2000) identified that adults felt unable to attend courses to improve their literacy skills for reasons such as lack of confidence and lack of time: the same reasons given by many of the respondents to the National Adult Learning Survey.

The following list represents some of the barriers that learners may experience before or during access to any learning.

- Low self-esteem
- Lack of confidence
- Transport difficulties
- Lack of time
- Limited availability locally
- Lack of knowledge about available courses
- Learners can feel uncertain about the appropriateness of a course or uncertain whether they will enjoy it or not
- Learners may not have sufficient qualifications to access a specific course
- Literacy or numeracy difficulties
- Ill health can impact on attendance and achievement
- Previous negative experience
- Cost of the course, materials and impact on other finances such as benefits
- Stereotyping
- Older adults may feel they are too old to learn something new. Other people feel that they are too slow to learn skills or that there is no point as they are coming to the end of their working lives
- Language skills
- Lack of positive role models
- Lack of support at home

- Peer pressures
- Lack of motivation: the 2005 National Adult Learning Survey (DfES, 2006d) identified that if individuals cannot see the benefits of learning they are not likely to access it
- Prior achievement or lack of achievement
- Family responsibilities, including childcare and care for elderly relatives
- Lack of or confusing publicity materials
- Association of education with school
- Tomlinson identified that the structure of courses culminating with examinations can act as a barrier for many learners
- Mental health issues, including depression which is an acknowledged demotivator
- Lack of access to facilities
- Learning style: learners who prefer active or practical methods of learning may not be able to access theory or traditional methods of teaching
- Specific learning difficulties and/or disabilities can create barriers to learning where there are insufficient support mechanisms or inadequate resourcing
- Lack of flexibility

- Lack of appropriate programmes
- Boredom resulting from unstimulating teaching methods
- Poor building design may prevent access for some learners and may also remind other learners of school and associated negative learning experiences
- Return to a classroom is often seen as an admission of past failure
- Workplace practice: one study (OECD, 2003) identified that workplace practice was a key factor in adults accessing learning. The attitudes of an employer can either promote learning or be a barrier, in particular to older or low-skilled workers as there may seem to be no benefit for the employer in providing extra training to these groups
- Timetabling: learners can experience fatigue if they have specific learning difficulties and/or disabilities. Classes can clash with work. Shift workers may be able to access some classes but not all of them because of their shift patterns
- Cultural and religious barriers: learners may find it more difficult to concentrate during a time of fasting, such as Ramadan. Cultural traditions may also prevent men and women from mingling

10

In addition to these general barriers to learning, learners with literacy needs face additional barriers:

- They may feel that there is a stigma to admitting low levels of literacy.
- They may not recognise that they have a literacy need (it is an invisible need) or feel that the skills that they have are acceptable for a particular course or programme (it is a latent need).
- Learners with literacy needs may return to education to complete a vocational or work-related course. These learners often feel that they left English behind at school and can see no reason why they should study it further.

Overcoming barriers

Stop and reflect

This text is about literacy skills and knowledge. Consider some of the factors that motivated you to read this text.

Adults are more likely to respond to a programme of study if they feel it meets their needs. Some people may read this text not because they are particularly interested in the history of the English language or spelling strategies but because they need to pass the literacy test that is part of the requirements for QTLS. Some of the reasons identified may be personal ones; others may be related to the institution where you are studying on a course leading to your professional qualification. This last factor is linked to professional requirements and may also result from an employer requiring you to successfully complete your qualification.

Relevancy overcomes the socio-economic barriers that say that literacy post-16 is irrelevant. Age- and experience-related resources aimed at the right level of learning help create a positive as opposed to a negative learning cycle. Instead of feeling intimidated, bored or anxious, learners can see how literacy improves their achievement within their chosen vocational or academic setting.

Summary

- Everyone has a personal language history.
- The wider our experiences of language and literacy the wider the repertoire of language and literacy we can draw upon to match our use of language to audience and purpose.
- Children's acquisition of language is widely accepted to result from a combination of nurture and nature.
- There is a range of learning theories associated with adults.
- Learning theories can relate to three principal areas of psychology: behaviourism, cognitivism and humanism.
- Learning theories such as Kolb's learning cycle and Knowles's theory of andragogy relate to observed educational practices.
- Learning theories have strengths and weaknesses. No one theory offers a complete solution to supporting adult learners as they develop their literacy skills.
- In general terms, adult learners develop skills and knowledge where they can see relevance to their needs and experiences. This means that learning tends to be more effective if it is practical or problem-solving. They are more goal-orientated; they can be self-directed.
- Adults face a range of barriers that can be categorised in different ways.

- Tutors can draw on learning theories to find strategies to overcome some of the barriers that learners face.
- Literacy skills and knowledge need to be relevant to the learner and the learner's main programme of study.

Test your knowledge

10.1* Identify the barriers to learning faced by Tom and Anjim in the following two case studies. Suggest strategies to help them back into education and support their acquisition of language and literacy skills.

Tom is 18. He left school two years ago, with no qualifications. He signed up for a course at the local FE college. Even though he did not have to attend everyday he still found the commitment a hard one to make and he enjoyed the experience no better than he had enjoyed school. By Christmas Tom had dropped out of college. He did not like being referred for basic skills support even though he struggled with some of the written work expected of him. He found a job as a bricklayer's mate. Unfortunately he did not enjoy this work and had a poor record for punctuality culminating in unemployment. Tom does not know what he really wants to do although he does enjoy car mechanics. He does not think he needs to bother about literacy skills because he wants to work with his hands.

Anjim is in her mid-twenties. She comes from Pakistan. Her first language is Urdu and although she speaks some English she has difficulty with new words and her written English is not as fluent as her spoken English. She attended a short sewing course so that she could meet people, improve her language skills and also so that she could learn the skills necessary to make her own clothes. She thoroughly enjoyed the course, particularly the design element of the sessions. Her stitching skills have developed to the extent that friends and family ask her to help them with their sewing. She would like to extend her skills further and is sure that there must be a course that she could attend where she could learn to use sewing machines more creatively and also find out more about design and pattern-making skills. She is worried that her level of English is not sufficient for her to progress.

10

Where next?

Texts

Coffield, F., et al. (2004) *Should We Be Using Learning Styles? What Research Has to Say to Practice*, London: LSRC

Freeborn, D. (1993) *Varieties of English – An Introduction to the Study of Language*, London: Macmillan

Shrubshall, P. and Roberts, C. (2005) *Case Study Four*, London: NRDC investigate the methods by which instructional discourse can be interwoven with complementary therapy and personal care classes

Websites

http://tip.psychology.org/

www.campaign-for-learning.org.uk

www.dfes.gov.uk/readwriteplus

www.geoffpetty.com

www.teachernet.gov.uk

Specific learning difficulties and disabilities

The Specific Educational Needs and Disability Act 2001 (SENDA) drew education under the auspices of the Disability Discrimination Act (DDA) 1995, now amended by DDA 2005. These Acts make it unlawful to discriminate against disabled applicants, potential applicants or students. It enshrines the principle that learners with specific learning difficulties and disabilities should not be treated 'less favourably' because of their individual difficulty or disability. It also identifies the responsibility that educational providers have to make reasonable adjustments so that learners with specific learning difficulties and/or disabilities are not disadvantaged. People with the following difficulties are included: physical or mobility, visual, hearing, dyslexia, medical conditions, learning and mental health difficulties. This chapter is designed as an introduction to some of the learning difficulties and disabilities identified by SENDA, the DDAs and *Access for All* (DfES, 2000b). It is a starting point for vocational and academic tutors to consider the range of needs that they may encounter, the implications for teaching and learning strategies, resourcing and drawing on wider support mechanisms.

Snippet

> Almost one in five adults have a disabling condition, yet less than 3% of staff in FE declare that they have a disability, and the position in HE is little different. Those who are employed are concentrated in lower-paid positions. As a result, learners in the sector have little chance to see disabled staff as role models.
>
> Alan Tuckett in *The Guardian*, 10 April 2007

Minimum core element

A1

- The main learning disabilities and learning difficulties relating to language learning and skill development.

Some definitions

Taxonomy
Scheme/order based on a system of classification.

The World Health Organization created a **taxonomy** to define disability in 1980. These are the definitions that tend to be used when discussing issues of disability:

- Impairment is defined as 'any loss or abnormality of psychological, physiological or anatomical structure or function'. This definition would include loss of an eye or a limb, for example.

- Disability is defined as 'any restriction or lack of ability to perform an activity in a manner or within the range considered normal for a human being'. For example, it is considered normal for a human to see and to hear.

- Handicap is defined as 'the disadvantage for a given individual arising out of impairment and disability, that limits or prevents the fulfilment of a role that is normal (depending on age, sex and social and cultural factors) for that individual'.

This means that 'impairment' refers to changes in a person's body from the accepted 'norm' whilst disability refers to what someone can and cannot do. 'Handicap' is the reference to changes in the person's relationship with the physical and social environment. 'Handicap' is a word that is considered offensive by many people because of its historic usage and the suggestion of dependence.

● A medical model of disability

The taxonomy described above follows a medical model of disability. The 'problems' created by a disability are located within the individual rather than within the context of wider society. The implications of this can be explained through the following example. Imagine that you have a viral infection. You go to see a doctor. The doctor makes a diagnosis which labels your condition and then, hopefully, effects a cure. Much the same happens with disability under the medical model. Individuals are labelled by various professional groups and then the individual is treated. For example, some dyslexics find that they can read more easily if material is printed on a non-glossy paper. Some prefer pale blue, others prefer pastels in pink, green or yellow. Under the medical model of disability the individual is diagnosed and provided with a 'cure' for their difficulty that singles them out as different from everyone else in the group, who receives handouts printed on standard, and cheaper, white paper. The emphasis is put on there being something 'wrong' that needs to be corrected. The impact of this can be measured in terms of marginalisation, isolation and, in the view of some, oppression.

● A social model of disability

A second model of disability – the social model of disability – moves the focus away from the individual and locates the difficulties of disability within society. The definition of disability described by the social model of disability arose from Disabled People's International in 1981.

- **Impairment** – 'Lacking part or all of a limb or having a defective limb, organ or mechanism of the body'.

- **Disability** – 'The disadvantage or restriction of activity caused by a contemporary social organisation which takes little or no account of people who have physical impairments and thus excludes them from participation in the mainstream of social activities.'

Essentially, the social model of disability identifies society's failure to take into account the needs of individuals so that they can participate in society on an equal footing with everyone else. Thus if a someone who uses British Sign Language is unable to complete a course because there is no communicator, the responsibility lies within the organisation rather than the individual. If a blind person does not have access to communication appropriate for their needs such as Braille or large print, then the educational provider has denied them access to the information that they need.

The implications are obvious. The medical model is sometimes called the individual model or the charity model of disability whereas the social model of disability defines disability as a social state. Educational providers have a responsibility to be inclusive in their practices.

Language choice is one strategy that can be used to promote inclusivity. The term 'disabled learner' suggests an individual whereas the term 'the disabled' suggests a separate group of faceless, beings without identity. Other words like 'cripple', 'handicapped', 'invalid' and 'mentally handicapped' vary from confidence-sapping to plain insulting. Choice of language is not political correctness run mad: rather, it is about respecting individuals and avoiding creating barriers. If in doubt ask what phrase or term a learner prefers. Some people with hearing difficulties prefer the term 'hearing-impaired learner'; others prefer the term 'deaf learner'; some prefer the phrase 'partially hearing', still others prefer the term 'learner with hearing difficulties': ask, or check their application form. The language used by an institution and the wider population can create an atmosphere of inclusivity or otherwise. For example the phrase 'disabled toilet' should only refer to a toilet that is out of action. Toilet facilities are either 'accessible' or 'inaccessible' – simple as that.

11

Task

Find the policy and support documents provided by your institution. What forms of language do these documents use when learners with learning disabilities and/or difficulties are identified? Share your findings and discuss with your peer group.

SENDA and the DDA

Vocational and academic tutors need to be aware of three important Acts of Parliament relating to disability.

The Disability Discrimination Act (DDA) 1995 and also 2005 defines a disabled person as someone who has a physical or mental impairment that has a substantial and long-term adverse effect on his or her ability to carry out normal day-to-day activities. Day-to-day activities include mobility, manual dexterity, physical coordination, continence, speech, hearing or sight loss and memory difficulties. By 'long term' it means that the effect of the impairment has lasted or is likely to last for at least a year. Someone who has broken their leg would not be covered by the DDA, for example, nor would a learner with hay fever or alcoholism be covered by the Act. However, a hidden disability such as epilepsy or diabetes is covered by the law as the Act of 2005 extended protection to people with HIV, cancer and multiple sclerosis and other progressive illnesses. Part IV of the 1995 Act is about education and requires training providers to publish a disability statement or policy outlining the facilities made available for disabled learners by the provider.

The Special Educational Needs and Disability Act 2001 extended all the instruments of the DDA 1995 to education. Organisations have a responsibility to prevent staff discriminating against learners with a disability. This means that they should not be treated 'less favourably' than other people, and staff need to be aware that they should make 'reasonable adjustments' so that disabled learners are not placed at a disadvantage compared with other learners because of their disability. All aspects of educational providers' facilities and provision are included. There is no legal precedent for what the law means by 'reasonable.'

● Some aspects of education covered by SENDA

SENDA requires institutions and tutors to bring about changes to ensure that disabled learners are not placed at a substantial disadvantage. Many institutions carried out physical changes to landscapes and buildings when the Act became law. Ramps,

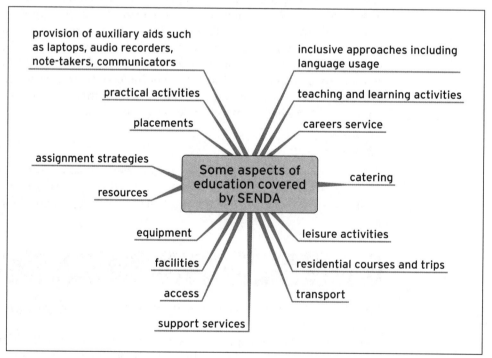

SENDA

Braille
System of raised
type represented
by dots.

lifts and automated doors were added to many organisations. Your own institution may have **Braille** signs and if there is a lift in operation an automated voice may indicate which level the lift has reached. Of course, these physical manifestations are just part of the package that a provider needs to implement to ensure parity for learners with specific learning difficulties and/or disabilities.

Task

Identify some of the adjustments that may reasonably be made and support mechanisms available to support learners with specific learning difficulties and/or disabilities. Consider your own organisation first. Share your findings with peers and add to your list.

The whole process and experience of educational provision needs to be considered. Educational providers encourage potential learners to share information about disability during the enrolment and interview processes. However, many learners may be reluctant to share their disability or even unaware that they have a learning need such as dyslexia, so it is important for vocational and academic tutors to make reasonable adjustments to their teaching and learning in order to cover a range of learning styles; chunk or structure activities to support learners who may have processing or memory difficulties or attention deficits. Recapping, routine, reinforcement and realistic expectations are all methods of making reasonable adjustment. In fact, they are all part of good practice!

The learners

11

Following the government White Paper *Learning to Succeed* (DfEE, 1999b) and *A Fresh Start* (DfEE, 1999a) a working group was established to identify the needs of learners with specific learning difficulties and disabilities. This was published in May 2000 (DfEE, 2000b). It identified the following groups of learners:

- People who are blind or visually impaired
- People who are deaf or hard of hearing
- People with mental health difficulties
- People with dyslexia
- People with physical difficulties
- People with learning difficulties.

Learners living with long-term conditions such as diabetes and epilepsy should also be considered. Many progressive illnesses are hidden but tutors still need to make reasonable adjustment where a learner has a need. Learners with diabetes may need to eat something during a session or may experience thirst requiring them to drink lots of fluid. Learners may have irregular attendance patterns because of medical requirements or ill health. Other learners may live with a condition that impacts on them socially, psychologically and physically but which does not impact on their general health. In all of these cases the focus should be on what the learner requires rather than the condition itself.

It is important to remember that all the groups of learners identified in the preceding paragraph are composed of individuals with different learning needs, strengths and weaknesses, just like any other learners. The following sections are an introduction to different groups of learners identified by *Freedom to Learn* (DfEE, 2000b) and the document *Access for All* (DfES, 2002b), which was created to support specialist literacy and numeracy tutors who deliver the core curricula but which provides useful and accessible information that is useful to vocational and academic tutors. Each section identifies some strategies that vocational and academic tutors can use to support individuals, although it is always best to find out from the learner what they would like.

● Learners who are blind or partially sighted

Louis Braille
Ray Charles
Stevie Wonder
Helen Keller
Claude Monet
James Thurber
Frederick Delius
Homer
John Milton
David Blunkett
Gordon Brown
Ella Fitzgerald
Sue Townsend

Moon
Another tactile system but with less complexity than Braille.

There are many different kinds of visual impairment. In 2000 there were approximately 1,670,000 people in the UK with visual impairment. It is important not to assume that someone registered blind lives in a world of total darkness. Vision may be blurred, peripheral or patchy, for example. The Royal National Institute for the Blind describes blindness as 'severely distorted vision'.

Learners with loss of sight will need a range of support, depending on the degree to which their vision is impaired. Comprehensive assessment of learning support required is unlikely to be provided by one single agency. Social services may make an assessment of communication needs such as the use of large print, tactile forms such as Braille or **Moon**.

Alternatively a learner may prefer information presented in an audio format. Hospital services may have made an assessment of low vision and lighting needs, such as even lighting and avoiding glare. The educational provider may have assessed support needs to be offered by the institution such as a note-taker or portable recorder, or other access technology such as voice-activated word-processing equipment. It is important for vocational and academic tutors to be clear about their role and to refer to other specialists for support (DfES, 2002c).

- Always make it clear who is speaking when beginning a conversation. You may think your voice is recognisable but this is not necessarily the case.

- Use verbal communication rather than body language. Pointing something out to a learner with a visual disability is not overly helpful. We tend to smile and nod to show that we are agreeing or affirming what someone is saying. Non-verbal communication should be replaced by voiced affirmation.

- Never walk off and leave a learner. They may not know that you have gone. It is better to finish a conversation by saying where you are going next or that you are going to let the learner get on with their work.

- Some learners simply require material to be enlarged, although many learners can read material that is printed clearly in a point 12 or 14 font.

- If work is enlarged it is helpful to remember that the learner may also require more table space so that they can work with the material.

- Learners often also express preferences for non-glossy paper, clear fonts without shadowing and a clutter-free presentation. Learners may use a magnifying glass or a light alongside the enlarged material.

- It may also be helpful to give reading to learners before they are required to use it during sessions. This gives them an opportunity to familiarise themselves with the content before the session. It also allows them to pace themselves in order to reduce eye strain.

- Handouts with spaces for answers may require extra space so that learners can complete their answers as their handwriting may be larger.

- Some learners require work to be transcribed into Braille or Moon. This means that forward planning is essential. Preparation cannot be left to the last minute.

- Other learners may make use of technology such as CCTV or prefer to use a computer monitor to enlarge materials.

- It is also possible to access keyboards with enlarged keys or to add Braille or Moon stickers to a regular sized keyboard. However, as with all adult learners, do not assume ICT knowledge.

- Some learners may need a note-taker.

- Learning needs to be provided in manageable chunks. It should be reinforced through auditory and tactile activities.

- Practical demonstrations should be shown and then broken down into small steps, depending on the needs of the individual learner.

- Keep things in identified places and do not change things around.

Each learner will have different experiences, needs and learning preferences. It is important to ask the learners what works best for them to ensure that information, notes and tasks are presented in an accessible format and at a time that is most appropriate for the learner to access and process the contents of what they have been given.

11

Beethoven

Alexander Graham Bell

Helen Keller

Eric Sykes

Halle Berry

Rebecca Anne Withey

Marlee Matlin

Lou Ferrigno

● Learners who are deaf or partially hearing

According to the report *Freedom to Learn* (DfEE, 2000b) there are 8 million people in the UK with some form of hearing loss. Some learners are born deaf. This group of learners is most likely to use British Sign Language (BSL) as their preferred language. Other learners are profoundly deaf or deafened as a result of accident, injury or as the consequence of illness. Other people are defined as hard of hearing; age is regarded as the most common factor for this type of hearing loss but each individual has their own story to tell. For example, Halle Berry is 80 per cent deaf in one ear as a consequence of a former violent partner's actions.

Each learner is different and should be consulted about their requirements. However, here are some introductory guidelines that may be helpful:

- Some learners may require communicators and note-takers if their language is BSL. Where possible it is important for the communicator and the tutor to be next to one another so that the learner can see both of them (or whoever is speaking). Allow for the delay of a 'three-way' conversation.

- A learner supported by a communicator will probably concentrate on their communicator. This does not mean they are not paying attention to you – the very opposite, in fact. However, tutors are used to interpreting non-verbal communication and it can be disconcerting when the tutor is not the focus of a learner's attention.

- Keep the content of your conversation and verbal presentations in a logical sequence. Do not jump from one subject to another as this makes your words harder to follow.

- Material should be provided ahead of the session to enable learners to process the information so that they can concentrate on the activities in the class.

- Video and DVD material should be given earlier with subtitles if possible. If subtitling is not possible, give the learner and their communicator an opportunity to watch the material before the session. Then when the material is viewed in class the communicator can sign the content and the learner will be able to switch their attention between the communicator and the material. Remember, the learner can only look at one thing at a time.

- Some learners may need support developing vocabulary in order to succeed in their vocational or academic area. It may be useful to be able to finger spell to help learners spell new words. Interestingly many learners with hearing difficulties spell much better than their peers. The reason for this is that they remember the shapes of words, so are not confused by homophones or possible phoneme–grapheme combinations.

- Use plain clear language. Make sure that the subject is established at the beginning of communication. Keep it clear and to the point.

- Ensure that handouts, worksheets and presentations are clear. Make use of 14-point font; keep sentences straightforward; use bullet points; give examples.

- Some learners may be able to lip-read. If this is the case, do not exaggerate what you have to say. Speak normally – do not exaggerate your facial movements, although you can slow down slightly. Do not cover your mouth, and make sure that you are standing in a clear light that does not cast a shadow over your face. Do not shout! Do not start writing something when you are talking to a learner who lip-reads. You will look down and then the learner will not be able to see you clearly. Beware talking whilst writing on a whiteboard. The learner will not be able to lip-read. It is also important to remember that it is difficult to lip-read. Some learners may only identify key words within a sentence, so they may not get much more than the gist of what is being said.

- Learners may not have an extensive vocabulary. Something as simple as the word 'avoid' could cause learners difficulty because they have not come into contact with the vocabulary before. They may need the word paraphrased to 'stay away from'.

- Learners who use BSL as their first language may need support writing in a standard English format. The reason for this is that BSL is a language in its own right. It has its own grammar that does not need 'little' words like articles and pronouns. Also, the word order is not necessarily the same as spoken or written English e.g. *name you what?* Rather than *what is your name?* Learners may also experience difficulty creating the plural form of words or the different tenses. This support may be provided outside vocational and academic sessions by a specialist member of staff. It is useful for vocational, academic and specialist support staff to work together to support the needs of individual learners so that they can achieve their programme of study.

- Learners who are deaf or partially hearing will not be able to access auditory materials as readily as their hearing peers. This may impact on their immediate understanding of lectures and presentations so that a transcript is necessary (provided by a note-taker or in handout form from the tutor).

- Lip-reading and interpreting can be tiring. Learners and their communicators may need to take regular breaks.

- Provide clear written instructions to support verbal instructions.

- Learners may need extra time to process information – allow processing and thinking time.

- Remember to gain the learner's attention before communicating with them. Some learners prefer a gentle tap on the shoulder, others may prefer the tutor to knock on the table in front of them. Ask the learner what they would prefer.

- Group work can be confusing. Make sure that everyone in the group follows the essential ground rule of speaking one at a time.

- Affirm and support learners with positive body language and expressions.

- Learners may require repetition and routine to help them remember information. Auditory input is an important factor in short-term working memory (as is visual input). Present manageable chunks of information, use repetition, recapping and visual reinforcement to support learner acquisition of skills and knowledge.

- Do not ask if the learner understands. Only really confident learners will tell you if they do not. It is better to ask questions to check for understanding.

One of the most important things to remember is that learners are individuals – not stereotypes: ask them what works best for them!

11

● Learners who have mental health difficulties

Vincent van Gogh
Richard Dadd
Sir Winston Churchill
Abraham Lincoln
Spike Milligan

Approximately 1 in 5 people experience mental health difficulties at some stage in their lives; this group includes people of all ages, races and backgrounds. Each individual's experience of mental health difficulties will be different. The spectrum of mental health difficulties is enormous. This chapter does not seek to provide an overview of all the different mental health difficulties that may be faced by learners:

Cary Grant
Robin Williams
Marilyn Monroe
Axl Rose
Charles Dickens
Sylvia Plath
John Cleese
Alanis Morissette
Stephen Fry

quite simply, there are too many. Depression is just one example of the diversity of mental health difficulties that exist, the different forms they can take and the responses that individuals may face.

There are varying degrees of depression and different types of depression; diagnosis may range from depression to bipolar disorder. Between 10 and 20 per cent of new mothers suffer from post-natal depression, according to the Depression Alliance. Other learners may be depressed at different times of the year; seasonal affective disorder (SAD) is linked to lack of sunlight and is increasingly recognised as a cause of lethargy and depression in many people. For some individuals depression is triggered by a single traumatic event; other people become depressed after prolonged exposure to a particular situation. Yet other individuals suffer from bipolar disorder (previously known as manic depression) with associated emotional highs and lows. For many people depression is temporary, for others it causes years of debilitating misery and for yet others it is something that must be lived with throughout their lives. Some learners may be diagnosed as depressed; others simply struggle with their symptoms without diagnosis or support. Some learners may be medicated, other learners may be receiving counselling, some may simply have been told 'to pull themselves together' or written off as 'lazy'. The way that people are labelled will depend on their circumstances and whether or not their need is recognised. The fact remains that whatever their diagnosis the learner is an individual with individual learning needs. It is wrong to assume that someone living with mental health difficulties also has learning difficulties.

Snippet

I'd never heard the word before, but for the first time at the age of 37 I had a diagnosis that explains the massive highs and miserable lows I've lived with all my life.

Stephen Fry talking about the diagnosis of his bipolar disorder in *The Secret Life of a Manic Depressive*, first screened on BBC2 September 2006

Many learners with mental health difficulties face barriers to learning created by anxiety, loss of confidence and lack of understanding.

Task

Create a list of words used in the popular media and by people in general to describe people or behaviour associated with mental health difficulties. Consider how these descriptions and words might impact on an individual if they felt the words and images were being used to describe them.

Words used to describe mental illness such as 'schizophrenic', 'mental illness' and 'paranoia' often have negative implications. Other, more colloquial, expressions such as 'looney', 'mad' or 'nuts' are derogatory and suggest that learners with mental health difficulties are unable to function logically or to learn. Stereotypical presentations of individuals suffering from mental health difficulties create an image of dangerous people leaving a trail of chaos in their wake. Learners living with mental health difficulties may face isolation and lack of social contact as a result of other people's fear of how the learner may behave. The report *Freedom to Learn* (DfEE, 2000a: 4) identified the fact that 'the main additional barrier for people with mental health difficulties is the widespread ignorance and prejudice about mental health.'

Other barriers to learning include anxiety, loss of confidence, mood change, difficulties making decisions, poor concentration and lack of memory resulting from medication. Other side effects from medication can involve thirst and restlessness. Learners who suffer from depression may be tired as a result of being unable to get to sleep, or waking up early in the morning. In addition, learners who have mental health difficulties may not attend every session because they have a 'bad day' or because they have an appointment with their service provider.

Barriers can be overcome in a variety of ways:

- A welcoming environment is important for learners who have become stressed simply walking through the doors of an educational institution. A friendly smile may make the difference in their attending again.

- Familiarity and consistency are important for many learners with mental health difficulties. It is important to be consistent in terms of location and staffing.

- Learners with mental health difficulties should not be forced to take risks.

- Alternative strategies may be required rather than direct questioning.

- Group work may need to be introduced gradually, or different tasks offering choices provided so that learners do not feel threatened.

- All learners need time and space to think through their answers. Everyone finds it stressful to be put on the spot.

- Some forms of assessment may be very stressful to learners with mental health difficulties.

- Learners will benefit from practice, reassurance and, if possible, from alternative forms of assessment.

- Some learners may be postgraduates, others may have very little experience of the education system. It is good practice to create ground rules for learning early in a programme of study, covering issues such as punctuality, handing in work, taking breaks and turn-taking during discussions. These ground rules should be printed and provided so that learners can refresh their memory of what is expected of them. This benefits all learners, not just those learners who may have mental health difficulties.

- In addition to a friendly welcome and reassurance it is also important to encourage learners to see their learning achievements. This may involve careful chunking of

11

activities so that learners can see their progress once they have practised a skill or acquired some knowledge.

- Plan for a variety of teaching and learning activities in small chunks of no more than twenty minutes so that learners have more opportunity to remember knowledge and skills.

- Learning programmes need regular recap opportunities for learners who have not been able to attend sessions or who may have memory difficulties.

- Tutors should be clear about their role. Tutors are not, generally, trained counsellors. It is important, however, to know what services and facilities an organisation provides.

These strategies benefit most learners regardless of whether they are living with mental health difficulties or not. The devices are designed to place the learner at the heart of the learning process. Placing the learner at the heart of the learning process also means that learners are independent. This means that support should be negotiated, flexible and consistent.

● Learners with dyslexia

Snippet

> I, myself, was always recognized . . . as the 'slow one' in the family. It was quite true, and I knew it and accepted it. Writing and spelling were always terribly difficult for me. My letters were without originality. I was . . . an extraordinarily bad speller and have remained so until this day.
> Agatha Christie

Leonardo da Vinci
Albert Einstein
John Lennon
Richard Branson
Whoopi Goldberg
Sir Winston Churchill
Orlando Bloom
Tom Cruise
Walt Disney
Agatha Christie
Cher
Noel Gallagher
Muhammad Ali

Dyslexia, or symptoms similar to dyslexia, affect approximately 10 per cent of the population, but to assume that someone has dyslexia because they cannot spell is erroneous. The definition of dyslexia is as follows:

> Dyslexia is a complex neurological condition that is constitutional in origin. The symptoms may affect many areas of learning and function, and may be described as a specific difficulty in reading, spelling and written language. One or more of these areas may be affected. Numeracy, notational skills (music), motor function and dyslexic learners' organisational skills may also be involved. However, it is particularly related to mastering written language, although oral language may be affected to some degree.
> (British Dyslexia Association, www.bdadyslexia.org.ukwhatisdyslexia.html [accessed 4 June 2007])

For vocational and academic tutors one of the most obvious signs of a possible need – and please remember that the learner may not have dyslexia or may not want to share their 'secret' with anyone else, including the tutor – is a noticeable difference between a learner's practical skills or verbal performance during taught sessions when compared with their written work. Learners with dyslexia may also show evidence of difficulties in some or all the following areas.

Spelling difficulties

Learners with dyslexia may make many more spelling errors than might ordinarily be expected. The reasons for this include:

- **Phonological awareness** (breaking words down to match the letters in the word to their corresponding sounds). Some learners with dyslexia will have little awareness of rhyme, syllabication or natural breaks in speech and written language. This means that many learners with dyslexia are unable to break new words down in order to learn how to say them, or to try to work out meaning based on another word with a similar root. Many learners with dyslexia rely on whole-word recognition when reading. It also means that they have difficulty breaking words down in order to spell them more efficiently.

- **Auditory discrimination** (recognising the difference between sounds – for example, 'hearing' the difference between sheep/cheap or between individual letters). Learners with dyslexia may confuse words that sound similar or which have similar construction.

- **Recognising letters or numbers**. The learner with dyslexia may confuse letters such as *b*, *d*, *p* and *q*.

- **Difficulty with recognising familiar words in print** or remembering how they are spelt.

Snippet

> One of the 'tests' for dyslexia is asking a learner to rearrange two words taking the first sound from each word and interchange them with the other word e.g. *car park* becomes *par cark*. This sound switch is called spoonerism – some people create spoonerisms accidentally but other people enjoy this kind of word game. Many learners with dyslexia dislike word games because they find them frustrating.

11

It is important to remember that some learners with dyslexia may have developed strategies to support their spelling, in which case poor spelling may not be immediately noticeable.

Sequencing difficulties

A learner with dyslexia may confuse or lose track of the order of letters, words or digits. Other indicators are difficulties sequencing days of the week or months of the year.

Reading difficulties

Reading difficulties include tracking words on the page and grouping sentences. Many learners with dyslexia are unable to 'hold' a number of words in their heads in order to gain meaning from a whole sentence. Instead they decode one word at a time. By the time they get to the end of the sentence they have forgotten the other words in the sentence and need to start over again. This means that they may have to reread passages several times in order to gain meaning from them.

Organisational difficulties

Organisation can be difficult. Planning written work can be a problem as can remembering when things need to be done.

Motor control difficulties

- **Fine motor control difficulties** including holding and controlling a pen may mean that the learner requires more time to write things down. Tutors should also be aware that many learners with dyslexia have developed strategies, such as extremely small or untidy handwriting, as a method of disguising their poor spelling or difficulty structuring sentences.

- **Gross motor control** difficulties may extend to clumsiness and a reputation for being 'accident prone'. Many learners with dyslexia may have experienced delay in learning to ride a bike.

Spatial awareness

- **Direction**. Learners with dyslexia may become confused about direction.

- **Telling the time**. Many learners with dyslexia may have learnt to tell the time using an analogue clock at a later stage than their peer group and some adults may still rely upon digital clocks in order to tell the time.

Memory processing

- **Short-term memory** difficulties mean that learners with dyslexia can have difficulty remembering verbal instructions and retaining information. Learners may also find it hard to concentrate or listen for long periods of time.

- **Automaticity**. This is the ability to carry out a learnt task without having to think about it – such as knowing that the letter 'f' follows the letter 'e' or that the capital of the United Kingdom is London. Learners with dyslexia may require up to one hundred more learning opportunities than their peers before they achieve automaticity. This means that a learner can study something one week and appear to have forgotten it by the following week. In terms of spelling, a learner with dyslexia may be able to spell a word when thinking about it or when they are concentrating out of context but will misspell the same word when writing it as part of a longer text where they are concentrating on the content of the text rather than the way it is structured or the way that words are spelt.

Learners may seem very able when taking part in discussion and spoken activities but their written work does not meet the same intellectual and academic standards as their spoken work. Learners may also have good days and bad days. As with everything else, stress and tiredness play a part in the effect that dyslexia may have. Learners may also lack confidence and self-esteem because of prior negative learning experiences and poor achievement during formal education.

 Snippet

It's such a relief to find out that I have dyslexia. It explains so much about the difficulties that I had at school. In the end my teachers thought I was just thick. If I'm honest I thought I was thick too.

A learner's response to being diagnosed with dyslexia. The same learner went on to achieve a first-class honours degree in computing.

It is also worth remembering that many of the signs of dyslexia indicated by the bullet points above are also indicators for unspecified learning difficulties, memory difficulties and dyspraxia, amongst other things.

Dyspraxia is another neurologically based syndrome commonly related to clumsiness resulting from both fine and gross motor difficulties but which also impacts upon auditory and visual perception as well as short-term memory and language skills. Other indicators of dyspraxia are difficulty using equipment such as scissors or tin openers and learning complex motor skills such as driving a car.

Another indicator of dyslexia is experiencing blurred letters or words on a page. Learners with dyslexia may have different experiences of printed formats, from slight blurring to letters becoming jumbled or words forming riverlets and 'streaming down the page'. The streaming may be so severe that the words seem to move or else a standard page of text seems to be composed of two columns of text when, in fact, there is only one. One of the causes of this blurring of print on the pages is scotopic sensitivity. It can also be an indicator of Irlen Syndrome. In both cases learners may benefit from the use of non-glossy papers. Black print on white paper can exacerbate scotopic sensitivity, so many learners prefer pastel papers or use a coloured acetate to overlay handouts and texts.

I think I might have dyslexia!

Having read through all the indicators for dyslexia it is quite possible that you may have recognised some of the indicators in yourself. There are a number of checklists that can help you determine whether you want to take your concerns further, including an online checklist offered by the British Dyslexia Association at **http://www.bdadyslexia.org.uk/adultchecklist.html**

Supporting learners with dyslexia

Strategies for supporting learners with short-term memory or language processing difficulties can include the following:

- Ensure that tasks are broken into manageable chunks that are achievable.
- Set SMART targets. Ensure that learning outcomes and tasks are **S**pecific, **M**easurable, **A**ttainable, **R**elevant and **T**ime-bound.
- Use multi-sensory strategies – visual, auditory and kinaesthetic strategies – to reinforce learning.
- Provide written instructions.
- Ensure printed materials are clear, have plenty of space and use a font that is clear. Ideally the letter *a* should look like a handwritten letter *a*, so fonts such as Comic Sans should be considered and should be point 12 or 14. Individual learners may have different preferences.
- Ensure that printed material is of a good standard.
- Support learners by providing a glossary and modelling its use.
- Help learners remember key spellings by using a variety of multi-sensory strategies. Do not try to teach a learner with dyslexia to spell phonetically. If the learner receives additional learning support, work with their tutor so that you are reinforcing the specialist input.

11

- Provide opportunities for recapping and reinforcing prior learning.

- Help learners access texts by using DARTs and the EXIT models explained in Chapter 3.

- Ensure that PowerPoint demonstrations have a pale yellow or blue tinted background to avoid white glare.

- Change activities every twenty minutes or so. Remember that learners may have difficulty concentrating for prolonged periods.

- Identify strategies to support learners as they develop their memory skills and model them.

Learners with physical disabilities

Snippet

Being unable to walk is an impairment, but disability results because electric wheelchairs are not readily available, ramps to buildings aren't fitted and cash machines are set too high in the wall.
French, S., 'Disability, impairment or something in between?' in Swain, J., et al. (1993) (eds) *Disabling Barriers - Enabling Environments*, London: Sage

Christopher Reeve

Franklin D. Roosevelt

Ian Dury

Stephen Hawking

Tanni Grey-Thompson

This category covers all learners with physical disabilities and not just wheelchair users. Each learner will have different needs and requirements. Some learners may find it painful to sit through a whole session and may need to get up and walk around every twenty minutes or so. Other learners may need extra time to complete assignments and examinations because of lack of fine motor control skills. The alternative may be for a note-taker to be provided or a tape recorder to be used. It would be sensible to give out more handouts to the whole class and provide board notes in a printed format the following week, to offer partially completed handouts and to make more use of group work in this context. These strategies would benefit the whole group.

Much of the guidance relating to working with wheelchair users relates to access and etiquette:

- Do not assume that the learner is unable to do basic physical tasks such as opening doors or going up ramps. Ask the learner whether they would like help or not. After all, how would you feel if you were able to do something perfectly well but someone else assumed that you were in need of assistance? If it happened often enough it would probably have a negative effect on your confidence or make you extremely cross. Equally, do not ignore the learner. It is better to ask and wait until you have received a reply.

- Speak directly to the learner, not to their support worker and try, where appropriate, to be on the same level as them. Ask what the learner prefers. If you are standing, try to stand back slightly so that the learner does not have to look up at you.

- Never assume that because a learner is a wheelchair user that they have a learning difficulty. The same applies to any other learning disability and/or difficulty.

● Learners with learning difficulties

The report *Freedom to Learn* (DfEE, 2000a) identifies some of the difficulties that may be experienced by learners with learning difficulties, including: poor short-term memory, processing difficulties, inability to speak or recognise written text – they may communicate better through symbols or signing and they may need specialist support. Many learners with learning difficulties have previous negative experiences of education and may also experience lack of confidence and low self-esteem.

- A programme needs to be interesting to the learner and relevant to the learner's needs.
- The programme needs to be flexible.
- Teaching and learning methods should include visual, auditory, kinaesthetic and tactile activities.
- Tasks should be broken down into small achievable steps.
- Activities should be carefully explained and structured.
- There is a need for routine, recap and reinforcement.
- Celebrate success.

● Learners with autistic spectrum disorders (ASD)

Autistic spectrum disorders (ASD) are a range of social and communication disorders including autism and Asperger syndrome. As with dyslexia, learners live with conditions ranging from mild to severe. When many people think of ASD they think of Dustin Hoffman's portrayal of the savant Raymond in the film *Rain Man*. In reality, the Centre for the Study of Autism believes that only (approximately) 10 per cent of people with autism demonstrate savant skills that allow them to excel in one area such as memory, calculation, drawing or music. Hoffman's portrayal did demonstrate the fact that many people with ASD can be unaware of body language and social boundaries. They use language literally, having difficulty with idiom, irony and word play. They may misinterpret what is being said because of difficulties recognising facial expressions, tone of voice and intonation. They may appear unresponsive as a consequence. They are also likely to work to routines and dislike working in groups.

- Use clear language. Avoid using figures of speech, sarcasm, irony, puns or using metaphors.
- Learners with autism may be unable to read non-verbal communication. Try to say clearly what you want, to affirm achievement and to draw conversations to a halt if the learner is unable to recognise the non-verbal signals that suggest that it is time to move on.
- In addition to being unable to read non-verbal communication, some learners with ASD may not be able to use non-verbal communication effectively e.g. they may avoid eye contact.
- Some ASD learners may not use phatic forms of communication. If you ask them how they are, then they will tell you rather than offering a formulaic response!

11

- Some people with ASD have no speech but may use a form of sign language, such as Makaton.

- Some learners with ASD may be sensitive to physical contact or have a dislike of anything they perceive to be unpleasant to touch. Some learners may dislike working with paint because of the sensation or because they dislike feeling unclean. Other learners may be sound sensitive. Some learners with ASD may try to block out the noise.

- Check understanding, and reinforce information or instructions by asking the learner to repeat them back if they are able or feel comfortable verbalising.

- Allow the learner an opportunity to think before answering or carrying out an activity.

- People with ASD often rely heavily on routine and repetition. Try to avoid changes of venue or accepted routines.

Learners are all individuals with different experiences and expectations. Try to avoid creating barriers or isolating learners from their peer group by situating them at the front of the class or to one side.

The majority of texts available relating to ASD relate to children. These can provide some useful information about support strategies but it is also important to remember the necessity of age-appropriate materials. If ASD is an area of interest, Daniel Tammet's (2006) autobiography provides an excellent starting point.

Supporting learners – a whole-organisation approach

Ofsted's guidance *Inspecting Post-16* (2002) identifies a number of generic factors that should be taken into consideration when supporting learners with specific learning difficulties and/or disabilities. They identify the need for individual learning plans and specialist support where appropriate as well as appropriate teaching environments. For example, a hard floor covering resulting in unwanted sounds would disadvantage a learner with hearing difficulties. Ofsted also identify the need for consistency across the learner's programme of study and effective use of specialist staff and equipment. These issues are whole-organisation issues.

Best practice

'In most effective colleges visited, irrespective of the type of college, the leadership of senior managers was the key factor in establishing a positive inclusive ethos.'
(Ofsted, 2007)

Summary

- Focus on the learner not the impairment.
- Remember that there are hidden disabilities. For example, people with diabetes will require a break during a long session and may need to eat something in a session. People with epilepsy may be sensitive to strobe lighting effects that feature on some film presentations.
- Establish a friendly, supportive relationship from the beginning to help with feelings of low self-esteem.
- Deal sensitively with personal information.
- Assume nothing.
- Ask the learner what works best for them.
- Try not to isolate the learner from the rest of their peer group by placing them at the front of the class or by sidelining them.
- Focus on what is needed to help the learner learn.
- Allow for setting-up time and regular 'catch-up' opportunities.
- Divide learning into small achievable steps. Set **S**pecific, **M**easurable, **A**ttainable, **R**elevant and **T**ime-bound targets.
- Chunk activities and use a variety of strategies to help with concentration and memory difficulties.
- Use multi-sensory strategies and a variety of teaching methods.
- Medication has side effects: drowsiness, low concentration levels and motivation, as well as mood swings (the afternoon is usually a better time for learning than the morning).
- Be aware of the stress and anxieties – provide practice, reassurance and, possibly, extra time whenever possible.
- Each learner is an individual. What works for one learner may not work for another.
- Plan ahead.
- Work with colleagues to ensure learners receive all the support and technology that is appropriate and available to them.
- Apply the principles of best practice to your teaching. All learners will benefit.

11

Test your knowledge

11.1 Read through the following case studies and then consider the questions that accompany them. You may wish to consider this question as part of a group.

Jamie uses a wheelchair. His access to one class is limited to entering the room and sitting at the table immediately in front of the door, because of movement restrictions imposed by equipment within the room and the numbers of learners attending the particular session. Although there are computers in this particular room Jamie does not use them as he feels that he causes inconvenience to other learners, who have to move themselves and their tables in order to allow him to reach them. This access, whilst not typical of the accommodation offered by the training provider, is typical of the unfriendly nature of the institution for those with physical difficulties. There are three lifts available for all learners and an additional lift for staff and learners with specific learning difficulties and/or disabilities. Jamie often stays in the classroom during break because this lift is full of staff, other students and their carers moving around the building. The lift is also situated in a lobby area behind heavy fire doors which Jamie is unable to negotiate without help.

Access to the resource centre has recently improved as a lift had been fitted and automated doors provided, giving learners with physical disabilities access to the collection for the first time without a journey through the front door of the institution, down a ramp and along the street (a real disincentive in bad weather) before re-entering the institution through a side door of the resource centre. However, if Jamie wants to access books on shelves above his reach, he has to ask a member of staff for help. All the magazines and journals are housed on the mezzanine level of the resource centre so Jamie is reliant on staff to fetch material for him. He feels that this creates difficulties for him as he is unable to browse through journals before selecting them. Although he finds the resource centre staff friendly and helpful, he often feels frustrated when he visits the resource centre.

a. Identify the barriers that Jamie faces.

b. Suggest strategies that could be implemented to overcome these barriers.

c. Do you feel that Jamie's educational provider caters adequately for the needs of disabled learners? What improvements, if any, do you feel could be made?

d. How far do you think that the institution in the case study complies with the DDA?

Arabella, who disclosed her mental health difficulties upon enrolment, said that she was prone to panic attacks and disliked the feeling of being closed in by desks, chairs and other learners once the class had started. Her husband escorts her from the car park to the classroom and collects her at the end of each session. She often arrives late because she feels intimidated by the number of learners moving through the main foyer of the college on their way to the first class of the day. She does not wish to work in groups or take part in whole-class discussion because she feels embarrassed and says she is 'too stupid'. She sometimes says that she should not come back because she is not learning anything even though her work is progressing and she is on target to pass the course. She is worried by the thought of taking the level 1 examinations. She often finds it difficult to concentrate because of the antidepressants she is taking.

a. Identify Arabella's main barriers to learning.

b. Identify some strategies that could support Arabella's learning.

Albert is a single father with twin sons. He works as a cleaner early in the morning and as security in a local nightclub whilst studying during the day. He is close to his extended family that usually helps with childcare. Albert would like to set up his own business as a joiner. However, he feels that he may not be able to do this despite his practical skills because of his problems with dyslexia. He would like to progress on to a business course but has admitted that he has difficulty taking notes and finds non-practical classes boring. Albert also has difficulty filling in forms and is worried that he would not be able to fill in the necessary paperwork if he started his own business.

a. Identify some of Albert's barriers to learning.

b. Identify some strategies to help Albert.

11.2 **a.** Consider your own places of work and take note of areas that you consider are easily accessible and inaccessible to disabled people.

b. Do you feel that your place of work caters adequately for the needs of disabled learners? What improvements, if any, do you feel could be made?

c. Locate your institution's equal opportunities policy. Evaluate the extent to which you feel it is being implemented.

d. How far do you think your place of work complies with the DDA?

11.3 *Access for All* (DfES, 2002b) is freely available either via the Internet or as a hardcopy (more information in Chapter 14). It was written to support tutors working within Skills for Life programmes. However, the strategies and suggestions it offers for supporting learners with specific learning difficulties and/or disabilities are useful for vocational and academic tutors. You will need a copy of *Access for All*.

Identify strategies to support the following groups of learners:

a. People who are blind or partially sighted.

b. People with physical disabilities.

c. People with learning disabilities.

11.4 Vocational and academic tutors are not expected to become expert in supporting learners with specific learning difficulties and/or disabilities. Each training provider should have access to specialist tutors and support facilities. Find out what facilities are available to support different groups of learners:

a. Inside your organisation.

b. External organisations.

Where next? 11

Texts

DfES (2002) *Introducing Access for All*, London: DfES

DfES (2002) *Access for All*, London: Basic Skills Agency. In addition to offering an overview of indicators and support strategies for learning with specific disabilities and/or difficulties, this text also contains a useful section on resources listing texts and websites that vocational and academic tutors may find useful if they wish to find out more about a specific disability or difficulty.

Hutchinson, J., Atkinson, K. and Orpwood, J. (1998) *Breaking Down Barriers: Access to Further and Higher Education for Visually Impaired Students*, Cheltenham: Stanley Thornes Ltd

Klein, C. (2003) (2nd edn) *Diagnosing Dyslexia*, London: Basic Skills Agency

Klein, C. and Miller, R. (1990) *Unscrambling Spelling*, London: Hodder & Stoughton

Klein, C. and Krupska, M. (1995) *Demystifying Dyslexia: Raising Awareness and Developing Support for Dyslexic Young People and Adults*, London: LLU

Lee, J. (2002) *Making the Curriculum Work for Learners with Dyslexia*, London: Basic Skills Agency

Minton, D. (1991) *Teaching Skills in Further and Adult Education*, London: MacMillan Education Ltd

Wertheimer, A. (2003) *Images of Possibility: Creating Learning Opportunities for Adults with Mental Health Difficulties*, Leicester: NIACE

Websites

www.autism.org.uk National Autistic Society

www.bdadyslexia.org.uk British Dyslexia Association

www.british-sign.co.uk

www.dfes.gov/readwriteplus

www.drc-gb.org Disability Rights Commission

www.dyslexiaaction.org.uk Dyslexia Action

www.dyspraxiafoundation.org.uk Dyspraxia Foundation

www.mencap.org.uk MENCAP

www.mind.org.uk Mind

www.niace.org.uk

www.radar.org.uk RADAR

www.rnib.org.uk Royal National Institute for the Blind

www.rnid.org.uk Royal National Institute for Deaf People (RNID)

www.scope.org.uk SCOPE

www.skill.org.uk SKILL: National Bureau for Students with Disabilities

12 World English and multilingualism

Many vocational and academic tutors are experiencing an increased contact with learners who use a language other than English first and who may speak English as a second, third or even fourth language. There are several reasons for this. One of the reasons relates to funding for courses; another lies in the fact that adult learners are known to prefer contextualised learning rather than language as a subject-based class. Learners functioning below entry level 3 benefit from language-specific classes. This helps them to orientate themselves, acquire essential language skills and gain in confidence.

Minimum core elements

A1

- Multilingualism and the role of the first language in the acquisition of additional languages.
- Issues that arise when learning another language or translating from one language to another.

World English

English is spoken as a first language in many parts of the world including the United Kingdom, Ireland, some Caribbean countries, Australia, New Zealand, Canada and the USA. These speakers are at the heart of the English language and estimates place the number of speakers in the region of 300 million (Crystal, 1995: 358). These varieties of English are used as standard forms in the countries where they are recognised. Their official status gives them prestige. They provide a model for what is normal in the English language because they are used by native speakers.

Monolingual
Speaking only one language

Many speakers in the UK are **monolingual**. Evidence from the NIACE report *Divided by Language* (Aldridge, 2001) confirmed that 62 per cent of adults whose mother tongue is English are unable to speak another language. However, in many countries it is normal to speak a number of different languages. Many countries also officially recognise a number of different languages as having equal prestige. For example Wales recognises Welsh and English; Canada recognises English and French as official languages; India recognises Hindi, English and fourteen other languages.

In these countries people can be, but are not always, multilingual. If someone is multilingual they are proficient and habitually use two or more languages.

There are about 750 million people who use English as a second language. English is often used as a second language because of factors such as tradition. English can also be used as a foreign language. Crystal estimates that there are 100 million people who speak English as a foreign language. This means that users are not fully proficient in the language other than for specific areas such as holidays or business. This command of language does not make the speaker bilingual or multilingual but it does give them the necessary linguistic skills to survive. Many asylum seekers and refugees are eager to learn English in order to survive.

It is difficult to identify whether some countries use English as a second language or a foreign language because it can be used for social as well as official purposes.

English has grown as a second language because of the following factors:

- English trade during the seventeenth and eighteenth centuries.
- English imperialism during the nineteenth and twentieth centuries.
- The impact of the US economy and technology. Computers and the Internet largely use the English language.
- Social and cultural factors such as music and literature. Also, many European countries access television programmes broadcast in English.
- English is the **lingua franca** for air-traffic control, diplomacy, academia and sport.

Lingua franca
A particular language used to ensure cross-group understanding.

One of the most important things to be aware of is that not all these speakers of English speak the same English. There are many varieties of English. An American will talk about an 'elevator' whereas someone in the UK will refer to it as a 'lift'. In addition to variations in vocabulary or lexis there are also phonological (sound) and grammatical variations.

Multilingualism

There are approximately 200 countries in the world of which 50 or so officially recognise more than one language. This suggests that multilingualism is the exception rather than the rule. However, there are 5,000 languages (Edwards, 1994: 1) which suggests that actually multilingualism is much more prevalent than monolingualism. In many countries it is a necessity to speak several languages depending upon the domain – work, travel, family, education etc. – that the speaker is functioning in. The speaker may have more linguistic skill with some languages than others. It will depend upon the context in which the language is used and the nature of the transaction.

Multilingual communities may develop as a result of political union. Switzerland has four official languages – German, Italian, Romansch and French. Canada's English and French languages reflect the dominant language identities of the two main groups of settlers who colonised the area. Other countries have multilingual communities because of arbitrary boundary decisions.

There are many different reasons why people become bilingual or trilingual etc. other than residing within a multilingual community. Sometimes bilingualism occurs because two people from different language traditions marry and need to learn one another's language in order to communicate. Other reasons for bilingualism include employment, religion, educational necessity, displacement due to natural disaster or **refugee** status, migration for economic reasons, family circumstances. In some instances a particular language is used to ensure cross-group understanding. A language used this way is called a lingua franca. In the past Greek, Latin, French and Arabic have filled the role of a lingua franca for specific groups of people with specific interests.

Refugee
Someone officially approved to stay in the UK.

 Snippet

I often attend meetings with my Japanese and Russian colleagues. They all speak English because the Russians don't speak Japanese and the Japanese don't speak Russian. I'm the only one who doesn't have to speak another language.

Heard on a Radio 2 discussion about teaching languages in schools. In this case English is the lingua franca for business transactions.

People may be able to switch between two or more languages without difficulty but it may be that one language has dominance. For some bilingual or multilingual learners though, there is a balance between the dominance of individual languages. These users of language tend to have grown up using multiple languages and have no preference as to which one they use. These language users have developed simultaneous bilingualism because they have been exposed to all their languages since birth. This is unusual. It is more normal for children to develop a language at home and then be exposed to a dominant language during their education. This is called consecutive bilingualism.

Bilingual learners, especially resettled learners such as refugees or migrant learners, tend to experience a language deficit in the language which has dominance where they live. In such cases it is also usual amongst younger multilingual speakers for the languages which are not normal to their everyday lives, and which are not habitually used home languages to become dormant because the young multilingual speakers choose not to use the language or languages which mark them as different from their peer group.

12

 Snippet

Student S is a bilingual twenty-year-old. She grew up speaking French and English. She happily used both languages until she entered full-time education. She came to recognise that her bilingualism marked her as different from her peers. By the time she was nine she refused to speak French even though her understanding remained intact. Visits to her French grandmother became difficult because she was unable to speak French in order to communicate with her French family. Since leaving full-time education Student S has travelled to and worked in France and has once again assumed a fully bilingual status.

Bilingual or multilingual speakers are able to use two or more languages for every-day transactions and communications. They may habitually move between languages during their conversations. They may incorporate vocabulary from one language into a sentence spoken in another language. This code-switching can extend to phrases and sentences. Sometimes a multilingual speaker is not aware of the switch; on some occasions a word may be more accurate or richer in one language than another.

Pidgins and creoles

This chapter has already looked at the idea of a particular language being used as a lingua franca to ensure understanding between participants in a particular domain. Edwards (1994) describes pidgin languages as another kind of lingua franca.

A **pidgin language** is a combination of two languages that has the limited function of allowing communication between the speakers of the different languages who often form a part of two distinct groups. This means that a pidgin language may not survive if one of the distinct groups leaves the area in which the pidgin is spoken. Crystal uses the example of pidgin French that was spoken in Vietnam. Once the French presence was removed, the use of pidgin declined. Other pidgins have expanded to cope with the needs of their users and gained recognised status, such as the pidgin used in Papua New Guinea.

Mother tongue
Language learnt from parents or carers during infancy.

Pidgin can evolve into a **creole**. This occurs where pidgin is used by speakers of other languages as a means of communication. Children born into these pidgin-speaking communities develop the language into a **mother tongue**. They expand the vocabulary and establish grammatical patterns. There are approximately 30 English-based creoles in the Caribbean of which Jamaican is the most widely used.

ESOL learners

ESOL
English for Speakers of Other Languages

The Moser Report – *A Fresh Start* (DfEE, 1999a) – suggested that approximately 1 million of the 7 million adults with literacy and numeracy difficulties spoke a first language other than English. The report *Breaking the Language Barriers* (DfEE, 2000a) published the year after the Moser Report, identified four groups of learners who need to develop their English Language skills:

1. Settled communities. This group may often work anti-social hours and have difficulty accessing regular language classes.

Snippet

English language skills are critical to the success of anyone living or working in this country.
Bill Rammell, Further Education Minister

Asylum seeker
Someone applying to stay officially in the UK.

2. Refugees and **asylum seekers**. More than 85 per cent of asylum seekers gained permission to remain in the UK. This group of learners face additional barriers to their learning. In addition to the trauma of fleeing their homes because of a natural disaster, political situation or civil war, they are likely to arrive in the UK on their own, live in poverty, live in temporary accommodation and often have medical problems including mental health problems. There will be stresses associated with applying for asylum. They may need to access the legal system and to be interviewed by the Home Office. Asylum seekers and refugees may hope to return to their own country as soon as possible.

3. Migrant workers. This group come to the UK in search of work or with the intent of learning English.

4. Partners and spouses of students, people who work in this country or individuals who have married someone who lives in the UK. This group may not feel an urgent desire to learn English because they have support from their partner or wider family network. However, they will need to learn English in order to take an effective role in the community, to gain employment and to support their own children's schooling.

Within this spectrum, learners have different experiences and educational backgrounds and different language backgrounds. For example more than 30 per cent of asylum seekers have qualifications at level 3 (A level equivalence) and higher. These learners can find their situation frustrating. In their own countries they often hold responsible jobs, yet in the UK they are unable to find a job that matches their skills. Individuals may have learnt some English as a foreign language during their schooling. They will also want to achieve different things for themselves – just like any other group of adult learners, in fact. Unsupported refugees and asylum seekers may feel that they need to learn English as a matter of urgency in order to survive.

A NIACE report (Aldridge, 2001) drew on findings from the Nuffield Languages Inquiry which identified the diversity of languages in use in the United Kingdom. It reported 307 languages in use by London schoolchildren. The NIACE report identified languages ranging from Armenian and Azerbaijani to Thai, Turkish, Twi, Urdu, Welsh and Yoruba.

12

Snippet

The current employment rate among people who do not have English as a first language is 58%, compared with 78% who do.
Liz Ford, *The Guardian*, 22 March 2007

The impact of poor English language skills means that speakers of other languages are unable to participate fully in the community, resulting in isolation and lack of self esteem; it affects employment and for many adults it means skill wastage. This can impact on individual stability and economic security. English language skills are now a necessity in order to gain British citizenship. All the groups of learners need to learn English.

Stop and reflect

Discuss some of the difficulties learners may experience during vocational and academic sessions if their first language is not English.

Learners face many difficulties. Some of the difficulties relate to language skills, other barriers are the same barriers as can be experienced by any adult learner. A final group of barriers relate to the cognitive and academic skills that learners have been able to develop prior to their arrival in the UK.

● Language barriers

- Learners using a language other than English as their first language may face many difficulties in accessing vocational and academic programmes.

- They may not be literate in their dominant language or they come from an oral rather than a written culture. This presents difficulties, as knowledge of grammar and written conventions in one language is a useful starting point for comparisons and development of grammar and written conventions in English.

- Learners who are literate in their own language may use alphabets other than the Roman alphabet.

- They may write right to left or down the page rather than left to right.

- This chapter has already identified that even where a speaker uses a variety of English, the lexis, pronunciation and grammatical structures of the speaker's form of English may vary. For learners who speak languages other than English as a first language these problems are magnified.

- Learners may be able to communicate effectively in English based on their experience of language within specific domains such as shopping, socialising and for their work. However, the vocational or academic course they are undertaking may be a new domain. They may struggle with technical terms and new words. They may need topic-based vocabulary and also classroom vocabulary e.g. *discuss*, *handout*, *experiment* etc.

- They may have difficulty translating from one language to another. Literal translations often occur where learners have used a dictionary definition and lost meaning in translation. They may struggle with grammatical forms e.g. the addition of the suffixes *-s* and *-es* to form the plural can be difficult for many learners writing in English. Learners may also have difficulty with punctuation.

- In addition there are other cultural factors. English uses idiomatic expressions that do not make sense if they are translated word for word e.g. *it's raining cats and dogs*. In addition native speakers make subtle use of language when they tell jokes or make an ironic comment.

- It is worth remembering that a learner's level of spoken English may be different from that of their written English. Some learners may have studied English as a foreign language. Initially they may feel that they have sufficient language skills but remember that received pronunciation is the standard form taught abroad. Native speakers use a range of accents and dialects that can be confusing.

Task

Identify the spoken communication skills that learners in your academic or vocational area need in order to succeed on their programme. Break these tasks into manageable chunks.

● Cultural barriers

- Learners may come from cultures where written English takes a form closer to spoken English. This may impact on their style of writing and their interpretation of texts.

- Non-verbal communication differs from one culture to another. It is important to use body language to support and affirm learners' progress but make sure that you're giving the message that you think you are!

- Learners may be used to a learning culture that is teacher-centred so may find more active learning strategies difficult to comprehend.

- Some female learners may not wish to work in classes that include male learners.

- Religious events often fall outside designated holiday periods and learners may also fast at different times of the year. This can lead to tiredness and lack of concentration as nightfall approaches.

Snippet

 It came as a big surprise that the desks were not arranged in rows and that we were not expected to learn lots of things by heart.
A learner commenting on the differences in teaching and learning methodologies

Stop and reflect

Consider the extent of your own cultural awareness.

12

● Other barriers

- Many refugees and asylum seekers have experienced traumatic incidents.

- Learners experience the same barriers as all other adults such as childcare responsibilities, shift work and cost of transport.

Snippet

 I want only – no police!' he says finally in English. As he goes, Teme sighs. 'Yeah, I dream at night of police and guards, too. But then I wake up and think, hey, I am in England, democratic, free!
Interviewee speaking to Libby Purves, 'Small mercies', _The Times_, 6 December 2006

Supporting learners who speak other languages

In order to support learners most effectively staff in different programme areas need to work as a team with specialist staff. Ideally all schemes of work should be looked at and tasks mapped to the ESOL core curriculum. Tutors should then be able to work together to develop or adapt material. Some learners may receive additional support in a vocational or academic class setting. Other support may be delivered at a different time but may relate to the language that learners encounter in their vocational and academic programmes of study. Different organisations take different approaches.

Some guidelines for vocational and academic tutors:

- Value the language skills that learners already have.
- Set the context for vocational and academic sessions in order to activate prior knowledge.
- Support understanding by repeating and rephrasing information and instructions.
- Identify key words in their context and on the board.
- Help to make meaning of spoken and written content explicit. Use pictures and diagrams where appropriate to clarify meaning.
- Allow learners to record lectures and presentations so that they can listen to the content again at home.
- Ensure materials are divided into short chunks.
- Support writing through modelling.
- Give guidance as to the content of specific types of writing. Offer writing frames that provide linking words, sequencing words or opening phrases as a support mechanism.
- Where appropriate consider joint construction of texts.
- Learners can draft work or make notes using their own language. This will enable them to concentrate on the skills and the knowledge to be acquired within a vocational or academic setting. Work that is to be handed in should then be translated into English.
- Introduce key vocabulary.
- Use dictionaries. Learners can extend their vocabulary in context. This means that learners will need to use a glossary or personal dictionary of words related to the context in which they are learning. It may also be useful to provide learners with example sentences to help them with the different structures that they come into contact with in vocational and academic settings.
- Group work can be an effective way for learners to practise their speaking and listening skills. It is important that group work activities are set up carefully. Too many instructions can be confusing. It is better to give simple instructions and repeat them. Ensure that the instructions have been comprehended and explain any words that learners may have difficulty with. This can involve modelling if the activity involves an experiment. There should also be clear outcomes for any group activity.

- Consider using role-play to allow learners to rehearse their skills in different situations. This needs to be set up carefully, with learners having access to the kinds of things that might be said in the role-play situation. Learners may also need cue cards to refer to in order to be able to carry out this activity.

- Use DARTs and the EXIT model described in Chapter 3 to support reading.

Stop and reflect

Consider how worksheets and handouts should be presented to be most effective for learners whose first language is not English.

Best practice remains at the heart of material presentation. Ensure that material is manageable. It is important that the text is not too dense and the font is clear. Material should be chunked with headings and subheadings. Use short sentences and bullet points to help keep handouts clear. It is also useful to identify key words, box important information, make use of planned repetition, use labelled diagrams and graphs that add to the meaning of the text. Avoid complicated sentences and lots of new words. It is better to introduce technical terms gradually rather than all at once.

Summary

- Millions of people speak English. For some it is a first language. For others it is a second, third or even fourth language.

- The reasons for this are historic, cultural, social, political and economic.

- Multilingual speakers are able to speak more than one language fluently.

- Sometimes people who spaeak different languages use a lingua franca to communicate effectively. In other situations a pidgin language may develop.

- If a pidgin language becomes the first language of a new generation, rules and a grammatical framework can evolve. If this occurs then the pidgin has evolved into a creole.

- People who speak languages other than English in the UK and who need to develop their English language skills fit into one of four groups: part of a settled community; refugees and asylum seekers; migrant workers; spouses and partners.

- Learners come from different educational backgrounds.

- The impact of poor language skills covers a range of social and economic issues.

- Learners on vocational and academic programmes may face a range of language barriers in addition to cultural and personal barriers.

- It is important to be inclusive.

- Effective learner support requires a team approach.

- Identify **S**pecific, **M**easurable, **A**ttainable, **R**elevant and **T**ime-bound targets.

- Use images, diagrams and demonstrations to support language-based content.

- Body language and gesture may be useful tools to affirm learner progress.

12

- Introduce key vocabulary gradually and reinforce it through handouts, exercises and activities.
- Offer scaffolds and models to support language development.
- Use multi-sensory strategies.

Test your knowledge

12.1 Explain what is meant by the following: mother tongue, pidgin, creole and lingua franca.

12.2 Read through the case study and then answer the accompanying questions.

Konrad is seventy-six. He wishes to attend a basic computer class on a Wednesday morning. He arrived in the UK in 1960. He has worked all his life in the steel industry. He speaks with a Central European accent but uses Sheffield dialect. He has always socialised within the Polish community and Polish remains the first language in the family home. Discussion reveals that his wartime experiences allowed for very little formal education.

a. Identify some of the possible barriers to learning that Konrad may experience.

b. Suggest some strategies that could be used to help Konrad develop his language skills alongside his computer skills.

12.3 Choose an activity that you use in your vocational or academic practice. Decide what difficulties multilingual learners might experience. Discuss your conclusions with a set of peers and identify some strategies to make the activity more inclusive.

Where next?

Texts

Deason, P. (1992) *Flexible Worksheets for Vocational ESOL*, Cambridge: National Extension College

DfES (2001) *Adult ESOL Core Curriculum*, London: DfES

Heaton, B. and Dunmore, D. (1992) *Learning to Study in English*, London: Macmillan

Websites

www.dfes.gov.uk/readwriteplus

www.learnenglish.org.uk The British Council

www.talent.ac.uk Information about ESOL found in PDCs and Projects

Skills auditing vocational and academic subjects

In many cases language and literacy skills are not formally taught as part of academic or vocational learning programmes. In addition to the requirements of their syllabus, lifelong learning practitioners should consider the language and literacy skills their learners need in order to achieve their qualification successfully. Tutors must decide how and where these skills are to be gained. For a training provider or institution to be truly effective the literacy and language needs of learners must be addressed at a strategic level supporting staff working at operational levels. Vocational and academic tutors are not expected to work in isolation: a whole-organisation approach is essential. This chapter is a starting point for vocational and academic tutors. It considers the range of literacy and language skills that different levels of qualification require; the need for assessment at an early stage in the teaching programme and the process for carrying out a skills audit to identify where literacy and language skills could best be embedded within specific programmes of study.

Minimum core elements

A1

- The different factors affecting the acquisition and development of language and literacy skills.
- The importance of context in language use and the influence of the communicative situation.

A skills audit

Best practice

'Effective learning in literacy . . .

- involves the learner
- makes sense to the learner and is recognised as something they need to learn
- fits with other learning
- takes the learner nearer to their goals.'

(DfES, 2004b)

A full skills audit is usually carried out by a course or programme team together with specialist *Skills for Life* staff. The audit is used to identify specific skills and levels of literacy, language and numeracy that learners need in order to succeed on the programme or course being audited. This reflects the importance of different teams working together to bring their different areas of expertise together to support learners.

Best practice

'The most effective support was relevant to the learner's main programme, achieved through close liaison between the support tutor and the subject teaching team or by integrating support into lessons. It developed transferable skills in literacy, numeracy and/or language.'
(Ofsted, 2007)

The National Qualifications Framework

There are currently eight levels of learning identified within the National Qualifications Framework which is overseen by the Qualifications and Curriculum Authority (QCA) in England. Each of the different levels recognises different skills, knowledge and understanding that learners must acquire to achieve qualifications within the secondary, lifelong learning and higher education sectors. Each level has a set of generic descriptive, although not prescriptive, characteristics and outcomes against which courses can be measured. The QCA accredits courses that meet required specifications. This ensures that there is parity between the different awarding bodies and types of qualification. It also ensures a clear route for progression and development. Most courses within the lifelong learning sector are pitched at one of these four levels described by the QCA:

- **Entry level** e.g. *Skills for Life* qualifications, Life Skills, Skills for Working life awards
  Learners are able to recognise and use basic knowledge and skills in a day-to-day situation. The range of ideas covered is narrow and the outcomes must be specific to a particular situation. There are repetitive processes involved. Learners may be closely supervised.

- **Level 1** e.g. GCSEs grades D–G,
  Learners develop basic knowledge and skills which they apply in everyday settings. Learners may be required to make limited choices at this level but they are carrying out familiar routines. There can be links to competencies for specific jobs.

- **Level 2** e.g. GCSEs grades A–C, NVQs, BTEC First Diplomas and Certificates
  Learners gain grounding in a specific subject or vocational area. They are able to apply knowledge and skills in varied contexts and make more choices with less guidance than the previous two levels. This is a skills-building level with learners taking more responsibility for their decisions, some of which may be unfamiliar.

- **Level 3** e.g. A levels, NVQs, BTEC National awards
  Learners require detailed range of knowledge, skills and understanding which they should be able to apply independently. Learners have moved from specific to general applications of their knowledge and skill and should be self-directed.

The level of support that learners need to develop their language and literacy skills will depend on the level at which a course or programme of study functions. It is also important to remember that learners will have strengths and weaknesses. Individual learners may have gaps in their knowledge which need to be filled.

Task

Identify a specific course or scheme of work.

a. What level should learners function at by the time they achieve the qualification?

b. List the literacy skills and attributes that you may need to support your learners in order for them to achieve this programme of study e.g. analyse information. It is important not to take any literacy skills for granted. Learners may have gaps in their knowledge. We all have strengths and weaknesses.

Awarding bodies identify the level at which a qualification is awarded. This information can be found in syllabi, on awarding-body websites and at **www.qca.org.uk**. The QCA provides an overview of the National Qualifications Framework, gives examples of courses at different levels and also maintains descriptors for each level.

Undertaking a literacy skills audit

A literacy skills audit identifies literacy skills and knowledge needed by learners in order to succeed on a particular vocational or academic programme. A skills audit is the first step in a process towards helping learners to succeed on vocational and academic programmes by supporting the development of literacy and language skills. The Rodbaston College case study (DfES, 2003c) provides a model for best practice with *Skills for Life* staff working with practitioners from vocational areas to identify opportunities to embed literacy, numeracy and language skills across the curriculum.

13

Stop and reflect

Consider the range of different teaching and learning strategies and generic type of content that require learners to apply literacy skills effectively in order to access academic and vocational courses e.g. use of specialist terminology, group discussions, skimming and scanning material to find information, active listening etc.

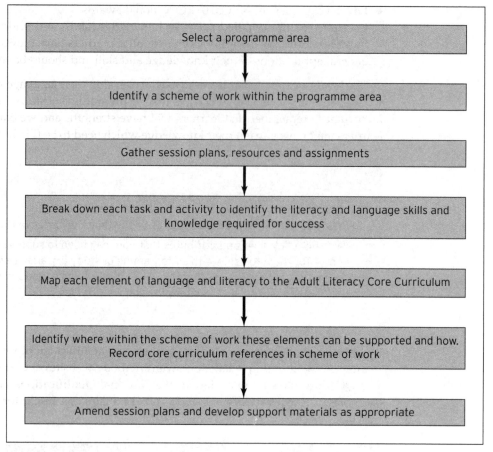

Skills audit flow chart

Teaching and learning activities, handouts, worksheets and specific tasks need to be broken down into component parts. The language and literacy skills of each of these components should be identified where they form a part of the process. Remember though, not all activities involve language and literacy skills! For example, giving an agricultural learner instructions to double dig a plot of land would involve speaking and listening skills as well as knowledge of the specialist term 'double digging' but the actual digging of the land would not require language and literacy skills or knowledge (it would require knowledge and understanding of estimation, which is a numeracy skill). Any teaching and learning strategies that require speaking and listening skills, such as listening to lectures and taking effective notes; participating in group discussions; following instructions; giving presentations; communicating verbally with clients, require learners to be able to draw on a repertoire of skills. Many vocational learners perform well during classroom discussion and practical sessions but are less confident when it comes to tackling theoretical components of a programme. Learners need to read material, which requires effective use of a variety of strategies so that they can extract information, comprehend and infer meaning. It is also worth identifying the range of writing that learners need to undertake such as note-taking, drafting and editing material for different purposes including essays, reports and official documentation. Of course, all of those skills follow on from the literacy skills that learners must initially access in order to interpret assignment briefs or prepare their answers to examinations. Many learners undertaking numeracy- and mathematics-based qualifications have difficulty with examinations because they are unable to extract the mathematical data that they are required to manipulate from the wording that surrounds the numbers.

Best practice

'The integration of basic skills and vocational skills helps learners to achieve challenging goals. In several lessons, learners were reading and understanding demanding specialist vocabulary and text relating to their vocational areas that were pitched at a much higher level than their assessed level of literacy. In a lesson on exotic animals, entry level learners were reading, writing and using specialist words, for example aquarium, chameleons, and amphibians, with confidence.'
(Ofsted, 2002)

Task

Either arrange to observe a session delivered by a peer or consider aspects of your own delivery. Identify and list the speaking, reading and writing activities required by learners to follow and successfully complete the objectives identified within the session.

Outcomes of a literacy audit

The results of the audit should be used to:

- map literacy and language skills to relevant activities within vocational or academic programmes;
- identify naturally occurring opportunities to support learners as they develop literacy and language skills.

Stop and reflect

Consider what a skills audit might prompt a review of within a course or programme of study e.g. criteria for entry to the programme.

An audit of literacy and language skills can have far-reaching consequences. It could influence initial and diagnostic assessment within a vocational or academic programme which in turn could result in an induction-week suite of activities being built into the programme. A skills audit can also lead to a review of the range of teaching and learning activities used; consideration of levels of reading required on a particular programme and review of assignment design.

13

The skills demanded of learners during the programme may need to be demonstrated at entry before the learner joins the programme; taught to those with some skills gaps through additional support, or taught to the whole group before or alongside the vocational activity that requires the skill.

Task

Many programme areas carry out induction activities to introduce learners to the vocational or academic area and also to identify the literacy levels at which learners are working. Share your induction activities with your peers. Discuss their purpose and effectiveness.

Task

Work with a group of peers to develop an effective induction programme for the your vocational or academic programme area.

Snippet

> **Programmes must prepare trainee teachers to identify and to take advantage of the opportunities within their own vocational or subject area to develop the literacy . . . and language skills of their learners**
> FENTO, 2004b

Summary

- Language and literacy skills are often assumed to be in place. Lack of these skills can impact on learner achievement.
- Successful embedding is the result of a whole-organisation approach.
- Subject specialist staff and specialist support staff work as a team to support the learning needs of individual learners.
- A skills audit is a tool for identifying the language and literacy requirements of a course or programme of study.
- All aspects of teaching and learning are covered by the skills audit.
- Tasks and activities are broken down into their component parts. These components may be mapped to the core curriculum and referenced on schemes of work.
- Strategies are identified to support the development of language and literacy skills within the vocational or academic context.
- A skills audit may prompt review of every stage of the learning cycle: criteria for entry, induction sessions, assessment techniques, learner support as well as teaching and learning methods and resources.

Test your knowledge

13.1* Read the cooking instructions for rice, given here. Break the task into its specific literacy skill components. Do not forget that for many learners words like 'simmer' and 'absorb' may be specialist terminology.

Cooking Instructions

On the hob

a. Empty the contents into the saucepan and add 425ml (3/4 pint) boiling water.

b. Cover the saucepan and simmer for 15-20 minutes or until the water is absorbed.

Tip: For extra flavour, fry rice in 1 tbsp of vegetable oil before boiling.

13.2 Look at these two case studies labelled a and b:

a.* You are teaching on a level 1 bricklaying course. Your learners need to know specialist terms so that they can follow your instructions during practical activities and so achieve success on the written part of their examination.

  i. Identify the specific skills that your learners may need to possess or develop, in terms of specialist vocabulary, to achieve their vocational qualification.

  ii. Suggest some strategies, demonstrating good practice, you could use that would support individual learners and benefit the whole class.

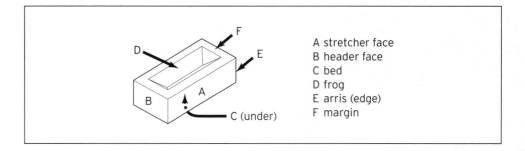

A stretcher face
B header face
C bed
D frog
E arris (edge)
F margin

b. You are teaching on a GCSE (level 2) history programme. Your learners need to go to the library to find out about the topic that they are currently studying. They need to select material and take notes on key events of the Peninsula War. They must then give a five minute presentation identifying their key findings.

  i. Identify the specific skills that your learners may need to possess or develop, in terms of specialist vocabulary, to achieve their vocational qualification.

  ii. Suggest some strategies, demonstrating good practice, you could use that would support individual learners and benefit the whole class.

13

Where next?

Casey, H., et al. (2006) *'You Wouldn't Expect a Maths Teacher to Teach Plastering . . .'*
Embedding Literacy, Language and Numeracy in Post-16 Vocational Programmes: The
Impact on Learning and Achievement, London: NRDC

Eldred, J. (2005) *Developing Embedded Literacy, Language and Numeracy*, London: NIACE

Marsh, A. (2007) *How to Undertake a Literacy Audit*, London: Basic Skills Agency, reference
A1027.

Websites

For examples, materials and case studies about embedding literacy and language into
vocational learning programmes visit the Embedded Learning Portal:

http://www.dfes.gov.uk/readwriteplus/embeddedlearning/

14 Adult literacy core curriculum

Success for All (DfES, 2002a) followed by the government's White Paper *Further Education: Raising Skills, Improving Life Chances* (DfES, 2006a) committed all vocational and academic tutors to addressing the literacy, language and numeracy needs of their learners within specific programme settings. For this process to be successful, vocational and academic tutors need to work closely with specialist literacy tutors and the *Adult Literacy Core Curriculum* (DfES, 2001a) to help ensure that learners achieve their goals and aspirations. The *Adult Literacy Core Curriculum* provides a benchmark mapped to national standards and guidance for specialist *Skills for Life* staff. It is useful as a tool for identifying the levels at which different skills can be embedded in vocational and academic settings and as a reference point for identifying strategies to support literacy and language acquisition. Lifelong learning practitioners are not expected to make detailed use of the different curricula but should be able to access the information contained in them. It is important to remember, though, that successful embedding is about more than mapping language, literacy and numeracy within specific programme areas to the core curricula: it is about supporting skill development in an academic or vocational setting where learners are more likely to recognise their own 'visible' or 'latent' needs.

Best practice	'The Skills for Life staff identify the opportunities for literacy, language and numeracy teaching; and vocational teachers ensure the materials are relevant to the subject areas. The development of good teaching materials comes from staff working together.' (DfES, 2003c)

The adult core curricula – an overview

In order to improve the quality and consistency of basic skills provision, the adult core curriculum was created. There are three curriculum areas: literacy, numeracy and ESOL. The core curricula documents are reference documents used by specialist tutors to underpin support for learners. It is essential for specialist *Skills for Life* tutors to use the core curricula documents to inform planning for individual learners and groups with language, literacy and numeracy needs.

- Learners fit into one or more of the different levels; Entry Level, divided into three sub-levels Entry 1, Entry 2 and Entry 3; Level 1; Level 2. The levels are progressive. They set out clear goals for learners and benchmarks against which literacy and language skills can be assessed. There is more information about the different levels in the previous chapter.

- The different levels are identified by and can be mapped across the national qualifications framework.

- The three different core curricula define the underpinning skills for literacy, numeracy and ESOL within levels as numbered elements as well as giving examples of tasks and of teaching and learning strategies that specialist tutors could use to support the development of particular knowledge or skills identified.

- Learners often have strengths that lift them into higher levels for some activities and skills gaps which mean their attainment for other activities are at lower levels. These learners have **spiky profiles**.

Spiky profile
Indicates that individuals have different skills, strengths and weaknesses.

- Learners with learning difficulties and disabilities who are building skills at a pre-entry level are supported by the *Pre-Entry Curriculum* (DfES, 2002d) which offers a framework of progressive literacy and numeracy milestones.

- The ESOL curriculum (DfES, 2001b) identifies standards of literacy and numeracy for speakers of languages other than English.

- Specialist tutors use diagnostic material mapped to the national standards to assess the learning needs of individual learners, negotiate SMART targets and individual learning plans (ILPs).

- Specialist tutors supporting learners as they acquire essential literacy, language and numeracy skills map teaching and learning activities as well as resources and handouts to the different elements identified within the curricula.

- The adult core curricula is supported by *Access for All* (DfES, 2002b) – a guide detailing strategies and techniques designed to make the literacy curriculum accessible to learners with learning difficulties and/or disabilities. Seven groups of learners with specific learning difficulties and/or disabilities are specifically referenced: learners who are deaf or partially hearing; learners who are blind or partially sighted; learners with mental health problems; learners with dyslexia and related difficulties; learners with physical disabilities; learners with learning difficulties and learners with autistic spectrum disorders. The advice contained in this document is useful to all practitioners working in the lifelong learning sector. *Access for All* offers an overview to the ways in which a specific learning difficulty or disability can impact on learning and suggests a range of approaches and strategies to support learners as they develop the skills they need.

 Snippet

> The standards for adult literacy, adult numeracy and ICT follow a common format and relate directly to the key skills of communication, application of number and ICT. They have also been developed to match the national curriculum requirements for English, mathematics, ICT and the national occupational standards for ICT.
>
> QCA http://www.qca.org.uk/596.html (accessed May 2007)

The literacy core curriculum

The curriculum is divided into three sections, covering: speaking and listening, reading, and writing. Each section is subdivided into different areas. Reading and writing are subdivided into text-level, sentence-level and word-level elements.

1. Speaking and Listening (SL)
   a. listen and respond (SLlr)
   b. speak to communicate (SLc)
   c. engage in discussion (SLd)
2. Reading (R)
   a. text (Rt)
   b. sentence (Rs)
   c. word (Rw)
3. Writing (W)
   a. text (Wt)
   b. sentence (Ws)
   c. word (Ww)

● Understanding adult literacy core curriculum referencing

When specialist tutors map skills and knowledge to the core curriculum, the area of knowledge is referenced, as are the subsection, the individual element and the level of the knowledge.

A specialist tutor can look up this reference in the *Adult Literacy Core Curriculum* (DfES, 2001a) to identify the skill that has been specified. In the case of the example given here the skill is: *'use reference material to find the meaning of unfamiliar words'*. The curriculum suggests examples of tasks that require this skill, and strategies to

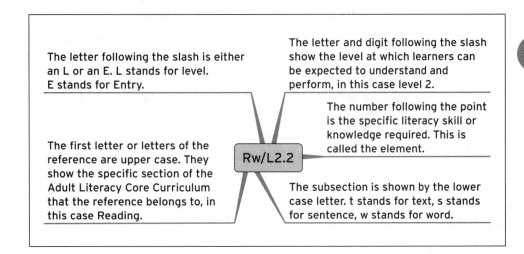

14

support the development of this skill. Alternatively a specialist literacy tutor can identify a task, break it down into component parts and then map the required skills to the curriculum e.g. if a vocational student was required to use a glossary at the back of a text to find the meaning to key terms, the core curriculum reference would be Rw/L2.2.

Tutors can refer to the same element in *Access for All* to identify areas of difficulty which may be experienced by particular learners, and strategies to support learners as they develop the skill identified within the element.

Best practice

'At Rodbaston College, Staffordshire all schemes of work and session plans are expected to include *Skills for Life*. This was one of the factors that led to the college receiving a Grade 1 for literacy in its Ofsted inspection in 2002. Specialist staff work with vocational tutors to ensure that planning is "informed by the national standards and the curriculum".'
(DfES, 2003c)

Where next?

Websites

The *Skills For Life Quality Initiative* offers an online tutorial for the ESOL, numeracy and literacy curricula as well as an introduction to the *Pre-Entry Curriculum Framework* and *Access for All*.

http://www.sflqi.org.uk/pdtraining/core_curriculum.htm

Free copies of the *Adult Literacy Core Curriculum*, the *ESOL Core Curriculum and Access for All* are available from:

The Basic Skills Agency Admail 524, London WC1A 1BR, tel: 0870 600 2400.

Alternatively, access the interactive *Adult Literacy Core Curriculum* with links to *Access for All* at **http://www.dfes.gov.uk/curriculum_literacy/**

The national literacy and numeracy standards can be accessed at **www.qca.org.uk**

It is also possible to search the Embedded Learning Portal for material that has been mapped to different levels:

http://www.dfes.gov.uk/readwriteplus/embeddedlearning/advancedsearch.cfm

Answers to Test your knowledge

Chapter 3

Solution to the investigate word search.

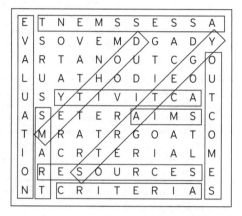

3.1 a. Consider your programme of study, texts and other literature that you have referred to; language used by colleagues and your peer group; official documentation. There are three specific areas that may produce different varieties of language: a professional lexicon used by practitioners in the lifelong learning sector; academic language used by the training provider delivering QTLS and finally your subject specialism will have words and phrases associated with it.

  b. Developing glossaries and using personal dictionaries are just two of the ways that you can develop whole-word knowledge.

3.2 a. There are specialist terms in most subject areas. Look out also for abbreviations and words which may have a slightly different meaning in your subject than they do in general use. It is also worth remembering that some learners may not know words that you assume they should. Learners who speak languages other than English may be in this situation including learners who use British Sign Language as a first language.

  b. In addition to glossaries and personal dictionaries, key words can be explained at the start of a session, discussed and written on displays and board work. Key words can also be noted on worksheets in much the same way as specialist vocabulary is identified in *Literacy for QTLS*. Key-word knowledge can be developed through matching activities, labelling diagrams, quizzes, cloze exercises and word searches.

3.4

Text	Primary purpose	Layout	Structure	Language	Intended audience
A newspaper article	Inform. Explain or describe.	Condensed text depending on whether the paper is tabloid or broadsheet.	Headlines and subheadings and by-lines. Images with captions. Tabloids have short paragraphs and maybe a quotation set in bold print whereas broad sheets have longer paragraphs and fewer images.	Tabloid: straightforward, use of puns and plays on words, present tense. Set out in a sequential order. Broadsheet may use more specialist terms – not so likely to pun.	General readership.
An advert	Persuade	Few words; images – colourful words placed where the reader is most likely to see them.	Simple – slogan and catchphrase; emphasis on image.	Emotive, descriptive, lists of three, rhetorical questions, use of I and we.	General.
An email	Depends on sender – could be any.	Clear headings providing key information.	From, To, Subject bars. Paragraph.	Can be informal, no greeting or closure. Use emoticons. Alternatively it can be more letter- or memo-like	Can be to one person or can be a circular sent to many people.
A fire notice	Instruct	Clear sequence – lots of white space.	A list	Short sentences using the imperative verb form (shut, close, leave).	Anyone using the location.
A class handout	Inform or explain.	Should be clearly set out, plenty of white space.	Headings, subheadings, bullet points – planned repetition.	Clear straightforward language, technical terms explained. Avoid overly complex sentences.	Learners who attended a specific session.

3.5 a. False – it is important to have all the authors so that the text can be traced. **b.** True – *ed.* is the abbreviated form of editor **c.** True. **d.** False. **e.** True. **f.** False – the edition e.g. *2nd edn* should be shown after the text title. **g.** True – *p.* on its own stands for a single page which should be identified.

Chapter 4

4.1 a. The leaflet would be of use to managers, tutors and anyone who wishes to know about the DDA.

    b. The handout is intended for trainees and learners who have little experience drafting paragraphs and essays.

    c. The session plan is of use to the tutor delivering the session, a cover tutor who may take over the group and to an observer either from a QTLS course, a line manager, a peer or an inspector.

4.2 a. Layout – headings and subheadings, lists and bullet points. Content – a summary of the information, key points, examples, a glossary of technical or specialist terms; at the very least they should be explained in a straightforward way. The language should be formal and impersonal. The sentences may be complex but they should be easy to follow.

    b. Layout should be straightforward – a single side of A4. There should be a heading. The mnemonic device may be emboldened or emphasised in some way. There should be space for the learners to make notes. Content – the text is explanatory. The mnemonic should be explained and illustrated by an example. There should be planned repetition and maybe a writing scaffold leading learners through the process. The word 'mnemonic' may be explained. The language should be simple. Sentences should be short or compound (these terms are explained in Chapter 4). There is no need for anything complicated. The language may be impersonal or it may make use of the second person – you – to involve the reader.

    c. The session plan will follow an accepted format. It may make use of bullet points. The content will identify aims, objectives, resources, timings, teaching and learning activities and have space for an evaluation. The language will be impersonal and use specialist terms which will not be explained.

4.4 a. a memorandum,

    b. an email

    c. an agenda

4.5 a. It is a letter.

    b. The features are the sender's address, the date the letter was written, a salutation beginning *Dear* followed by a name and a comma. The first line begins *Re:* and gives the topic for the letter. The next part is the body of the letter. The fact that there is a topic indicator shows that the language will be formal.

    c. The letter will finish with either *Yours sincerely* if the salutation is a named person or *Yours faithfully* if the salutation is *Dear Sir*, *Dear Sirs* or *Dear Sir/Madam*. The final piece of information on the letter will be the sender's signature and their role within the organisation that is sending the letter, if appropriate.

4.6 a. has a high register. It is rather formal.

    b. is somewhere in the middle of the register, whilst

    c. is getting lower on the register.

Chapter 5

5.1 a. Coordinating conjunction   but, and, or, as well as, therefore

        Subordinating conjunction   until, while, since, although

    b. i. Time, ii. Condition, iii. Opposition iv. Cause and effect

5.2

Regular verbs	Irregular verbs
account, categorise, contrast, describe, devise, discuss, extend, organise, outline, produce, rate, recognise, select, summarise.	build (built), choose (chose, chosen), find (found), teach (taught), tell (told), write (wrote, written)

The past tense of irregular verbs is formed by a vowel change in the middle of the word (a medial vowel change) or by an -en ending which is part of the Old English inflective system.

5.3 Subject + verb + object + adverbial phrase.

5.4 a. *I am going*. This is a complete sentence.

    b. *The learners* + verb + *different reading strategies*. The verb could be *considered* or *used*.

    c. *Go!* is complete. The subject is inferred because it is an imperative use of the verb.

    d. Subject + *is at the end of the corridor on the second floor*. This is incomplete. There are any number of options as to what the subject could be.

    e. Subject + verb + *more vocabulary than others*.

    f. *It is important to adapt language to the audience*. This is complete.

    g. *Entry-level learners only* + verb + *classes*. Although of course, most people understand what this means as it stands.

Chapter 6

6.2 b. Kolb (a name); learning cycle (a common noun describing a process); abstract conceptualisation (abstract noun); anadragogy (a learning theory – not named after anyone); UNESCO (acronym for United Nations Educational Scientific and Cultural Organisation – a proper noun); education; self-actualisation; Disability Discrimination Act (statutes require capitalisation); Sir Claus Moser (this is someone's name and title – in other words, it is specific to a particular person so it should all be capitalised. However, if a title is used without a name next to it, it becomes lower case – *The Duke of Devonshire* but *The duke's home is Chatsworth House*); English (a language – so needs a capital); literacy (does not need a capital unless it is part of a specific qualification with the word *literacy* in the title); DfES (Department for Education and Science is a proper noun).

6.3 True, False, True.

6.4 (a), (c) and (m) are examples of the listing comma. The comma separates items in a list: words or phrases. (b) and (e) are examples of the way that the comma is used to mark off names – these can be either proper nouns or generic names. (d) is an example demonstrating how a pair of commas can be used to place extra information in a sentence rather than using brackets. (f) and (g) show that a comma is used to show the point where narrative changes to direct speech or back again. Narrative simply means the story. (h) shows how a comma can mark an aside. In this case the aside turns the statement into a question. (i) Commas are used to mark off phrases within sentences beginning with a participle – *searching* is a present participle. (j) and (l) emphasise points of view. (k) separates the subordinate clause from the main clause. Remember the main clause makes sense on its own but the subordinate clause cannot stand alone. It needs the main part of the sentence next to it. The pause lets the reader know that the main clause follows.

6.5 The first letter of each sentence should be capitalised.

    a. How well do learners achieve? (A direct question)

    b. Learners at Top Trainees continue to achieve excellent success rates. (Check that the proper noun – the name of the organisation – has been capitalised)

    c. Attendances continue to improve with 92 per cent of learners on daytime courses attending 100 per cent of sessions.

    d. The organisation consistently achieved excellent overall success rates.

    There should be no exclamation marks used even though the writer may wish to emphasise the statements made in (c) and (d). This is a report. It is a formal piece of writing requiring a balanced approach: it should not contain exclamation marks demanding emotion from readers or suggesting emotion by the writer.

6.6 The advice day, which was held at the end of October, provided a chance for year 11 pupils to sample the course available to them in the lifelong learning sector.

For most of the visitors it was their first visit to a college and an ideal opportunity for them to find out about which courses they wanted to study. Lecturers were available to speak to and provide guidance throughout the day. Each department produced displays and presentations; potential students were shown around the college as well.

Courtney Jones said that the day was a positive vehicle for advertising the diverse range of courses and facilities that the college had to offer.

6.7 Programme Manager: salary £20,000 pa (plus expenses and pension contribution)

Work with young people, 14-19 years, delivering exciting enterprise learning programmes; widening participation is an essential component of the job.

Enterprise Intiative has an opportunity for an exceptional candidate to be responsible for organising the delivery of business and enterprise programmes to young people in the lifelong learning sector across the county. The role will encompass all aspects of successful programme delivery, including coordination and presentation on the day, plus supporting work such as training volunteers and teachers, as well as pre-event preparation.

The successful applicant will work with business volunteers, teachers and young people to ensure that all benefit from the successful delivery of Enterprise initiative's education programmes.

Chapter 7

Correct answers to the cut-and-match exercise:

Plant name and word journey	Original name	Meaning
Dandelion Middle English via Old French	Dent-de-lion	Lion's tooth
Garlic Old English	Garleac	Spear leek
Orchid Originally Greek borrowed by Latin; used by 17th century botanists	Orkhis	Testicle
Tulip Originally a Persian word borrowed by the Turks, then Latinised and used in 16th century England via the Lowlands	Dulband	Turban
Cowslip Old English	Cuslyppe	Cow's slimy dropping
Daisy Old English	Doegseage	Day's eye
Lupin Latin	Lupinum	Wolf-like
Pansy A loan word from France in the 16th century; modern spelling evolved in the 18th century	Pensee	Thought

7.1   The answer is 16. Many (spell + ing) (rule + s) are (link + ed) to (add + ing) (suffix + es) to (word + s).

7.2   **a.** between/among

     b. outside

7.3   **a.** -al creates an adjective e.g. someone may have a *visual* learning style.

     b. -nomy related to the law e.g. *astronomy* relates to the laws governing the stars, *economy* relates to the laws governing resources, *autonomy* relates to the way people govern themselves, a *taxonomy* relates to laws created by classifications.

7.4   **a.** re + view, multi + culture + al, develop + ment + al, multi + sense + ory, in + flex + ible, assess + ment, re + assess + ed.

     b. Breaking the words down creates more manageable chunks that are more likely to be spelt correctly. Patterns can be identified and applied.

     c. There is no change to the root word when the prefix is added. When a suffix beginning with a vowel is added to a root word that ends with e and where the stress is on the last part of the word, the e is dropped (remember that there are exceptions to every rule - *useable* does not fit the expected pattern, for instance.)

7.5 **To** is a preposition – it gives direction or position e.g. *They were going to a family learning centre.*

Too is part of something called an adjectival phrase; it gives additional information to an adjective e.g. *They were too late for enrolment.*

Two is a number e.g. *one, two, three.*

Help learners by asking prompting questions, help them identify patterns and groups, direct them to examples of correct use so that a model is provided.

7.6 All staff are reminded that **new** (adjective describing the state of the registers) registers must have a course code. Staff who do not **know** (verb) the relevant code should contact **their** (belonging) line manager for clarification.

It is **our** (belonging, not a time) policy that students cannot be enrolled until a course code is provided. They will not be **allowed** (verb giving permission) to remove materials from the resource centre and will not **be** (verb, not buzzing insect – interestingly people are less likely to get this homophone wrong) certificated **where** (location) they have **passed** (verb, not a time) portfolio **based** (verb giving past tense rather than half of an infinitive) courses.

7.7 prob-ab-ly, re-mem-ber, ex-per-i-ence, pro-fes-sion-al, a-chieve-ment, suf-fic-i-ent, con-clu-sion, can-did-ate, part-ic-i-pant.

Chapter 8

8.2 a. They were (subject–verb agreement),

   b. I did (formation of the past tense),

   c. It isn't (formation of negatives),

   d. those books (use of demonstrative pronoun),

   e. We went … but did not find anything (double negative).

   Introducing the Grammar of Talk (QCA, 2004) identifies that speakers who use dialect forms make use of non-standard grammar. The errors in these examples are not acceptable in a written format but for spoken discourse, excepting formal situations, their meaning is transparent.

8.6 a. First it is important to activate learners' prior knowledge. This could be through a mind map, a snowball activity or a KWL grid. Explain things in a logical sequence. Use sequencing words such as *first, then* and *finally* to help give structure to what you are saying. Identify key words and phrases. Give examples. Use visual aids (so long as they are not cluttered). Ask questions to check understanding and conclude by summarising what you have said.

   b. Ask students to listen to and then recall the main points of a talk.

Chapter 9

9.1 The paralanguage provides additional information that the words alone do not offer.

   a. The first version of *bedtime* is a statement; it could be neutral, clipped or light depending on the parent's frame of mind. The child's response could be surprise or it could turn the question into a plea to stay up beyond the appointed time. The exclamation mark on the final bedtime turns it into a command or there may be an increase in volume.

9.2 a. Anger   **b.** Happiness   **c.** Surprise   **d.** Fear   **e.** Disgust

9.3 a. Shrugging can mean anything from *I don't know* to *I'm not interested* depending upon the context in which it is used. It can signify that someone is fed up or that they do not know the answer.

b. Hand rubbing could show that someone is looking forward to an event – in can be a gesture of excitement or alternatively if the hands fold round each other rather than being a palm-to-palm rub it could mean that the person is either worried or cold.

c. Leaning against something like this is an open gesture and suggests calm confidence. A teacher might use this stance.

d. If someone stands with their hands on their hips it could mean that they are angry or exasperated. It could also mean, if they are female, that they wish to emphasise their shape!

e. Steepling fingers together can show that someone is thinking, or if they are speaking it tends to suggest that they feel superior in terms of knowledge to the people around them.

9.4 a. The orientation of these two people suggests that they do not know one another. They are trying to keep their personal space intact. They do not wish to communicate.

b. These two people may or may not know one another but they are in a position that requires eye contact, so they are positioned for communication.

c. This is a traditional classroom layout. It suggests the tutor is going to be in charge and that the learners are there to listen.

d. The horseshoe shape is more informal. It puts the tutor and the learners on a more equal footing and also allows the possibility of group discussion.

Chapter 10

10.1 Tom would benefit from an introductory course in mechanics. Aspects of theory and record-keeping could be gradually introduced. His literacy needs to be situated in mechanics in the first instance but it needs to be carefully structured so that he does not become demotivated.

Anjim should seek advice about the kind of sewing courses available in her area.

Chapter 13

13.1 The first thing that the reader needs to be able to do is skim the instructions and recognise that they are instructions – the subheadings, numbers, use of imperative verb form and short sentences indicate this. The reader then needs to read in detail from start to finish. If they fail to do this, then the tip for extra flavour is lost because it is out of sequence. The reader needs to recognise and understand specialist terms including *hob*, *simmer* and *absorbed*. The reader needs to understand abbreviations. The reader also needs to understand that the conjunction 'or' in the second point gives an element of choice.

13.2 a. Learners will need to learn the specialist terms – some, like *arris*, are new words and should be used instead of the more familiar word *edge*. Other words may be familiar but they have a different meaning in a specialised context. Learners should be able to understand what the words mean and spell them correctly. The activity illustrated is a DARTs-type activity and requires reconstruction of the text by labelling. This is a useful strategy. Learners could also be required to create personal glossaries of specialist terms. Tutors could model good practice by using the correct term, initially followed by an explanation or paraphrasing into more straightforward language.

Glossary

Accent The way words are pronounced, usually according to geographical but also social location.

Accommodation The speaker changes the way that they speak in order to sound more like or to imitate the listener. The speaker will use words, syntax and grammatical constructions that they feel that the listener will be more likely to understand.

Acronym The initial letters of a phrase or name are used to form a new word e.g. *vat* (said as a word) is an acronym for *value added tax*.

Action plan Document to plan progress towards learning goals. The outcomes of action plans should be SMART.

Adjacency pairs Turn-taking and expected patterns within transactions e.g. 'How are you?' The expected response is 'Fine, thanks.'

Affix Addition to the beginning (prefix) or end of a word (suffix) to change the meaning of the word or to change the grammatical group to which the word originally belonged.

Ambiguity This is where there is more than one meaning to a sentence. The reader cannot be sure what the writer intended. It may be because of the order of the words or the way that they have been punctuated.

Asylum seeker An asylum seeker is someone who has made an application to stay in the UK but the Home Office has not yet reached a decision.

Audience Intended readership of a text.

Automaticity A skill that is automatic. It does not need to be thought about. An example of automaticity is the knowledge that the number eleven follows the number ten, without having to think about it or count forward.

Bias Favour one point of view rather than remaining neutral on a topic.

Bibliography A list of literature that has formed background reading during the course of study for a particular assignment.

Braille A system where letters and common words or phrases are represented by different combinations of six raised dots arranged in three rows of two columns. It is a tactile system. Braille is created on an electronic Braille printing machine or by hand with a style and frame.

Clause This is a group of words that has a subject and a verb. If the clause makes sense on its own, we tend to think of it as a simple sentence. There are two kinds of clause: main and subordinate. A main clause can stand alone as a sentence. A subordinate clause does not make sense on its own: it needs its main clause in order to make complete sense.

Cloze exercise A passage is presented with key words removed. These words may be given in a word bank at the top or the bottom of the page. Learners predict the missing words using their knowledge of the topic (the context) and the existing sentence structures as cues.

Colloquial Informal style of speaking containing abbreviated forms and some dialect words.

Context The situation in which language is used.

Cue The means by which the reader is able to decode the text.

Deixis Expressions which cannot be understood unless the context in which the expression is used is known e.g. one-word answers in response to a question such as *mine, here* and *tomorrow.*

Derivation The original source of a particular word.

Descriptive grammar Grammar is used to describe the way people are currently using language. It is non-judgmental, unlike prescriptive grammar which sets out rules that must be followed.

Diagnostic assessment Diagnostic assessment is a focused assessment identifying strengths, weaknesses and knowledge/skills gaps. It provides detailed information that can be used to inform an individual learning plan.

Dialect Words, phrases and grammatical constructions peculiar to a geographical region, specific social strata and/or occupation.

Domain The context in which a particular form of language is used e.g. work, home, religion.

Dominant literacy A form of language that is regarded as having prestige and which is used by formal organisations within society such as education, law and religion.

Elaborated code The ability to switch between different forms of language to suit audience and purpose.

ESOL English for Speakers of Other Languages.

Etymology The study of the derivation or history of words.

Fillers A form of paralanguage used to fill gaps between speech such as 'er' and 'um'.

Genre In literature a genre refers to the type of text such as poetry, drama and prose. It is now used more widely to describe different types of the written form including non-literary texts such as lists and letters. Genres have recognisable forms.

Grapheme Letter. Grapheme–phoneme links describe the way in which sounds relate to written letters.

Group noun The name given to a specified group of people or things e.g. *a herd of cattle.*

Harvard referencing A system for identifying literature by name and date.

Ideolect A personal speech pattern, but not part of an accent.

Idiom An expression that has meaning but not what it literally says. For example the idiom 'look on the bright side' does not mean that someone is looking into the sunshine; it actually means that they are being positive about something that has not gone according to plan.

Imperative The form of the verb that gives orders, commands and instructions e.g. *Sit!*

Implicit If the meaning of something is implicit it is unwritten but can be understood from the language that the writer uses. The reader is able to infer meaning.

Infer Read meaning into the words beyond what is written in the text.

Inflection The use of word endings to vary the word class to which a word belongs. Old English was a highly inflected language. Modern English uses far fewer word endings. The remnants of Old English inflections sometimes create spelling irregularities.

Initial assessment An assessment that gives an indicator of the levels that a learner is currently working at. Initial assessment which identifies a general level is often followed by diagnostic assessment.

International phonetic alphabet The limitation of the alphabet used in the United Kingdom is that there are not enough letters for every sound that we are capable of making. The IPA provides a symbol for each sound that is made. This means that it can be used to provide a phonetic transcription of the way that individual words sound.

Ipsative assessment Independent self-assessment allowing individuals to reflect upon their own strengths and weaknesses and set their own learning goals. Self-assessment can take different forms, including self-testing, self-rating and reflective questioning. This skills audit contains elements of these different forms of self-assessment.

Jargon Specialist or technical vocabulary used by small groups of people as a shorthand to communicate effectively without lengthy explanations e.g. *ipsative assessment*. Unfortunately many people use unnecessary jargon to sound more knowledgeable than their listeners or to fill space e.g. *blue sky thinking*.

Key words Words that are essential for understanding and being able to communicate about a particular subject e.g. *formative* and *summative assessment* are key words that must be understood in order to understand and discuss assessment strategies.

Kinesics The study of the way in which people move to communicate information or emotion non-verbally.

Leakage Non-verbal communication, of which the speaker is unaware, that usually contradicts what the speaker is saying. Common famous examples of leakage are those that signal that a speaker may be lying but leakage can, just as easily, show underlying anxiety or lack of confidence.

Levels The National Qualifications Framework (NQF) identifies the level of skill and knowledge that different qualifications require and the levels at which qualifications will be recognised by employers and educational providers. Qualifications are grouped together by level. For example, level 1 is pre-GCSE; level 2 is GCSE grade C and above; level 3 relates to qualifications such as A levels and BTEC Nationals.

Lexical features Specialist vocabulary or vocabulary that is not standard English e.g. dialect forms.

Lexis Another word for vocabulary.

Lingua franca A particular language used to ensure cross-group understanding.

Literacy The dictionary definition of literacy is the ability to read and write. However, as UNESCO explains, 'literacy is a plural concept, with diverse literacies shaped by their use in particular contexts' (UNESCO, http://portal.unesco.org/education).

Literal Words in a text are interpreted in a way which everyone understands. There are no hidden meanings. Instructions and explanations are taken literally.

Marginalised literacy Non-standard form of language that is not recognised by influential institutions within society.

Metacognition Thinking about what is involved in a task or process and planning to carry out the different stages before undertaking them.

Miscue analysis This term is usually applied to diagnostic assessment used to identify the language processing difficulties experienced by struggling readers. Effective tutors also make analysis of the different kinds of difficulties learners have with spelling patterns and grammatical construction. This means that the cause of learner difficulties can be pinpointed and effective support provided.

Mode Another word for purpose e.g. *inform, instruct, explain* or *persuade*. Remember texts/spoken language can have more than one purpose; the primary purpose is the most important although there may be secondary purposes behind a piece of writing as well.

Monolingual Speaking only one language.

Moon Another tactile system but with less complexity than Braille. It is composed of raised letters tilted at different angles. The letters look more like the ordinary Roman alphabet that people with sight use.

Morpheme A morpheme is the smallest unit which has meaning. Some morphemes are words. Other morphemes are affixes. An unbound morpheme makes sense on its own. A bound morpheme has to stand next to another morpheme in order to make sense.

Morphology The study of the way words are formed and their functions.

Mother tongue Language learnt from parents or carers during infancy.

Object The object of a sentence, or the person or thing on the receiving end of the action carried out by the subject of the sentence e.g. *The tutor listened to the learner*. The learner is the object of the sentence because the teacher is carrying out the action.

Orientation The way people position themselves in relation to others.

Paralanguage All the voiced communication devices that work alongside speech e.g. tone, pitch and volume.

Parse Make an analysis of a sentence by identifying the different units, or features of language, within it such as subject, verb and object.

Phatic language A communication that has little literal meaning. The transaction is a social exchange.

Phoneme The smallest unit of sound. There are approximately 44 separate sounds in English.

Phonetics The symbols used to represent the sounds of a language. The international phonetic alphabet (IPA) provides a symbol for each individual sound.

Phrase This is a group of words that do not make sense on their own but they can be used as a building block to help build up meaning in a sentence.

Plagiarism The term used to describe the outcome when writers use the words or ideas from a text that they have read and do not reference the source, making it look like their own work. This can be accidental or intentional.

Posture The way someone stands or holds themself when they are sitting e.g. slouched, or upright.

Pragmatics The features of conversation that people take for granted but which can be confusing to people who do not speak English as a first language. Pragmatics refer to the codes of communication that people use when they make language choices.

Pronoun Words like *I*, *you*, *he*, *she* and *it* which are used to replace nouns (naming words) in sentences. This often improves the flow of a text because it reduces repetition.

Proper noun The names of specific people, places and times of the year.

Prosody features The sounds created alongside the words in speech such as pitch, tone, intonation and rhythm.

Proximity The physical distance between people. Edward Hall identified four spatial zones where people place themselves depending upon how well they know one another and what is culturally acceptable. Proxemics is the study of the way people use space in order to communicate.

Punctuation The signposting device for the written word. We use punctuation as a cue for grouping words and for identifying context. It is an effective device for avoiding ambiguity because it works with grammar to clarify meaning. In order to use punctuation effectively, the writer creating the text needs to know and use the conventions that apply to punctuation.

Purpose The writer's intention. There are many categories of purpose including entertainment, information and persuasion. Texts can have primary and secondary purposes.

Reference list A list of texts identifying complete information about works which have been cited during a piece of writing. It is different to a bibliography. The bibliography identifies all the texts that have been studied including background research.

Refugee Someone whose claim to stay in the UK has been accepted by the Home Office.

Register The level of formality or informality of a piece of writing depending upon its context and purpose. The concept of register was first introduced in the 1960s by the sociologist Basil Bernstein.

Restricted code Having only a limited variety of language to choose from rather than being able to switch between dialect forms and standard English as appropriate for the audience and purpose. An elaborated code is the opposite of this.

Rhetorical devices These are techniques that speeches and other forms of persuasive writing use to persuade listeners and readers towards the viewpoint of the text. Devices include lists of three, alliteration (the initial sound of two or more words is the same – e.g. a *tongue twister*) to emphasise points, using quotations or statistics, using *I* or *we* to involve the audience.

Rhetorical question The speaker or writer asks a question but does not expect an answer. The question is a device that signposts the topic addressed by the speaker or writer.

Scanning Reading a text in search of specific words or information e.g. searching for a specific name on a register or looking for a specific topic in a textbook.

Semantic cues Using knowledge of context to work out the meaning of a text.

Semantics The study of how language communicates meaning. Modern semantics studies the ways in which words and sentences create meaning in specific contexts.

Situated literacy A literacy practice associated with particular locations, such as work or religious beliefs. Language and form that belong to a specific location e.g. the ability to follow a knitting pattern requires a situated literacy.

Skills audit A personal skills audit identifies the level and type of skill demonstrated by individuals. A skills audit is also a term used in an educational setting to identify the levels and skills required to achieve a particular learning programme.

Skills for Life A term used to describe provision for adult literacy, numeracy and English for speakers of other languages launched in 2001 following the findings and recommendations of Moser's report *A Fresh Start*.

Skimming Reading a text quickly to gain the gist of what the text is about.

Slang Words that are considered to be non-standard either because they are used by specific groups of people to communicate among themselves or because the words are too new. Examples of slang include describing the police as 'the fuzz', a difficult exam as 'solid' or, if it is very difficult, 'well solid'.

Soft goals/targets These goals/targets are subjective because they are related to emotions, often confidence. For example, a trainee has bad memories of learning grammar from their school days. The trainee may feel concerned that they cannot tackle grammatical frameworks successfully. The action plan that this trainee produces will require them to break grammatical frameworks into small but manageable chunks. One of their long-term goals will be to overcome their confidence barrier.

Speech divergence The opposite of accommodation. A transaction between two speakers will result in the two speakers using different modes of speech, emphasising their own idiolect and using words that reflect different register and knowledge to the other person. These two speakers are not on the same wavelength!

Spiky profile Individuals have different skills, strengths and weaknesses. It is unusual for someone to be equally strong in all areas. There will be peaks and troughs, hence a spiky profile.

Standard English A prestige dialect used in formal situations.

Style The way it which language, structure and content are organised.

Subject In grammatical terms a subject of a sentence is the person or thing carrying out the action. *The tutor marked the work*. In this example the tutor is the subject of the sentence. The tutor is carrying out the action.

Substituting Non-verbal communication is used to replace a verbalised message.

SWOT analysis SWOT is an acronym. This means that each letter is the first letter of another word in this case **s**trengths, **w**eaknesses, **o**pportunities and **t**hreats. The analysis requires individuals or organisations to reflect on the four different categories, for instance the skills audit requires reflection related to the minimum literacy core.

Syntactic cues Using knowledge of grammar and word order to help work out the meaning of a text.

Syntactical features The way in which a speaker (or writer) uses grammar. Dialect speakers do not always use standard syntax.

Syntax The order in which words are placed in a sentence to give them grammatical meaning.

Tag question A short question such as 'isn't it?' following a statement which changes the statement into a question.

Taxonomy A scheme or order based on a system of classification.

Text Any written form ranging from a few words to a novel.

Transportable literacy Skills and knowledge that can be used in different situations and contexts e.g. the ability to change reading style depending on the purpose of text and reason for reading. Processes tend to be transportable as do the frameworks of language. Understanding that instructions are sequenced and that instructions can be used differently depending on their context are transportable skills.

URL A URL is another name for a website address. Each website, each page, each directory and each file on the Internet has a unique address to enable web users to find the different resources available. The term URL is an acronym. It stands for uniform resource locator.

Usage The way in which language is currently used, including construction and meaning.

Varieties of language A language form that is distinct from other forms of the language.

Bibliography

Texts

Aitchison, J. (1999) (5th edn) *Teach Yourself Linguistics*, London: Hodder & Stoughton

Aldridge, F. (2001) *Divided by Language: A Study of Participation and Competence in Languages in Great Britain Undertaken by NIACE*, Leicester: NIACE

Bandura, A. (1977) *Social Learning Theory*, Englewood Cliffs, NJ: Prentice Hall

Barton, D., Hamilton, M. and Ivanic, R. (eds) (2000) *Situated Literacies*, London: Routledge

Basic Skills Agency (2000) *Getting Better Basic Skills: What Motivates Adults*, London: Basic Skills Agency

Beard, R. (1987) *Developing Reading 3–13*, London: Hodder & Stoughton

Bernstein, B. (1975) *Class Codes and Control*, Vol 3, London: Routledge and Kegan Paul/Paladin

Besser, S., et al. (2004) *Adult Literacy Learners' Difficulties in Reading: An Exploratory Study*, London: NRDC

Birdwhistle, R. L. (1970) *Kinesis and Contact*. Philadelphia: University of Pennsylvania Press

Borwick, C. and Townend, J. (1993) *Developing Spoken Language Skills*, Egham, Surrey: The Dyslexia Institute

Boud, D. (1995) 'Developing a typology for learner self assessment practices.' *Research and Development in Higher Education*, 18, 130–5. Available at www.education.uts.edu.au/ostaff/staff/boud_publications.html (accessed 12 January 2007)

Bragg, M. (2003) *The Adventure of English*, London: Hodder & Stoughton

Brown, L. (ed) (2002) (5th edn) *Shorter Oxford English Dictionary*, Oxford: Oxford University Press.

Brown, H. and Brown, M. (1992) (2nd edn) *A Speller's Companion*, Wigton: Brown and Brown

Bryson, B. (1991) *Mother Tongue*, London: Penguin

Burley-Allen, M. (1995) *Listening: The Forgotten Skill*, New York: John Wiley & Sons

Burt, A. (1983) *A Guide to Better Punctuation*, Cheltenham: Stanley Thornes

Bynner, J. and Parsons, S. (1997) *It Doesn't Get Any Better: The Impact of Poor Basic Skills on the Lives of 37-Year-Olds*, London: Basic Skills Agency

Bynner, J. and Parsons, S. (2000) *Use It or Lose It? The Impact of Time Out of Work on Literacy and Numeracy Skills*, London: Basic Skills Agency

Carbo, M., Dunn, R. and Dunn, K. (1986) *Teaching Students to Read Through Their Individual Learning Styles*, NJ, USA: Prentice-Hall

Carroll, L. (2003) *Alice Through the Looking Glass and What Alice Found There*, London: Penguin

CBI (2006) *Working on the Three Rs: Employers' Priorities for Functional Skills in Maths and English*, London: CBI

Cowley, S. (2004) *Getting the Buggers to Write 2*, London: Continuum Books

Cox, B. (1991) *Cox on Cox: An English Curriculum for the 1990's*, London: Hodder & Stoughton

Crystal, D. (1987) *The Cambridge Encyclopedia of Language*, Cambridge: Cambridge University Press

Crystal, D. (1995) *The Cambridge Encyclopaedia of English Language*, Cambridge: Cambridge University Press

Crystal, D. (2003) *Rediscover Grammar*, Harlow: Longman

Crystal, D. (2004) *The Stories of English*, London: Penguin

Cullup, M. (1999) *Brush Up Your Grammar*, Tadworth: Right Way

DES (1975) *A Language for Life* (The Bullock Report), London: HMSO

DES (1984) *English From 5 to 16* (Curriculum Matters 1), London: HMSO

DES (1988) *Report of the Committee of Inquiry into the Teaching of English Language* (The Kingman Report), London: HMSO

DES (1989) *English for Ages 5 to 11* (The Second Cox Report), London: HMSO

Dexter, T. (1802) *A Pickle for the Knowing Ones or Plain Truth for a Homespun Dress*, Newburyport, MA: Self published

DfEE (1998) *The National Literacy Strategy: Framework for Teaching*, London: DfEE

DfEE (1999a) *A Fresh Start: Improving Literacy and Numeracy (The report of the working group chaired by Sir Claus Moser)*, London: DfEE

DfEE (1999b) *Learning to Succeed: A New Framework for Post-16 Learning*, London: DfEE

DfEE (2000a) *Breaking the Language Barriers (The report of the working group on English for speakers of other languages (ESOL))*, London: DfEE

DfEE (2000b) *Freedom to Learn: Basic Skills for Learners with Learning Difficulties and/or Disabilities*, London: DfEE

DfES (2001a) *Adult Literacy Core Curriculum*, London: DfES

DfES (2001b) *Adult ESOL Core Curriculum*, London: DfES

DfES (2002a) *Success for All: Reforming Further Education and Training – Our Vision for the Future*, London: DfES

DfES (2002b) *Access for All: Guidance on Making the Adult Literacy and Numeracy Core Curricula Accessible*, London: DfES

DfES (2002c) *Basic Skills for Adults with Learning Difficulties and/or Disabilities: A Resource Pack to Support Staff Development*, London: DfES

DfES (2002d) *Adult Pre-Entry Curriculum Framework*, London: DfES

DfES (2003a) *21st Century Skills: Realising Our Potential*, London: DfES

DfES (2003b) *Skills for Life: Focus on Delivery to 2007*, London: DfES

DfES (2003c) *Delivering Skills for Life Case Study: Rodbaston College, Staffordshire*, London: DfES Publications

DfES (2004a) *Equipping our Teachers for the Future*, London: DfES

DfES (2004b) *Delivering Skills for Life: The National Strategy for Improving Adult Literacy and Numeracy Skills. Raising Standards: A Contextual Guide to Support Success in Literacy, Numeracy and ESOL Provision*, London: DfES. Available at www.dfes.gov.uk/readwriteplus

DfES (2006a) *Further Education: Raising Skills, Improving Life Chances*, London: DfES

DfES (2006b) *National Primary Strategy*, http://www.standards.dfes.gov.uk/primary/ (accessed 4 June 2007)

DfES (2006c) *Independent Review of the Teaching of Early Reading (The Report of the review chaired by Jim Rose)*, London: DfES.

DfES (2006d) *National Adult Learning Survey 2005*, London: DfES

Dunn, R. (2000) 'Learning styles: Theory, research and practice', *National Forum of Applied Educational Research Journal*, 13(1): 3–22

Dunn, R. and Dunn, K. (1978) *Teaching Students Through Their Individual Learning Styles: A Practical Approach*, NJ, USA: Prentice-Hall

Edwards, J. (1994) *Multilingualism*, London: Routledge

Ellis, R. and McClintock A. (1991) *If You Take My Meaning: Theory into Practice in Human Communication*, London: Hodder & Stoughton

FENTO (2004a) *Addressing Language, Literacy and Numeracy Needs in Education and Training: Defining the Minimum Core of Teachers' Knowledge, Understanding and Personal Skill*, London: FENTO

FENTO (2004b) *Including Language, Literacy and Numeracy Learning in all Post-16 Education*, London: FENTO

Flavell, L. and Flavell, R. (2000) *Dictionary of Word Origin*, London: Kyle Cathie Ltd

Flower, L. and Hayes, J. R. (1981) 'A cognitive process theory of writing', *College Composition and Communication*, 32: 365–87

Fordham, N. W. (2006) 'Crafting questions that address comprehension strategies in content reading', *Journal of Adolescent and Adult Literacy*, 49 (5): 390–7

Forgas, J. P. (1989) *Interpersonal Behaviour: The Psychology of Social Interaction*. Oxford: Pergamon Press

French, S. (1993) 'Disability, impairment or something in between?' in Swain, J., et al (eds) *Disabling Barriers – Enabling Environments*, London: Sage.

Further Education Funding Council (FEFC) (1996) *Inclusive Learning: Report of the Learning Difficulties and/or Disabilities Committee*, London: FEFC

Gardner, H. (1993) (2nd edn) *Frames of Mind: The Theory of Multiple Intelligences*, London: Fontana Press

Gardner, H. (1999) *Intelligence Reframed. Multiple Intelligences for the 21st Century*, New York: Basic Books

Gration, G. N. (1989) *Communication and Media Studies*, Cheltenham: Nelson Thornes

Hall, E. T. (1973) *The Silent Language*, New York: Anchor Press

Hamilton, M. and Hillier, Y. (2006) *Changing Faces of Adult Literacy, Language and Numeracy: A Critical History*, Stoke on Trent: Trentham Books

Harris, R. and Savitzky, F. (eds) (1988) *My Personal Language History*, London: New Beacon Books

Harrison, R. (1993) 'Disaffection and access', in Calder, J. (ed) *Disaffection and Diversity. Overcoming Barriers to Adult Learning*, London: Falmer, p. 2

HMIe (2005) *Developing Writing Through Reading, Talking and Listening*. Livingstone: HMIe, from www.literacytrust.org.uk as a pdf or http://www.hmie.gov.uk/documents/publication/dwtrtl.html

HM Treasury (2006) *Review of Skills: Prosperity for All in the Global Economy: World Class Skills*, London: TSO

Honey, P. and Mumford, A. (1982) *Manual of Learning Styles*, London: P Honey

Jarvis, P. (1995) *Adult Education and Lifelong Learning*, London: Routledge

Johnson, S. (1775) Preface to his *Dictionary of the English Language*, downloaded from http://andromeda.rutgers.edu/~jlynch/Texts/preface.html (accessed 3 February 2007)

Kennedy, H. (1997) *Learning Works: Widening Participation in Further Education*, Coventry: FEFC

Kipling, R. (1990) *The Complete Verse*, London: Kyle Cathie Ltd

Knowles, M. S. (1990) *The Adult Learner: A Neglected Species*, Houston: Gulf Publishing

Kolb, D. A. (1984) *Experiential Learning: Experience as the Source of Learning and Development*, Englewood Cliffs, NJ: Prentice Hall

Labov, W. (1972) *Sociolinguistic Patterns*, Philadelphia: University of Pennsylvania Press

Lee, J. (2002) *Making the Curriculum Work for Learners with Dyslexia*, London: Basic Skills Agency

Lifelong Learning UK (2006) *New Overarching Professional Standards for Teachers, Tutors and Trainers in the Lifelong Learning Sector*, London: Lifelong Learning UK

Lowth, R. (1762) *A Short Introduction to English Grammar*, London: Publisher unknown

Maxted, P. (1999) 'Understanding barriers to learning', *t Magazine*, July 1999, (www.tmag.co.uk)

McArthur, T. (ed) (1992) *The Oxford Companion to the English Language*, Oxford: Oxford University Press

Myers, G. E. and Myers, M. T. (1985) *The Dynamics of Human Communication*, New York: McGraw-Hill

Neill, S. (1991) *Classroom Nonverbal Communication*, London: Routledge

Office for National Statistics (1998) *The International Adult Literacy Survey*, London: ONS

Ofsted (2002) *Inspecting Post-16 Basic Skills in Literacy and Numeracy, with Guidance on Self-Evaluation*, London: Ofsted

Ofsted (2006) *The Annual Report of Her Majesty's Chief Iinspector of Schools 2004/2005* can be accessed at: http://live.ofsted.gov.uk/publications/annualreport0405/4.2.5.html

Ofsted (2007) *Current Provision and Outcomes for 16–18 year old learners with Learning Difficulties and/or Disabilities in Colleges* can be accessed at: www.ofsted.gov.uk

OECD (Organisation for Economic Cooperation and Development) (2003) *Employment Outlook: Towards More and Better Jobs*, Paris: OECD, www.oecd.org (accessed 4 June 2007)

Parsons, S. (2002a) *Do I Want to Improve my Reading, Writing or Maths?* London: Basic Skills Agency

Parsons, S. (2002b) *Basic Skills and Crime*, London: Basic Skills Agency

Parsons, S. and Bynner, J. (2002) *Basic Skills and Social Exclusion: Findings from a Study of Adults Born in 1970*, London: Basic Skills Agency

Pinker, S. (1994) *The Language Instinct*, London: Penguin

QCA (1998) *The Grammar Papers: Perspectives on the Teaching of Grammar in the National Curriculum*, London: QCA

QCA (2004) *Introducing the Grammar of Talk*, London: QCA, downloadable from: www.qca.org.uk

Rawlinson, G. E. (1976) 'The significance of letter position in word recognition' Unpublished PhD thesis, Psychology Department, University of Nottingham, Nottingham, UK

Reece, I. and Walker, S. (2000) (4th edn) *Teaching, Training and Learning: A Practical Guide*, Sunderland: Business Education Publishers

Rogers, A. (2002) (3rd edn) *Teaching Adults*, Maidenhead: Open University Press

Shannon, C. E. and Weaver, W. (1949) *The Mathematical Theory of Communication*, Urbana: University of Illinois Press

Skills and Education Network (2004) *Guide 2 ... Engaging Adults: Overcoming the Barriers to Adult Learning*, London: Learning and Skills Council

Skinner, B. F. (1973) *Beyond Freedom and Dignity*, London: Penguin.

Tammet, D. (2006) *Born on a Blue Day*, London: Hodder & Stoughton

Trudgehill, P. (2000) (4th edn) *Sociolinguisitics: An Introduction to Language and Society*, London: Penguin

Truss, L. (2003) *Eats, Shoots and Leaves*, London: Profile Books Ltd

Tusting, K. and Barton, D. (2003) *Models of Adult Learning: A Literature Review*, London: NRDC

UNESCO (2003) *Literacy as Freedom*, Paris: UNESCO

Wainright, G. R. (2003) *Teach Yourself Body Language*, London: Hodder Education

Wray, D. and Lewis, M. (1997) *Extending Literacy: Developing Approaches to Non-Fiction*, London: Routledge

Websites

http://tip.psychology.org/
www.askoxford.com
www.autism.org.uk
www.bbc.co.uk/skillswise
www.bdadyslexia.org.uk
www.bl.uk
www.british-sign.co.uk
www.campaign-for-learning.org.uk
www.dfes.gov.uk/readwriteplus
www.drc-gb.org
www.dyslexiaaction.org.uk
www.dyspraxiafoundation.org.uk
www.geoffpetty.com
www.learnenglish.org.uk

www.mencap.org.uk
www.mind.org.uk
www.mrccbu.cam.ac.uk/~mattd/Cmabrigde/
www.plainenglish.co.uk
www.qca.org.uk
www.radar.org.uk
www.rnib.org.uk
www.rnid.org.uk
www.scope.org.uk
www.sflqi.org.uk
www.skill.org.uk
www.talent.ac.uk
www.teachernet.gov.uk

Index

Note: Page references in **bold** relate to Glossary